D0818910

Women Encounter God

Theology across the Boundaries of Difference

Linda A. Moody

ORBIS BOOKS
Maryknoll, New York 10545

The Catholic Foreign Mission Society of America (Maryknoll) recruits and trains people for overseas missionary service. Through Orbis Books, Maryknoll aims to foster the international dialogue that is essential to mission. The books published, however, reflect the opinions of their authors and are not meant to represent the official position of the society.

Copyright ©1996 by Linda A. Moody

All rights reserved. No part of this publication may be reproduced or transmitted in any form or by any means, electronic or mechanical, including photocopying, recording or any information storage or retrieval system, without prior permission in writing from the publishers.

Queries regarding rights and permissions should be addressed to: Orbis Books, P. O. Box 308, Maryknoll, New York 10545-0308.

Published by Orbis Books, Maryknoll, NY 10545-0308
Manufactured in the United States of America

Library of Congress Cataloging-in-Publication Data

Moody, Linda A.
    Women encounter God : theology across the boundaries of difference
/ Linda A. Moody.
        p.   cm.
    Includes bibliographical references and index.
    ISBN 1-57075-082-3 (alk. paper)
    1. Feminist theology.   2. Womanist theology.   3. Mujerista
theology.   I. Title.
BT83.55.M66   1996
230'.082—dc20   96-31157
                                                                              CIP

This book is dedicated to
the memory of my father, Dean Arthur Moody;
my grandmother, Bernice Lyndal Moody;
and all the orphans and widows of war.

May we live to see the day when we study war no more and, instead,
study ways to get along with those who see things differently.

Contents

Acknowledgments

I WANT TO THANK Benjamin A. Reist, Clare B. Fischer, and Margarita Melville for their support and encouragement. I also want to thank Robert McAfee Brown and Gustavo Gutiérrez, from whom I learned much as their teaching assistant. Other former professors I want to thank include Claude Welch, Durwood Foster, Walter Shurden, Larry McSwain, Richard Cunningham, Glen Stassen, Paul Simmons, and Andrew Lester. Edwina Hunter, Will Coleman, Vera Long, Marge Thomas, Bill Thomas, Julia McKay, and many colleagues at Mills College, too numerous to name individually, have been supportive through the years, all in different ways. Special thanks go to Emilie M. Townes, Elizabeth A. Say, and Sheila Briggs, who read earlier versions of this manuscript and provided helpful suggestions and comments. My appreciation is also extended to Garen Murray, my research assistant, and Mary Vinci, my office assistant. I am also grateful to Sue Perry of Orbis Books for her editorial guidance. Finally, I appreciate the support of my mother, Barbara Ellen Caton, and the home away from home provided by my brother and sister-in-law, Danny and Denise Moody.

Introduction

MARY DALY's *The Church and the Second Sex*, first published in 1968, was one of the key works that opened the doors for a feminist theology of liberation in the United States. With its publication, women doing theology began to understand their mission as no less than the liberation of theology itself.[1] Along with Daly, Rosemary Radford Ruether, Carol Christ, and others began a radical feminist critique of the doctrines and practices of Christianity. Central to this critique was the notion that theology, under the guise of neutral, objective scholarship, was actually a theology written by white males from a white male perspective. The perspectives of women had largely been lost to theological scholarship. Daly issued a call for a radical rethinking of the ways that theology had been constructed, so as to give room for the development of a new theology that would take seriously the experience of women.

Less than a decade after Daly and others began to describe what they termed as women's experience of God, a new critique appeared. In 1979, Audre Lorde drafted a response to Daly's newest work, *Gyn/Ecology*. Lorde's critique appeared in what has come to be understood as a groundbreaking work for women of color, *This Bridge Called My Back* (1983). Published as "An Open Letter to Mary Daly," Lorde challenged Daly for having lifted up only white women's experience, advocating white, European images of the Goddess and ignoring such darker African Goddesses as Afrekete, Yemanje, Oyo, and Mawulisa.[2] Just as male theologians were criticized by Daly for generalizing their own experience to be "human" experience, so Daly herself was criticized for generalizing white, middle-class women's experience as normative for all women. Lorde's argument for the particularity of Black women's experience was heard echoed in the arguments of Black feminist theorists bell hooks and Patricia Hill Collins.[3] In the area of theology, similar arguments for the particularity of the experience of women of color and

1

ethnic women could be heard among Hispanic, Latin American, African-American, Asian American, and Native American women.[4]

Currently, a new phase of constructive liberation theology is underway as women in differing sociocultural, racial, and ethnic contexts seek to move forward to develop new theological understandings of God that come from their own experience. While white women have often referred to their theological writings as feminist, African-American women in the United States have taken up Alice Walker's term "womanist"[5] to describe their own particular type of Black feminist scholarship. Similarly, many Hispanic women in the United States have consciously chosen the term *mujerista*[6] (from the Spanish word for woman, *mujer*), to describe their own type of theologizing, which takes into account their experience of sexism, racism, and classism.

In this work, I hope to contribute to yet another phase in contemporary constructive theology as women doing theology begin to listen to the theological insights and critique developed by women from differing cultural contexts. This process can be aided by insights from the "third-world"[7] peoples of the United States—those marginalized by race, class, and other factors—who offer a method of feminist critical analysis of difference that will allow each of these theologies to speak with the clarity of its own voice without blurring the distinctions that characterize the uniqueness of its own context. Equally important to this multicultural theologizing is the ability to discern commonalities between the many ways that women in differing social contexts understand God and the workings of God in their lives.

This work will briefly trace the early critical work as women doing feminist theology have sought to understand God in nonpatriarchal ways. Primarily, it will explore women's constructive efforts to understand God from feminist and liberation perspectives. While the discussion of women's understandings of God is a current topic of virtually all feminist liberation theologies, I will focus on the work of white feminists in the United States, Hispanic and Latin American women doing liberation theology, and womanist scholars of religion in the United States. In each category I look at how differing women understand God. Thematically, I will explore issues of God language, God's power and liberation, immanence and transcendence, and relationality and embodiment.

Clues to Women's Multicultural Theologizing

In searching for a biblical narrative to help us in our efforts, one that is woman-centered, liberating, embodied, and relational, the covenant between Naomi and Ruth comes to mind. There is significant evidence that women of very differing cultural contexts are interested in this concept. White feminist Mary Hunt, womanist Delores Williams, and Latin American theologian Tereza Cavalcanti, among others, all offer the covenant between Ruth and Naomi as a model for friendship.[8]

Each of these theologians, all of whom come from widely differing cultural backgrounds, looks to the story of Ruth and Naomi for inspiration. The story of the book of Ruth begins as Elimelech marries Naomi, a Hebrew woman. A famine at home in Bethlehem causes them to go with their two sons to the Land of Moab, probably somewhere in what is now southwest Jordan. Having just left her homeland and traveled to a new country with a different cultural and belief system than her own, Naomi is shocked to find that her husband has died. "How will I raise these two sons?" she must have asked herself. Somehow she managed to raise those children, who then grew up and married Moabite women, Ruth and Orpah. As if it were not enough to leave her homeland and lose her husband, Naomi then is faced with one of the most painful experiences one can have. Not one, but both her sons died.

Naomi must have been beside herself. Where would she live? How would she support herself? Ruth and Orpah were grieving widows. For a time, Naomi, Ruth, and Orpah decided to live together, even with all their differences. Then Naomi heard that the famine had subsided in Bethlehem and decided that she would return. She told both her daughters-in-law to return to the houses of their mothers.

Orpah and Ruth made different decisions. Orpah went back home. Ruth made known to Naomi her intention to follow her to Bethlehem. Of particular interest are the words Ruth said to Naomi:

> Do not press me to leave you, or to turn back from following you; for where you go I will go; where you lodge I will lodge; your people shall be my people, and your God my God; where you die I will die, and there will I be buried. (Ruth 1:16, 17a, NRSV)

These words may offer women doing contemporary constructive theology a model for cross-cultural theologizing. Before accepting this covenantal model at face value, however, several questions must be asked. Is the relationship between Ruth and Naomi mutual and reciprocal, or are Ruth's words to Naomi evidence of a one-sided relationship? Does Ruth give up her own culture, history, family, and God in order to honor those of Naomi? Is this yet another example of the patriarchal God of Israel silencing the god(s) of others? If we are to transpose the covenant between Ruth and Naomi into the contemporary scene as a model for women doing the-

ology across the boundaries of difference, several parallel questions immediately come to mind. What will happen to my own identity if I follow you
into your theological terrain? Will my own identity be sacrificed in the
process? What will happen to those distinctives that make my theology
unique if I promise to honor your God? Will I end up sounding like a theological parrot if your God is my God? Or even worse, will I be accused of
theological misappropriation? What will happen if I promise that your people will be my people? Will my own people desert me? Will your people
reject me? Will I end up a theological nomad with no place to call home?

Sharon Welch's ethic of risk may be helpful at this point.[9] Welch's point,
particularly for white women, is that at this juncture in the history of feminist ethics, it is critical to be willing to risk entering the wilderness of unfa-
miliar cultural terrain, to risk the possible criticism which may ensue, for to
fail to risk moving beyond difference is to continue to live and move in the
same terrain that has fostered racism, ethnic oppression, and cross-cultural
misunderstanding to date.

It should be noted that Jacquelyn Grant raises a critical question regarding the use of the term "covenant." She brings a hermeneutic of suspicion to
notions of reconciliation, community, and covenant:

> All too often, notions of reconciliation, covenantal relationship, uni-
> ty, and community mirror those in the system of domestic service
> relationships. The needs of one group (partner) are universalized in
> such a fashion that those on the topside of history are the beneficia-
> ries of the system; and those on the underside of history are mere
> victims of the relationship.[10]

Grant prefers the term "discipleship" to describe the hard work of justice
making. I want to emphasize that when I use the term "covenant" as a possible model for women doing theology across the boundaries of difference,
I am not talking about the type of oppressive relationship described by
Grant, which might rightly be called pseudocovenantal. I am referring,
instead, to a mutually reciprocal relationship and to an ethic of justice making that governs the love, friendship, and hard work of those living in
covenant with each other. The questions raised in the model provided by
Naomi and Ruth will be further explored in chapter 5 to determine the
helpfulness of this covenantal model for the contemporary constructive
theological enterprise among women. If women from differing cultural
contexts accept the notion that God is a covenanting God who can bring
together women from very differing cultural backgrounds, such as Ruth
and Naomi, we have a possible basis for mutual, shared theological reflection across the boundaries of difference.

Differences and Commonalities

There are important distinctions in the various ways that white feminist, *mujerista*, and womanist theologians reflect on God. These might be represented by a white feminist emphasis on God/dess as opposed to patriarchal notions of God, Latin American women's emphasis on God as the God of Life and source of joy, and the womanist use of slave narratives that call on God as the liberator who has come to set women and men free from the bonds of slavery and racial oppression. In addition to pointing to clear differences such as these in the three theological traditions, I suggest that there are important similarities in women's conceptions of God that have emerged in the independent strains of white feminist, *mujerista*, and womanist theologies. These similarities include the understanding that one site of God's embodiment in the world occurs in women's lives as they struggle for justice, that God is fundamentally relational and acts as the one who calls us into relationality with each other, and that God serves as a key source of empowerment for women in the struggle for liberation. These commonalities in ways of perceiving God may be able to serve as a point of focus for a much-needed emerging intercultural theological dialogue among women.

Contributions to Women's Constructive Theology

There are three significant contributions this project hopes to make to women's constructive theology. First, with the exception of collaborative anthologies, such as Carol Christ and Judith Plaskow's *Weaving the Visions* or the anthology of Letty Russell, et al. , *Inheriting Our Mother's Gardens*, little has been published in which women from differing liberation theology contexts attempt to dialogue with one another. A new effort has just begun, even as recently as a panel entitled "Appropriation and Reciprocity"[11] given at the 1991 meeting of the American Academy of Religion, for women to begin to think of appropriate ways to engage in shared theological reflection. Sharon Welch's *Communities of Resistance and Solidarity: A Feminist Theology of Liberation*, Susan Thistlethwaite's *Sex, Race, and God*, and Ann Kirkus Wetherilt's *That They May Be Many: Voices of Women, Echoes of God*[12] offer helpful methodologies for white women taking seriously the work of women of color and/or women of differing ethnicities. In this work, I place into dialogue the insights from white, Hispanic and Latin American, and African-American women doing theological reflection on God, examining the commonalities among their theologies and those differences which are intrinsic to each. As part of the task of bringing these theologies into dialogue with one another, I highlight previously untranslated work from Latin American women doing liberation theology.

A second significant aspect of this work is that it seeks to put the voices of white feminist, *mujerista*, Latin American feminist, and womanist theologians into contact with the voices of feminist theorists in order to see how insights from each respective field might contribute to the others.

Finally, I will offer a constructive proposal for incorporating mutuality and difference as keys for the development of intercultural shared reflection on God among women of very different class, religious, racial, ethnic, and sociocultural backgrounds.

Method

Several basic precepts of liberation theology will be in operation in the course of this book. Among these, I make use of Ricoeur's notion of a first and second naivete and a hermeneutics of suspicion as a basis for feminist inquiry.[13] Second, I employ the methodological principle of the hermeneutical privilege of the poor and oppressed, first made popular in Latin American liberation theology,[14] in looking at the way class issues affect women's views of God. Third, I give importance to the notion of race as a starting point for contemporary cultural and/or theological reflection.[15] Fourth, I make use of the method of liberation theology based on a feminist sociology of knowledge that grants to women the hermeneutical privilege to declare as nonauthoritative those scriptural texts oppressive to women.[16] Finally, I consider the insistence on praxis as the starting point for theological reflection, first made popular in Latin American liberation theology, an important tool for examining the ways that women view God.[17]

The primary method I employ in this project will be a critical and comparative analysis of white feminist, *mujerista*, Latin American feminist, and womanist theologies, particularly emphasizing a feminist critical theory of difference. This theological exploration of women's varying ways of understanding God is part of a larger discussion of a feminist critical theory of difference, a theory that accepts the notion that women's differing sociocultural, religious, economic, and political contexts produce particular understandings of reality that may not be shared cross-culturally, thus pointing to the importance of the concepts of "difference" and "particularity" in constructing knowledge.

In designing a methodology for conducting the critical and comparative analysis of three different types of theology, the works of U.S. third-world feminist theorist Chela Sandoval, theologians Ada María Isasi-Díaz and Elsa Tamez, and theorist Rosemary Tong are helpful. Chela Sandoval describes the problem as twofold. First, we must understand the ways in which what she terms "hegemonic [white] feminism" has contributed to the invisibility of women of color. Thus she cites the move by U.S. third-world feminists to label what had come to be known as "the second wave of feminism" of the 1970s as "the white women's movement."[18] According to Sandoval,

> this renaming teaches us that it is impossible to utter the word "woman" as if it holds some common, unified meaning. Every woman is subject to very different desires, values, and meanings that have been shaped—not only by her experience of sexuality and gender—but by her particular experience of the intersections of race, culture, and class.[19]

Second, it is important to allow the particularities of the experiences of differing groups of women to stand on their own, rather than attempting to level all differences in order to achieve an artificial archetypal definition of reality that only serves to mask real difference and to make marginalized persons invisible. This insistence on difference as a central tenet of U.S. third-world feminists is not intended to create divisions where none exist, but rather simply to allow the real differences that exist among women to be given voice. In Sandoval's words,

> United States Third World feminists are pointing out the differences that exist among all women not in order to fracture any hope of unity among women but to propose a new order—one that provides a new possibility for unity without the erasure of differences.[20]

In looking at white feminist, *mujerista* and Latin American feminist, and womanist conceptions of God, I will draw on what Sandoval has termed "the method of oppositional consciousness,"[21] which informs the theory, method, and praxis of United States Third World feminists, a consciousness that has arisen in the context of intentional opposition to powers of domination and subjection. For this reason, I have structured this book to treat as separate entities the theologies developed by white feminists, *mujeristas* and Latin American feminists, and womanist scholars of religion, noting the distinct contributions of each before attempting to enter into any discussion of possible commonalities among them.

I conclude with suggestions for ways in which feminist theology and feminist theory can interact so they can incorporate the categories of difference and commonality in the effort to develop an understanding of

women's varying views of God in contemporary feminist constructive theology. These suggestions will point toward a methodology for doing theology across the boundaries of multicultural difference as women continue
to reflect on God and the ways God acts in women's lives.

A Personal Note on Boundary Crossing

I want to follow in the footsteps of womanist Delores Williams, who in
the preface to her recent work *Sisters in the Wilderness* states, "I have come
to believe that theologians, in their attempt to talk to and about religious
communities, ought to give readers some sense of their autobiographies."[22]

The unspoken assumption of my research into white feminist,
mujerista, Latin American feminist, and womanist conceptions of God is
that in order for our world to survive, we must find ways to communicate
across the boundaries of difference. If women doing theology are to contribute to resolving the many problems we face, I believe we must find
common, even sacred ground for doing multicultural work.

How did I come to this basis for my work? I have chosen to focus on the
theologies of white feminists, *mujeristas* and Latin American women, and
womanists for two reasons. One is that the vast majority of material published by women on liberation theology comes from these three groups.
This is not to dismiss the important work of Asian, Asian American, Native
American, African, and other women making significant contributions to
constructive liberation theologies. A second reason, perhaps more critical,
is that I have spent a good deal of my life working, living, and struggling in
community with other white feminists, African-American friends and colleagues, and Latin American friends. My involvement with this project
began more than twenty years ago when I developed friendships with Black
women from the southern part of the United States and with Latin
American children in Venezuela. It may be helpful to tell a bit of my story.

I come from a family of Kentucky tobacco farmers and construction
workers—people who had never had extra money. But there was always
enough. We were taught to be thankful for what we had and to feel for those
who had less. I come from folks who love the land, plant gardens, grow
much of their own food, raise a hog or two and maybe a few calves—proud
people who live by folk wisdom, common sense, a good bit of ingenuity,
and a fair amount of trial and error. I am the only person from my family to
go to college. While my mother completed high school, my father didn't.
My grandmother made it through the eighth grade. My grandfather had a
sixth-grade education.

In terms of my racial, ethnic, and cultural heritage, I think of myself as
white, although some members of my family have darker skin than others.

When my brother and aunt stay in the sun a while, it requires a far stretch of the imagination to see how, with their skin pigment, they are of Irish or English descent, though this is supposed to be our heritage. I was told as a child that we were part Native American, although my mother and aunt now disagree about this. Our family tree is unhelpful at this point because it doesn't go back very far; my father was adopted and my mother's father was raised by an uncle. As an adult I learned that my grandmother's grandmother was a Jew from Germany, which caused scandal in one part of the family and pride in my mother, who simply said, "I knew it." Why we should have been surprised when my grandmother's name was Ruth Naomi I do not know. I am more interested in deconstructing notions of race and ethnicity than in blindly accepting the categories invented by the U.S. Census Bureau. I also do not find all our current designations of race and ethnicity to be helpful or accurate.

In terms of our class background, our family story is like the one told in *The Dollmaker*.[23] My grandpappy and other relatives were poor tenant farmers, sharecroppers as they were known in other parts. They were part of the Hillbilly clan that moved from Kentucky up to Michigan to try to make a better life. Twenty-five years later, my family went home for good, back to Kentucky near where they were born. My mother bought an old farmhouse in Aliceton that used to belong to a cousin. My grandpappy bought a little house above the Rolling Fork River, where he took me fishing and trapping whenever we could sneak away. Pappy taught me to shoot his pistol and shotgun down at the river, and I learned to drive a stick-shift, a 1936 Chevy pickup, in his pig lot. Later when they moved to Gravel Switch, population two hundred or so, my mother, Pappy, and Aunt Kathryn lived in three houses next to each other beside the railroad tracks. Given the way I was brought up and the values I was taught, as well as the vast quantities of iced tea and fried chicken I have consumed, I suppose I can best be identified as Hillbilly American at heart. Though I may not have as much of a Kentucky accent as the rest of my family, having only lived in Kentucky part of my life, I do hate to wear shoes.

While these are my roots, I have spent much of my life educating myself out of the class background of my grandparents and even parents. Living in many worlds, speaking many languages, developing intellectual understandings of the "other," and forming bonds of friendship across the boundaries of difference is a theological, ethical, and political commitment of two decades of living, working, researching, befriending, and loving. Much of this world-traveling[24] began in Kentucky.

In speaking autobiographically, it may be useful to refer to a lecture given by Mary E. Hunt on the work of Sylvia Marcos, a Mexican psychotherapist who believes that in discovering the sources of our own oppression, we are often led to a position of solidarity with others whose oppression may be different from our own.[25] Marcos speaks of two distinct phases in this process.[26] "Primary rebellion" takes place as we initially recognize our own oppression and rebel against the injustice of it. "Permanent rebellion" is the experience that takes place as our initial understanding of our own oppression leads us to understand the oppression of others and prompts us to work to rid the world of other forms of injustice. Hunt refers to those in permanent rebellion as "lifers for justice."[27]

My own transition from primary to permanent rebellion was solidified as I played softball in the rural parts of Kentucky as a teenager, for it was there that we spent long summer nights—Black and white women together —swaying in the breezes of country porch swings, or standing late into the night until dew set on empty softball bleachers, listening to the crickets and katydids and the comforting rhythms of neighboring cows chewing their cuds. Together, we Kentucky women in the early 1970s integrated the softball leagues; integrated our lives; came home to each other in ways we will never forget; forgave each other for the sins we did not know we would commit; came to love each other in ways we will live out for the rest of our lives. With an unspoken covenant with each other to love across the boundaries of difference, we disbanded our segregated softball teams—the Mustangs, P-ville Women, the Springfield Gals. Instead we all became Heifers—proud, strong women, committed in friendship to the idea that beyond the slavery of our shared histories, women can love each other across the color line. I have described this experience elsewhere as follows:

> In those days, I played on teams with other white women. We would drive over to Lebanon or to Springfield to play against Black teams, aware of our differences and the stereotypes that separated us. And at the same time, there was a real sense of sisterhood as we got together. We always brought soda by the six pack and they brought potato chips for after the game or vice-versa. One year, by some miracle, when it came time to form teams, the rosters were not formed along racial lines. We became an integrated softball league, a process none of us quite understands to this day. It was not an easy process. People talked behind our backs. Some folks wouldn't speak to us. Nonetheless, we had picnics and went to tournaments together. Julia came to my house and I went to hers. It was a magical time when the Spirit entered into our history together and brought about radical change. To this day, the friendships formed out of that experience are some of the strongest friendship ties I have. In becoming teammates and then friends with Black women, in being invited to their homes and in having them come to mine, I began to unlearn some of the

racism of our society. That early moment of solidarity with women of color has since led to other such moments when through the mystery of the Spirit, change has come.[28]

This story indicates the genesis of my relationship with African-American women from the South. It does not attempt to describe other aspects of my relationship with African-American women and their communities. I am not entirely sure why in college in the early 1970s—long before it became a badge of courage or political correctness for a white woman to take ethnic studies courses—I took an English course in Black Poetry, a linguistics course in Black dialect, and in 1972 I wrote a paper on the noticeable absence of women and Black folk in the textbooks used in a local elementary school. Though I was an active member in a very white Baptist church in Ann Arbor, I also attended a Black church in town. Back in Kentucky sometimes I went to a Black church with my friend Julia. I did these things simply because I thought it was important to learn something about Black culture and intellectual life. Some twenty years later when I had just begun a Ph.D. program, I spent one summer reading the major works of Zora Neale Hurston, certainly not because they were on the required reading list for comprehensive exams in Systematic and Philosophical Theology and Philosophy of Religion at my school! I read Hurston's work for a very simple reason: I heard several African-American friends and colleagues mention her name and her work, and it was obvious to me that it was important. I had never heard of her, and I didn't want to appear ignorant. In the years between Black Poetry 102 and my self-taught summer crash course in Zora Neale Hurston were many, many American Baptist clergy women's annual conferences and regional meetings, a prime locus for witnessing firsthand the ways that white women ministers continued to practice racism and cause divisions between white women and women of color in our denomination. In the midst of those conferences, and in the midst of much struggle, emerged several cherished friendships which crossed the color line.

My relationship with Hispanic communities began with a foreign-language requirement for college. I chose Spanish over French, German, or Latin because I thought that it made sense to learn a language that was spoken by a large group of people in the United States. A high school teacher took a group of us to Spain and to Mexico and it was then I decided to major in Spanish in college. At the University of Michigan I met Gustavo, whom I would have married except that he didn't want to live in the United States, and I didn't want to be a Venezuelan politician's wife, so we had to give up on our relationship after four years of trying. I spent one of those four years living in Venezuela, working in an orphanage part of the time and teaching school the rest. I fell in love with a little boy named Kimito, a fifteen-year-old named Hildemaro, and two twins whom we simply called "Las Morochas." It was from Alfredo that I learned the most Spanish, because he loved to tell jokes and couldn't bear for me not to get the punch line, so he would repeat them over and over until I got it.

The time in Venezuela was critical in terms of my career. I had gone to Venezuela with a very conservative mission and had studied with the Summer Institute of Linguistics—which has loose ties with Wycliffe Bible Translators—with the thought of becoming a Bible translator in the jungles of Venezuela. A master's degree with training in linguistics and a cross-cultural emphasis made me a perfect candidate. What I saw when I got to Venezuela made me change my mind. The mission's work with the Tucana-Panore and Yecuana-Makiritaré Indians was to teach them the Bible. The only hitch was that in order for the missionaries to obtain Venezuelan visas, they had to promise the Venezuelan government that they would teach the Bible in Spanish rather than in the native languages of the Indians. This was part of the government's cultural program for the tribes who had so far resisted Westernization. The Indians I saw still wore only loincloths and painted their bodies. The missionaries saw this as an opportunity and brought Western cloth along with their Spanish Bibles. Seeing the faces of the Indians, who looked perfectly happy speaking their own languages and wearing comfortable clothing for the jungle heat and humidity, I simply knew in my heart that we were wrong and that I didn't want to be any part of the cultural program of the government or the mission. It should be easy to see why I was later attracted to the theologies of liberation coming out of Latin America. I had witnessed the effects of colonization firsthand.

There is perhaps one more part of my personal story that I should share. I finished a master's degree in teaching English as a second language and left Venezuela in 1976. In the twenty years between then and now, I've continued my own work in multicultural settings in a number of ways. For nine years I worked as director of a program teaching English as a second language and providing job training to refugee women from more than thirty countries and language backgrounds, and I served on the board of a refugee resettlement agency in the San Francisco Bay area for five years. For several years I also served as the international student advisor at the college where I now teach. One of my former students, Selly Castillo of Venezuela, has generously offered to provide the Spanish translations for this project. My point is that my commitment to living and learning and working across the boundaries of difference is a life-long commitment. This book is the continuation of a path I have been on for many years. While no doubt I will make mistakes in this project, it has been part of a journey I am committed to make—encountering God across the boundaries of difference.

In Mary Hunt's lecture, referred to above, she stated that it is precisely the process of coming together with others different from ourselves, this moving from primary to permanent rebellion, that will lead us into liberation, into equality and mutuality.[29] Hunt's definition of church as an "unlikely coalition of justice-seeking friends"[30] challenges our notion of church as sanctuary, as a place to escape the world, to be with others who sing and pray like we do. If we take seriously the relationality of God and the embodiment of God in our world, as this book proposes, and if we allow the Covenanting God to bring us into covenant with each other, we may find ourselves in "unlikely coalitions," expanding our circle of friends and acquaintances so that we know and understand people who are quite different from ourselves and take action to live in solidarity with them. I see this as our hope for the future.

I want to close with a story from my Kentucky softball days. Dick Sinkhorn would drive his van from Mitchellsburg through Perryville, up Aliceton Road to Gravel Switch, and on to Lebanon, stopping to pick us up on roads like Quirk's Run, Cranetown, Tatum Lane, and the Beech. One evening we were headed to Greensburg for a softball tournament and were not sure where the ballpark was. We stopped and asked an old farmer how to get to the park. He paused, spit tobacco juice, then looked toward town and the setting sun and said, "All the way out and all the way on through." I can't tell you how many times over the years we've laughed at the lack of specificity of his directions. Yet the man's words were wise ones. He trusted we would find our way.

As we face what has been called the "sunset of the 20th century,"[31] those farmer's words can help us find our way to the unknown place of our shared future. To get there together, we're going to have to go all the way out beyond the places we've known and all the way on through.

1

Contemporary White Feminist
Conceptions of God

MARY DALY's 1968 publication of *The Church and the Second Sex* marked the beginning of a new era in contemporary theology in the United States, as white feminists began to critique traditional theology, based on their own experience of God and humanity. This chapter will introduce some of the initial concerns raised by white feminist theologians, giving particular attention to their critique of traditional conceptions of God and the ways God relates to humanity. This critique focuses on the symbolic nature of God language. Mary Daly and Rosemary Radford Ruether, for example, each reject the patriarchal rubric of God language because they came to understand the strong hold it has over women's lives. If women are to see themselves as creatures made in the divine image, the language used to speak of God must reflect more than male symbolism.

In essence, this early critique, inspired by the women's movement of the 1960s and early 1970s, represents a turning point for women doing theology. This early work was highly critical of abstract, philosophical notions of the God "above." Daly's work focuses on a nonstatic concept of God as verb, Be-ing, engaged in actions of weaving, spinning, and sparking women to take the courage to live their lives as whole selves. Ruether's rejection of an abstract, transcendent God takes the form of an image of God as Primal Matrix, generator of life, source and wellspring of renewal. This God is intricately involved in the lives of women, leading them on their journey into wholeness, just as the God of the exodus led the Jewish people toward the Promised Land. As they rejected male ways of doing theology, white feminist women sought to discover the nature of women's ways of doing theology and of speaking of God.

Much of the early work of white feminist theology in the United States sought to critique the white male theological tradition for its failure to address the concerns of women. The importance of this early critical work, particularly its deconstruction of white male conceptions of God, cannot be overemphasized. At the same time, it is important to acknowledge the significant ways that white feminist theology was influenced by the white male theological tradition, for there is considerable evidence of direct borrowing of white male theological images and methods, which were to become limitations of this early white feminist work and cause for its critique.

The Relationship of White Feminist Theology to White Male Theology

One cannot speak of the early years of white feminist theology in the United States without noting the work of Mary Daly. While Mary Daly has moved out of the realm of feminist theology into feminist philosophy and theory, she made significant contributions to the field of feminist theology in her early work. These contributions include her ground-breaking critique of the patriarchal nature of the Christian church, her analysis of the ways in which the church has contributed to the oppression of women in society, and her contructive suggestions for new understanding of the female nature of God. The result of Daly's initial critical and constructive work is that it opened the doors for other women to begin to question church tradition, the role of scripture, and the place of women in church and society.

Mary Daly begins *Beyond God the Father*, published in 1973, by noting how her thought has changed between the publication of this text and that of her earlier work, *The Church and the Second Sex* (1968). She describes these five years as "intense living on the boundary—a veritable full generation of change measured by the accelerated time flow of this age."[1] In describing her situation as one "on the boundary," she links herself with the tradition of Paul Tillich, who had used the term earlier to describe his effort to span the fields of theology and philosophy, the worlds of Europe and the United States, and even the nineteenth and twentieth centuries.[2]

Mary Daly, who holds doctoral degrees in both theology and philosophy and has taught courses in both disciplines, was educated in Europe and in the United States. In addition to her work being "on the boundary" *between* the fields of philosophy and theology, Daly also notes that it is "on the boundary" *of* these "(male-created) disciplines . . . because it speaks out of the experience of that half of the human species which has been represented in neither discipline."[3] Like Tillich, she develops a new language for speaking from the boundary existence. Using his method, her early work sought to correlate theological answers with pressing social concerns, which in her case involved the dismantling of patriarchy. Moving into self-proclaimed exodus from the church, Daly inherited both the excitement and the difficulty of living within the tradition which Tillich termed "the boundary."

Because Daly relies heavily on Tillich, it may be helpful to briefly introduce some of the areas of Tillich's thought that may be of interest to feminist and liberationist readers. For Tillich, no moral or religious system can be absolutized. The spirit of the Reformation must live on in order for theology to reflect the concerns of all involved. This Protestant Principle appears in Tillich's willingness to criticize the church and society, in his use of historical critical methods, and in his insistence that the church cannot be interpreted apart from the culture in which it exists.[4] Feminist liberation theology shares Tillich's commmitment to theology speaking critically about the church and about social conditions of oppression.

A second area of Tillich's thought that is attractive to feminist and liberation theologians is his view of religious authority. Unlike Karl Barth, Tillich is willing to use extrabiblical sources for theology.[5] Tillich takes seriously the history of religion and culture. He is open to mysticism, and he gives "an important place" to the category of experience in his theological method.[6] Similarly, many feminist and liberationist theologians argue for the use of extrabiblical sources and give importance to the category of women's experience.

A third aspect of Tillich's theology that is of interest to feminist thought is his concept of language and symbol. Willhelm Pauck and Marion Pauck believe that it was, in part, out of an effort to communicate with poor parishoners, seminary students, and the laity that Tillich came up with a new language for expressing existential concerns.[7] This is one area of common ground between Tillich and feminist liberation theologians, who likewise have argued for the need for theological language which is accessible to the people.

Even more important for feminist theology is Tillich's understanding of symbol. Tillich feels that religious symbols live and die. This radical openness to religious symbols leads him to suggest the need for a re-examination of the doctrine of the trinity that takes seriously questions about the maleness and femaleness of God, a concept which he develops in the third volume of his *Systematic Theology*. Many women have taken up Tillich's suggestion that new symbols for God need to arise, symbols which reflect both the male and female aspects of the sacred.

One final aspect of Tillich that is interesting to feminist thought will be mentioned. Though Tillich maintains the ultimacy of Jesus as the Christ throughout his systematic theology, he grows in appreciation of other world religions as his thought develops and as he has opportunities to travel to cultures as diverse as Greece and Japan.[8] Liberationist and feminist theologians, likewise, are growing in their appreciation of non-Christian religions.

Throughout *Beyond God the Father* Mary Daly freely uses the language and concepts of Paul Tillich. While various parallels between the thought of Tillich and Daly could be cited, including her borrowing his notions of "courage in the face of nothingness" or his anthropology related to the "centered self," what is most germane to this discussion is Daly's concept of God, which can be directly traced to Tillich. Daly is well aware that Tillich belongs to that tradition of theological and philosophical thinkers who espouse a notion of God as "being-itself." Along with the image of God as "being-itself," Tillich uses a second image of God as "power of being."[9] Each of these images appears in Daly's writings. In fact, she credits Tillich's attempt to avoid hypostatization of God and reflects positively that "his manner of speaking about the ground and power of being would be difficult to use for the legitimization of any sort of oppression."[10] Affirming both the transcendent and immanent aspects of God, she writes, "The power of being is that in which all finite beings participate . . . this power is in all while transcending all."[11] This "power of being" is a nonstatic concept for Daly, for God is a verb. God is Be-ing. Daly's critique of Tillich's use of the term "power of being" is that Tillich does not make explicit the possible demonic use of God language to oppress women.

Incorporating Tillich's major metaphor into her own thought, Daly develops the idea of God as Being in detail.

> Why indeed must "God" be a noun? Why not a verb—the most active and dynamic of all? Hasn't the naming of "God" as a noun been an act of murdering that dynamic Verb? And isn't the Verb infinitely more personal than a mere static noun? The anthropomorphic symbols for God may be intended to convey personality, but they fail to convey that God is Be-ing.[12]

Describing this dynamic God, Daly uses Tillich's category of "nonbeing" as the antithesis of being. The Verb of Verbs is intransitive. It is not necessary to have an object limiting itself. "That which it is over against is nonbeing."[13] In her later writings, Daly becomes quite imaginative in describing the actions of her dynamic God. In *Gyn/Ecology* these activities are described as Spinning, Sparking, and Spooking.[14]

A second area of common ground between Tillich and Daly involves their understanding of symbolic language about God. Symbols participate in the reality to which they point. While a sign can be changed arbitrarily to meet the needs of a given situation, symbols cannot be so manipulated. As Tillich has noted, "the symbol grows and dies according to the correlation between that which is symbolized and the persons who receive it as symbol."[15] According to Tillich, a religious symbol can die "if the correlation of which it is an adequate expression dies. This occurs whenever the revelatory situation changes and former symbols become obsolete."[16]

That Daly fully incorporates Tillich's understanding of the life and death of symbols can be demonstrated by comparing her discussion of symbol in two separate works. In the earlier work, *The Church and the Second Sex*, Daly cites Tillich's understanding that "symbols, like living beings, grow and die."[17] In the later publication, *Beyond God the Father,* she makes a similar comment, this time without crediting Tillich. Here she writes, "religious symbols fade and die when the cultural situation that gave rise to them and supported them ceases to give them plausibility."[18]

Even the title of Daly's work, *Beyond God the Father*, takes up the Tillichian notion that the traditional symbols for the divine need to move beyond purely masculine conceptions of God. As familiar as Daly was with Tillich, she no doubt had read the section of Volume III of his *Systematic Theology* in which Tillich suggests the need for an alternative "over against a one-sided male-determined symbolism."[19] He offers the concept of "ground of being" as inclusive of "the mother-quality of giving birth, carrying, and embracing," a symbol offered "as a way of reducing the predominance of the male element in the symbolization of the divine."[20] That Tillich was able, as early as 1963, to talk about God in these feminist ways is quite remarkable. In some real sense, the God "beyond" father which Daly attempts to articulate is a continuation of a project begun by Tillich, whose influence clearly played a part in her early theologizing.

Where Tillich and Daly differ is that Tillich believes that such symbols as the Fall and the Christ as New Being are living symbols. Daly, on the other hand, feels that these symbols have lost all meaning for women. She specifically criticizes Tillich for analyzing the Fall as estrangement, without seeing the inherent notion of oppression of women in the symbol of the Fall. Similarly, she criticizes his view of New Being as a symbol of centeredness and wholeness because he fails to address the question of how a male can function as savior for women.

> Tillich abstracts from the specific content of the symbol, which functions to justify oppressive societal structures. Once again, there is no notice taken of the fact that the medium is the message. . . . If the symbol can be "used" [in the oppression of women] and in fact has a long history of being "used" in that way, isn't this an indication of some inherent deficiency in the symbol itself?[21]

Rejecting the symbol of the male savior, Daly argues that women must be the bearers of the New Being if patriarchy is to be overcome.

It seems clear that one of the sources which contributed to theological reflection in Mary Daly's early work was Paul Tillich. While it is easy to trace Tillich's influence in Daly because of the many explicit references to his work, I believe there are also striking parallels, although perhaps not direct borrowings from Tillich, in the thought of another key white feminist theologian, Rosemary Radford Ruether.

Catholic theologian Rosemary Radford Ruether is one of the most prolific writers of feminist theology in the United States. Her work in the fields of theology and history have guided many readers to re-examine the nature of the Catholic church, to remember the important contributions of women throughout the centuries, and to understand the role of God language in shaping our understandings of our world and our relationship to each other and all creation. I begin this comparison between Ruether and Tillich by looking to Ruether's understanding of God.

The language about God espoused by Rosemary Radford Ruether in *Sexism and God-Talk* (1983) is similar to Tillich's notion of God as the ground and meaning of being. She describes the "root human image" of the divine as "Primal Matrix, the great womb within which all things, Gods and humans, sky and earth, human and nonhuman beings, are generated."[22] This image, which first appears as the Goddess in the ancient Near East, "survives in the metaphor of the divine as Ground of Being."[23] Like both Tillich and Daly, Ruether rejects the notion of God as transcendent being removed from human experience. For Ruether, the divine as Primal Matrix is no distant, transcendent God; instead, Primal Matrix is described as "beneath and around us as encompassing source of life and renewal."[24]

A second comparison of Ruether's and Tillich's views of God is that both see God as the author of both the actual and the potential. Ruether's God/ess as Primal Matrix is more directly linked with the God of the exodus and with the tradition of God as Liberator and Redeemer than as God the Creator. Her God/ess is not the one who has created the present disorder, but rather the one who is to lead us out of this disorder into new life. This God is one who both embraces the ground of our being and drives us toward new potential and hope. "The God/ess who is the foundation (at one and the same time) of our being and our new being embraces both the roots of the material substratum of our existence (matter) and also the endlessly new creative potential (spirit)."[25]

Third, the goal toward which God moves the individual is strikingly similar between Tillich and Ruether. Tillich speaks of the movement and return toward a centered self. Ruether similarly claims that the God/ess leads us "to the converted center, the harmonization of self and body, self and other, self and world."[26] Here, she seems to take this notion of centeredness further in the direction of relationship and community than Tillich does. However, it can be argued that her notion of a harmonized self is similar to Tillich's idea of a centered self and is basic to her concept of centered-ness with others and the world.

Fourth, Tillich and Ruether purposefully choose metaphors for the Christ that transcend the male/female dichotomy. For Tillich, this meta-phor is one of self-sacrifice or service. According to Tillich, "self-sacrifice breaks the contrast of the sexes."[27] While most often Ruether views Jesus as prophet and as liberator from the existing social and religious hierarchy, she also speaks of Jesus as servant. Like Tillich, it is important for Ruether that the image for the Christ transcend sex roles. "His ability to speak as lib-erator does not reside in his maleness but in the fact that he has renounced this system of domination and seeks to embody in his person the new humanity of service and mutual empowerment."[28] From Ruether's point of view, "the maleness of Jesus has no ultimate significance."[29]

One final point of comparison between the theologies of Tillich and Ruether can be made. When speaking of conversion, Ruether again uses the notion of centeredness that appears in the thought of Tillich, although she develops the ideas of women's centeredness much more than he does, to be sure. While not wanting to give up the category of service, Ruether is clear that service for women is problematic. Too often women have become "suf-fering servants" through loss of identity, abuse, and exploitation. Women's conversion, then, involves "a turning around in which they literally dis-cover themselves as persons, as centers of being upon which they can stand and build their own identity."[30] This grounded self, aware and in touch with her anger, can move on to mutual service with others that is not self-deny-ing or self-destructive.

We can see that there seem to be clear links between the thought of early white feminist thinkers and the work of white male theologians such as Paul Tillich, even as these women sought to differentiate their work from that of their male predecessors. This relationship can best be seen in the language that Daly and Ruether use in describing God as "being," "power of being," and as the source of centeredness; in their search for meaningful symbols that arise and take on life in the context of contemporary women's lives; and in Ruether's identification of the essential nature of Christ as being rooted not in his maleness but rather in his identity as one who transcends sexual categories.

In looking at the early period of white feminist theology, one discovers a problem. On the one hand, early white feminist theology sought to high-light the ways in which it differed from its predecessors, particularly as it moved away from male language for God and developed new images of God as female. On the other hand, early white feminist theology was dependent on prior theological tradition as a springboard for its critique. Two aspects of this critique are significant. First, as mentioned in the introduction, was the stinging critique of Mary Daly's work by Audre Lorde, who aptly noted that just as white male theologians had produced a God portrait that strongly resembled their own, so white feminist theologians had created an image of God/dess that was fair-skinned, European in origin, with values strongly resembling those of middle-class white U.S. culture. The darker-skinned God/dess of Middle Eastern, African, or South American origins did not appear in this early work. In 1985, Delores Williams issued a similar critique of one of Rosemary Radford Ruether's articles. "Just as Christian patriarchy only makes visible and valuable the concerns of men, Ruether only gives visibility and authority to the concerns of white, non-poor feminist women."[31] Williams criticizes Ruether for describing the constructive work of contemporary theology as being "the repentance of sexism, exodus from patriarchy, and entrance into a new humanity."[32] Williams is critical of Ruether for failing to address the need for repentance of racism and classism, in addition to repentance of sexism.

A second critique of this early type of theologizing lies in the identification of white feminist theology with white male theology. It is easy to see how this type of theology, with its origins in the academy, using tools of philosophical and theological reflection developed in Europe, was primarily devoted to analysis and critique rather than praxis. It was largely silent on issues of race and class and, as such, it repeated many of the mistakes of white male theology by privileging one group's experience—white, middle-class women—over the experience of poor women and women of color. One point I would like to make, however, is that women such as Daly and Ruether were pioneers in the academy, and their very presence in classrooms and hallways was a type of praxis for which we would do well to be grateful. *Mujerista* theologian Ada María Isasi-Díaz has indicated that, given the lack of Hispanic theologians in the academy and the pressures to "be everything to everybody," she considers the work of *mujerista* academic theologians to be praxis.[33] Given the oppressive conditions for women doing theology at the time of Daly and Ruether's early work, I believe that their stories of survival, different though they may be, provide a kind of historical praxis that has been crucial.

While we acknowledge the more academic tendencies of some early white feminist theologians, it is important to note that this critique is not intended to dismiss the important contributions of their early work. Many women writing during this period were actively involved in various types of praxis without necessarily making this praxis the central theme of their writing. It is important to remember Nelle Morton's work in civil rights; Letty Russell's work with the urban poor in East Harlem; Beverly Wildung Harrison and Rosemary Radford Ruether's work for justice within church systems and structures; Anne McGrew Bennett's work with the peace movement and women's organizations; and Emily Culpepper's work in the civil rights, peace, and lesbian and gay liberation movements. In addition, many unacknowledged women, Catholic and Protestant alike, working without the title of theologian, have spent their lives working in the trenches for justice.

One of the ongoing tasks of white feminist theology is to critically evaluate its reliance, conscious or otherwise, on the white male theological tradition, its methods and assumptions. Another is to remember the legacy of praxis of white feminist theologians and to examine alternative ways of being involved with praxis at the grassroots level. There exists at the professional level a wide gap between theologians and pastoral ministers, particularly those in the local parish. If theologians believe in the necessity of "doing" theology, as opposed to merely thinking or writing about it, it might behoove us to be in more direct conversation with those doing theology in the form of ministry. Finally, we need to develop new sources for constructive theological efforts. In chapter 5, I will offer suggestions for how white women might further develop their own source materials for theological reflection.

The Contributions of Sallie McFague and Carter Heyward

Epistemology and Method

In looking at the work of white women doing constructive theology in the United States, Sallie McFague and Carter Heyward stand out as key figures whose work offers possibilities for those interested in doing theology across the boundaries of difference. The epistemological and methodological contributions of McFague and Heyward, as well as their constructive efforts to develop new God language, lead to an appreciation of the role of experimentation and imagination in the theological enterprise.

In the context of an age of militarism and exploitation of the earth, Sallie McFague asserts that in our contemporary nuclear age, we need to ask new theological questions and we need to understand God in new ways.[34] Her methodology and epistemology follow from this commitment to find new ways of relating to God and each other. McFague's first major work, *Speaking in Parables* (1975), describes the parable as "a prime genre of Scripture and certainly the central form of Jesus' teaching."[35] McFague understands the parable as the place where "the transcendent comes *to* ordinary reality and disrupts it." In saying that God comes *to* ordinary reality, she is locating God *within* the ordinary realm of reality rather than somehow outside or above this world. Through Jesus, the "parable of God," and through Jesus' teachings in the form of parable, God comes to us.[36] McFague understands parable as metaphor. She writes,

> Parables are stories, of course, but of a particular kind—stories that set the familiar in an unfamiliar context, which is also what a metaphor does. A metaphor is a word used in an unfamiliar context to give us a new insight; a good metaphor moves us to see our ordinary world in an extraordinary way.[37]

She makes an important epistemological assertion when she claims that "metaphor is a way of *knowing*, not just a way of communicating." Metaphors about God provide a way of knowing God. This knowing is a uniting of "language, belief, and life—the words in which we confess our faith, the process of coming to faith, and the life lived out of that faith."[38]

In McFague's epistemology, coming to know God is both tentative and processive. Depicting the revelatory/conversion experience as a lifelong process, McFague argues, "Christian belief must always be a process of coming to belief—like a story—through the ordinary details of historical life."[39] Because of the open-endedness of the process of coming to know God, one never "arrives" in this life at anything more—or less—than seeing in the mirror dimly. This imperfect, linguistically speaking, not-yet-complete understanding leads to theological reflection that also is prone to human imperfection. Therefore, theological reflection on God is "a risky and open-ended kind of reflection." She follows Paul Tillich and Simone Weil in asserting that "there are no explicit statements about God."[40] We can understand God only through reflection on the metaphor or story. Assertions about God must be made "lightly" and "indirectly."[41] Recognizing the "inconclusiveness of all conceptualization when dealing with matters between God and human beings,"[42] McFague in her later works begins the tentative process of conducting "thought experiments" on the possibility of speaking metaphorically of the world as God's body, and of God as mother, lover, and friend.

Another important aspect of McFague's understanding of metaphor is that metaphor uses embodied language grounded in the ordinary experiences of life. She writes,

> Metaphorical language is a mirror of our own constitution: the unity of body and soul, outer and inner, familiar and unfamiliar, known and unknown. Metaphorical language conveys meaning through the body of the world. It makes connections, sees resemblances, uniting body and soul—earthly, temporal, ordinary experience with its meaning.[43]

McFague is making two important claims here. First, she proposes that God is understood gradually and that one comes to belief processively.

Second, she calls for embodied language to describe the ways that God comes to us in ordinary reality. These dual assertions make it possible for her to move beyond the claims of rationalism and assert that the process of coming to understanding is not merely an intellectual process.

> On the contrary, metaphoric meaning, insisting as it always does on a physical base, is inclusive meaning which overcomes the distinctions of mind and body, reason and feeling, subjective and objective. Another way to say this is that metaphoric meaning is a *process*, not a momentary, static insight; it operates like a story, moving from here to there, from "what is" to "what might be."[44]

In summarizing McFague's epistemological and methodological contributions to a contemporary, constructive understanding of God, three elements are key. First, she insists that knowledge of God is tentative and processive. Because our understandings of God are tentative at best, our metaphors should likewise be tentative. An open-endedness characterizes this epistemology and allows McFague to experiment with different models and metaphors for God in each of her works.

A second epistemological contribution is McFague's emphasis on the relational aspects of knowledge. In fact, McFague privileges relationship as the "root metaphor" of Christianity. This view of relationality affects the entire theological enterprise, which for McFague is not to describe God as an abstract entity separate from all else, but rather to understand God in relation to humanity and all creation. This concern for relationality ultimately leads her to reject such patriarchal metaphors for God as father and king, focusing instead on such relational metaphors as God as friend, mother, and lover. Each of these contributions will prove valuable in developing language for God that may relate to the theological language being developed by women in other parts of the world.

Finally, like many liberation theologians, McFague employs an epistemology that refuses to distinguish between knowledge and action. In using the metaphor of Jesus as a parable of God, McFague asserts that Jesus was the one who both knew the will of God and did the will of God. Metaphor, for McFague, is a way of knowing that involves action. For her, parables are important because they connect knowledge of God's will and the command to act in accordance with God's will. The command to "go and do likewise" in the parable is an intrinsic part of the parable itself. Therefore, theology and ethics, action and reflection, cannot be separated.

The metaphor of the world as God's body, which McFague favors in her 1993 "thought experiment," allows her to speak of embodied knowing and doing. This organic model of the universe provides hope, according to McFague, precisely because "embodiment may move us not only toward a more biocentric and cosmocentric perspective but also toward a more inclusive sense of justice for the needs of *all* (embodied) human beings."[45] As in liberation theology perspectives, the epistemological assumption that knowledge comes *through* praxis leads McFague to make immediate claims on human ethical behavior. "In an embodiment ethic," she writes, "hungry, homeless, or naked human beings have priority over the spiritual needs of the well-fed, well-housed, well-clothed sisters and brothers."[46] Herein lies the strength of McFague's model of the world as God's body. It gives us hope, and it gives us something to do.

Another white feminist theologian whose contributions are helpful is Carter Heyward. In *Our Passion for Justice: Images of Power, Sexuality, and Liberation* (1984), Carter Heyward describes her view of the role of the theologian in speaking of God. She uses the metaphors of "explorers," "diggers," "artists," and "reformers" to describe the task of feminist theologians. She writes,

> We do not "do theology" for the sake of "doing theology" but rather because we who experience God moving within, between, and among us believe that we must try to articulate what it is that we experience, in order to point to and lift up the presence of God here and now and in order to live and speak *in* God, *through* God, and *by* God, rather than simply *about* God.[47]

This description of the role of the theologian points to Heyward's conviction that theology is not done impartially, objectively, or speculatively. Feminist theology "is not a system of dogmas, doctrines, and categories, but rather a revelation of a living God whom we believe to be Godself defiant of all static, rigid categories and concepts."[48] Heyward explores this "defiant" God as she breaks with theological tradition and attempts to lay new groundwork for theological images of God.

Critical to understanding Heyward's epistemology is this rejection of the notion that the task of theology is to engage in objective, neutral, or abstract speculation about the nature of the divine. Heyward wants to distance herself from all speculative, objective, highly rationalistic attempts to understand God apart from God's relationship to humanity. She rejects notions of God's "set-apartness" and impassivity as "completely useless to us." This distant, unchanging "God" is not God but rather "a destructive controlling device, manufactured in the minds of men who have bent themselves low before ideals of changeless Truth, deathless Life, pure Spirit, perfect Reason, and other qualities often associated with the patriarchal 'God.'"[49] For similar reasons, Heyward also rejects the "God above God" or "Essential God-Man" of liberal Christianity, whom she also sees as unaffected by the realities of human joy and suffering.[50]

To counter a tradition that has devoted itself to classifying and catego-
rizing the attributes of God, Heyward offers the possibility that God is a
"surprise."[51] Heyward emphasizes that it is impossible for us to categori-
cally identify the nature of God as has been attempted in classical theological investigation. Instead, she advises that "God is warning us that we had
best not try to find our security in any well-defined concept or category of
what is Godly—for the minute we believe we are into God, God is off again
and calling us forth into some unknown place."[52] The importance of this
theological statement is that it does not simply refer to traditional ways of
doing theology, but rather it speaks of an experience of discovering God in
unlikely places. Heyward cautions that if we look for God in earthquakes
and fires, God will be found in the silence of meditation, or if we seek
out God in silent meditation, "God will be shouting protests on the
street. . . ."[53] The locus of theological investigation is not rooted in scripture or in text, but rather in the unlikely, surprising places in which an
enigmatic God manifests Godself in the world.

This "surprising" aspect of God is developed in a section of *Our Passion
for Justice* called "The Enigmatic God." Here she depicts a God who cannot
easily be pinned down, one who resists our efforts to define, characterize, or
label God once and for all time. God's answer to Moses about the name by
which Moses should refer to God was simply "I AM WHO I AM." Heyward
suggests the possibility that this statement, rather than being a riddle, could
perhaps be a simple, straightforward statement of God's refusal to conform
to our expectations. It is not easy for us, suggests Heyward, to accept this
elusive quality of God. In her words, "I AM WHO I AM is hard to bear."[54]

Not unlike McFague's "thought experiments," Heyward's method is one
of tentative experimentation. Heyward uses a technique of imagination and
hypothesis to wonder about the nature of God. She often invites the reader
to "re-image" God or Jesus in a new way. For example, Heyward asks us to
question notions we have of the unchanging, timeless, absolute character of
God. For the biblical basis of her challenge to this traditional concept of
God, she looks to the relationship between Jesus and God. She begins by
noting that while Jesus grows, God also grows. "God is parent in that God is
resource for Jesus' growth in power. But it may be equally appropriate . . . to
image God as Jesus' child, whose growth in the world Jesus facilitates."[55]
Heyward then asks us to "re-image" a God who is "touched, healed,
instructed, rebuked, and comforted by Jesus."[56] This methodological technique is aimed at getting us to open new possibilities to imagine. It is striking in that it seeks to cut through centuries of church dogma that make the
idea of "touching" God seem blasphemous.

At other times, Heyward simply raises questions without providing
definitive answers. For example, in writing of our understanding of God,
Heyward asks:

But what if:

In seeking to feel better, we are avoiding God's moving us toward growth?

In seeking God always as light we are missing God as darkness?

In avoiding change, we are missing God's plea for us to move into the wonder of some unknown possibility?

In perceiving God as our Father, we are refusing to be nurtured at the breast of God our Mother?

In seeing God only in our own colors, shapes . . . we are blinded to God's presence in others' colors . . . ?

In looking for God in the magnanimous . . . we are overlooking God in the most unremarkable places . . . ?

In perceiving God always in that which is sacred . . . we are failing to see God in the secular . . . ?[57]

Rather than making assertions, Heyward, like McFague, employs the technique of asking questions, drawing upon the imagination, raising possibilities, opening opportunities for understanding God in new ways. This linguistic and methodological technique, in part rooted in a "hermeneutic of suspicion" that enables her to ask questions not only of the biblical text but of traditional theological doctrine, is characteristic of those feminist and liberationist theologians who understand their current challenge as more to raise questions than to provide neat answers.

A second assumption that informs Heyward's methodology stems from a rejection of the dualistic understandings of reality that have informed much of traditional theology. She feels such language has hindered our understanding of God. For Heyward, God is not light as opposed to darkness, God is not life as opposed to death, God is not rational as opposed to irrational, God is not Father as opposed to Mother, God is not spirit as opposed to flesh, and neither is God spiritual as opposed to sexual. Heyward criticizes those theologies that propose this dualistic split in the nature of God, for in them spirituality is used "as a weapon employed tenaciously against death, darkness, chaos, woman, and sexuality."[58]

A third explicit assertion about her theological method in this early work is that the hermeneutical norm for her use of source materials and the authority granted to them is the love of one's neighbor as oneself.[59] Using this methodological principle, Heyward admits certain biblical source materials and rejects others, attempting to establish "what is 'of God' and what is not."[60] Heyward later expands this notion of love of neighbor as she grants justice a normative status in theology. For Heyward justice is understood as "right-relation between and among people, relation of mutual benefit, created by mutual effort."[61] Theological resources such as the Bible, doctrine, the field of systematics, church discipline, and polity are to be measured by the extent to which they are useful in bringing about justice and ending oppression. In fact, all doctrine and belief must be subject to the normacy of justice. This hermeneutical norm is rooted in Heyward's concept of a "just god/ess."[62] For Heyward, God is the source of justice, resource for justice, maker of justice, and justice itself.

A fourth methodological principle concerns the centrality of praxis. She writes, "I am seeking solidarity—good strong relation—in Christian praxis, if not in theological language. What we do together is more critical than whether we recite the same creed."[63] Here praxis is given greater importance than theological assertion. The focus of theological investigation on God, then, is earthbound for Heyward. She writes that theology "is not a cerebral exercise; it is a passionate effort to express and evoke human activity. Its appropriate focus is earth, not heaven. And it is not about God as God is in Godself, but rather about us as we experience God."[64] A "here and now" urgency can be heard between the lines of Heyward's writing as she attempts to speak of the need for immediate action to bring about mutuality in relation.

This fourth methodological distinction can be seen in the following words:

> I submit that *all* constructive theology is done in the praxis of life experience and that feminist theology pays special attention to life experience in sexist society. The experience of sexism provides the ground on which we stand as we reflect on, and articulate, theological meaning and value.[65]

Similar to other white feminist theologians, such as Daly and Ruether, Heyward places the experience of sexism at the center of her theological analysis. This starting place will be critiqued by those who argue that this type of analysis tends to mask the different experiences of white women and women of color and those of middle-class and poor women, an argument that will be examined in detail later.

A fifth methodological presupposition characteristic of Heyward's "critical theology of liberation" is that she makes the claim that it must be done on the basis of a "hermeneutic of suspicion."[66] Here Heyward cites Juan Luis Segundo as the main articulator of a hermeneutic of suspicion in liberation theology. However, she adds her own questions to those posed by Paul Ricoeur, Segundo, and others in reading critically behind the text. Heyward makes the claim that

> feminist theology moves beyond the main streams of Latin American liberation theology . . . in explicating the physical human body as absolutely central to the "hermeneutical circle." All experiencing of

our experiences . . . [is] done in relation to how we experience, feel, think about, and *live* as bodies.[67]

In claiming the importance of embodied theology, Heyward demonstrates that she shares similar concerns with some of the women authors of Latin American liberation theology, who, as we will see, also explore the importance of the body in doing theology.

Sixth, Heyward claims that body-centered, feminist theology is sensual/sexual in nature. The sensual and sexual spirituality she describes is rooted in "our experiences of our body-yearnings/feelings/needs for relatedness/connectedness with other participants in the world."[68] This point is key in understanding one of the major metaphors she uses for God's activity as yearning for relationship with humanity.

Following her notion of the centrality of the body in doing theology, Heyward makes a seventh methodological claim, that "feminist theology is fundamentally relational, . . . a broadly *ecumenical* enterprise."[69] This understanding of the relational aspect of doing theology is related to her idea that all striving for meaning in a feminist context must be done in community. Speaking of the corporate nature of theological reflection, Heyward writes, "The new meanings bestowed upon old words are fruits of corporate search and struggle. If these words release some power, it is not because they are mine. It is because they are *ours*."[70] Here Heyward's thinking is much more in line with Latin American liberation theologians than her white feminist counterparts in the United States, whose theological reflection has been more individualistic in nature. Like U.S. Hispanic and Latin American women doing theology, Heyward insists that theological work derives its meaning from the struggles of the community.

I have detailed some of the epistemological and methodological principles governing the work of McFague and Heyward because their conceptions of God and humanity are directly tied to these assumptions about epistemology and methodology. Similarly, it is important to see how their notions about the relationship of knowledge and action and their assertions about the role of experience, for example, play into their conceptions of God and ethical human behavior.

McFague's Relational God

In her second major work, *Metaphorical Theology: Models of God in Religious Language* (1982), McFague begins constructing tentative, experimental models for understanding God, suggesting that relational models are the most appropriate. This argument "rests in understanding the root-metaphor of Christianity as a relationship, not a state of affairs, between God and human beings."[71] In looking for models of God other than the patriarchal model of God as father, McFague believes it possible to find models of God that are liberating to women. One important model she explores is the model of God as friend.

God as Friend

In constructing the model of God as friend, McFague wants to move not only beyond patriarchal metaphors for God, but also beyond parental images for God as the primary metaphor for understanding the relationship between God and humanity. McFague offers the model of God as friend somewhat tentatively, for she herself admits that the metaphor falters at the point of communicating the creative powers of God. While God is the source of our life, "friends are not the source of each other's lives."[72] I am inclined to disagree with McFague on this point, for it seems to me that as friends, we can indeed be sources, wellsprings of love and God's creative power in each other's lives.[73] She also cites other limitations of the metaphor: it is too individualistic, it does not adequately express the leadership capacity of God, it is unable to fully express the dimension of awe necessary in explaining human relatedness to God, and it may not express the depth of God in a way similar to Tillich's "being-itself." Despite these limitations, McFague is interested in experimenting with the metaphor of God as friend, an enterprise that seems highly worthwhile.

McFague points to biblical authority for the model of God as friend. She finds support for this notion in the Book of Isaiah, where Abraham is referred to as God's friend (Isa. 41:18); in Jesus' saying that there is no greater love than laying down one's life for one's friends (John 15:13); and in Jesus' reference to the Son of man as the friend of tax collectors and sinners (Matt. 11:19). She also cites passages referring to companionship, fellowship, and partnership with God as further evidence for the model of God as friend.[74] McFague is particularly drawn to this notion of God as friend, for this conception of relationality leaves human responsibility intact. Together, in friendship, God and humanity are engaged in acts of salvation and reconciliation. This God is the companion who calls us into a relationship of companionship with each other as we work within our own communities and with persons of differing nationalities, cultures, and backgrounds for the well-being of our world. This notion, that together in friendship we can participate in the salvation of our world, is one that holds great hope in the realm of multicultural religious dialogue.

God as Mother

In McFague's third work, *Models of God: Theology for an Ecological, Nuclear Age* (1987), she moves further in trying to find new models for

God. McFague seeks to experiment with alternative models to both the patriarchal image of God as father and to the imperialistic, triumphal models of God that she believes have contributed to the contemporary situation in which our entire world and life systems are threatened by nuclear warfare and ecological nightmares. Here McFague experiments with the image of God as mother. Making a distinction between that which has been culturally prescribed as "feminine" and that which is biologically female, McFague suggests that the metaphor of God as mother relies not upon stereotypes of maternal tenderness and sentimentality, but upon the female experience of gestation, birth, and lactation.[75] This mother God, represented in the concept of "agape," is engaged in the activity of creation and establishes an ethic of justice to care for the world. This world includes all her created beings and the entire ecological system as well.

In looking at McFague's model of God as mother, we need to be clear that McFague is aware of the limitations of the model. She is aware that not all women physically bear children, and she does not want to normalize such activity. In addition, she intends the female parental model not as a replacement for the father image of God, but as an alternative possibility that needs to be complemented with other nonparental images of God. She is particularly drawn to this metaphor because it holds the possibility of undercutting the dualistic split of mind and body that is central to much of Christian theology. The birth metaphor makes clear that God and the world are not of radically different natures. McFague also demonstrates the parental nature of love by insisting that a mother's love does not stop with birth. The creating God is also the judging God. Her ethics are those of justice, as she is concerned for all her human children and for the rest of creation as well. This "mother-judge" is actively engaged in the task of establishing justice in the here and now, an action crucial in this age in which nuclear and ecological disaster are not remote possibilities, but real threats to our world.

God as Lover

A third relational image McFague offers is that of God as lover. Here God is seen as lover not of particular individuals but of the world. The model of salvation provided by this image is of God the lover and the world as beloved participating together in salvation. This model guards against the passivity that McFague believes has led us to the brink of nuclear disaster. The primary activity of this lover God, who is represented as "eros," is that of salvation, with healing as the primary ethical task. This model, when seen in conjunction with other models of God, reinforces the relationality between God, humanity, and the world. No dualism between body and spirit is present. Instead, God is seen as the one who calls on humanity, God's beloved, to move toward creative, ethical solutions to today's real problems.

Carter Heyward and Relationality

Another aspect of the theme of relationality and God can be seen in Carter Heyward's work. In the opening lines of her dissertation, published as *The Redemption of God: A Theology of Mutual Relation* (1982), Carter Heyward writes of our yearning toward God and each other. She writes, "I want 'God'. And I will hold onto 'God' until you and I touch, until we are able to realize our power in intimate and immediate relation."[76] Here she hints at the theology of mutuality that her work hopes to construct. The God Heyward "wants" is a God connected to humanity, immediately available, and known often in the relationship between two human beings who share love.

In beginning to talk about Heyward's constructive proposals for God, it is important to note that Heyward's God project is writ quite large. Rejecting traditional understandings of God, she explains that the God whom she affirms is a feminist God. This God/dess

> is not a projected construct of hierarchical power, control, posses-
> sion, and jealousy. Such a God does not demand obedience for the
> sake of obedience. Such a God does not obliterate Canaanites, deni-
> grate sexuality, and despise women—in Israel, in the church, and in
> the so-called "pagan" glorifications of female power through the
> image of the Goddess. Such a God is as truly the Goddess as she is
> God, she who bears a close resemblance, for example, to Asherah
> (Canaanite Goddess of sexuality) as to the Hebrew God of righteous-
> ness, Yahweh.[77]

One aspect of Heyward's God project involves naming feminist images of God, as she believes that it is particularly important for women to discover these images. Among the feminist terms she uses for God are Mother, Sister, amazon, and wisdom. While Heyward finds it important to name God in female terms, she does not preclude the possibility of masculine images for God having value. An example of the ways that she offers a female view of God without denying the male aspects of God can be seen in the following ambiguous use of gender imagery. "We are here with God—our Baker-woman Mama, our tender Papa, our sister-brother-lover God who, when she comes, comes with power!"[78] Other relational terms she uses are Broth-er, Father, and Friend.[79] Using the term Friend for God enables Heyward to speak of "befriending" God. Because of the centrality of praxis in her theology, Heyward insists that the appropriate human response to God as friend is justice, for in the act of loving humanity, we befriend God. These are images with which Heyward feels comfortable, as opposed to more traditional images such as king, victor, husband, and judge.

God in Relation to the Poor, to Women, and to the Outcasts

In looking at available biblical materials to ascertain more about the nature of God, Heyward discovers a fourth category of images that speak of God as the God of justice. She cites biblical notions of God's justice for the poor, for women, and for outcasts.[80] As has been mentioned, one important aspect of Heyward's work is to find names for God that are female-positive, justice-oriented, and nonhierarchical in nature.

God's Relationality Transcending among Us

More important to a discussion of relationality in Heyward's thought is her departure from traditional understandings of God's transcendence. This discussion is critical to her thought and provides one of the most valuable resources for doing theology across the boundaries of difference. Heyward rejects any understanding of God's transcendence that posits an "otherly" dimension of God, that which is above and beyond human experience, at the expense of understanding God as vitally involved in human activity and in the world. Her rejection of traditional notions of transcendence is primarily based on the hierarchical power dynamic on which it rests. This dynamic, as described by Heyward, involves

> a god at the top, he who has been imaged in christian tradition as "Father, Son, and Holy Spirit," who before the worlds began, . . . knew the plot, how it would begin, how it would end. An "Almighty God," the essence of whose power is control. This is the "transcendent God" whom many of us reject, not in the first instance because he is portrayed as male, but rather because he . . . represents a use of power that neither we in our own lives today nor Western history itself from our perspective can testify to as creative or redemptive.[81]

According to Heyward, traditional notions of the trinity reside not in the reality of a God who would call us into mutual relation with one another, but rather in "a projection of men who are stuck—concretized in their experience of what it means to rule and be ruled."[82] Because of these male projections about God, "so too is their god stuck, sealed fast by the limits of particular cultural movements and assumptions that have been historically shaped by male domination, white supremacy, and economic exploitation."[83]

Heyward's critique is aimed at a hierarchical power dynamic purported to be essential to the very nature of God, a dynamic that in turn fosters oppression in the world, as subordinates are controlled by those who presumably know best. Heyward rejects outright this hierarchical understanding of God, men, women, children, slaves, and the animal world in descending order of power; traditional understandings of transcendence are rejected as well because they foster this type of hierarchical thinking, which has done little to remedy oppression in the social, economic, or political realm. Therefore, the "Almighty God" must be replaced with an image of God as the "power of mutual relation."[84]

In addition, Heyward critiques the dualism on which traditional understandings of God's immanence and God's transcendence are based. She rejects the notion of God's immanence as that aspect of God we can experience and comprehend, and God's transcendence as the unknowable, mysterious "God beyond God". Instead, she offers the concept of a God *who is at once immanent and transcendent*, crossing the boundaries of racial, gender, and class differences, among others.

In contrast to earlier conceptions of transcendence, Heyward offers a new definition of transcendence based on the metaphor of transcendence as a bridge. She defines transcendence as the experience "in the constancy of God's 'crossing over' between and among us."[85] Heyward explains:

> To transcend means, literally, to cross over. To bridge. To make connections. To burst free of particular locations. A truly transcendent God knows the bounds of no human life or religion. Such a God is not contained within holy scriptures or religious creedal formulations. No one person, no group of people, has a hot-line to a god who is actually transcendent, for God is too constantly, too actively, moving, crossing over from my life to yours, and from ours to theirs, to become our source of special privilege.[86]

God does not belong to any particular individual or group, but rather is seen as the power that brings all living beings—human and nonhuman alike—into relation. Transcendence is that aspect of divinity that "drives us, yearns for us, moves in us and by us and with us in the coming to know and love ourselves as persons fundamentally in relation, not alone."[87]

A Relational Trinity: God as Lover, Beloved, Spirit of Love

Heyward's notion of the intrinsic relationality of God leads her to a critique of traditional patriarchal language in the symbolism of the trinity.

She believes that the key to understanding the trinity lies in the relationality of the three persons. She rejects out of hand the traditional understanding of trinity as Father, Son, and Holy Spirit, in part because of the power dynamics discussed above and in part because of its moorings in patriarchal language and hierarchy. Heyward describes the metaphor of the trinity as "a homophilial/homoerotic image of relations between males."[88] Despite the thoroughly sexist nature of trinitarian theology, however, Heyward finds a possibility for feminist theology in the impulse of relationality behind these patriarchal images. Speaking of the trinity as "an intuition of ultimacy in relation," Heyward finds cause for hope in proclaiming a God who is "internally relational."[89] Heyward takes this notion of relationality at the core of God's being so seriously that she is able to state that "God is nothing except in relation."[90]

Thus, rather than rejecting the notion of trinity altogether, Heyward experiments with the possibility of rethinking this doctrine in new ways. One of the ways she experiments with language about the trinity is to use expressions such as "God the Lover, the Beloved, the spirit of Love that binds the Lover to her Beloved."[91] Heyward's relational trinity is ". . . the creative, liberating, and sanctifying Spirit that draws us together in right relation."[92] Heyward explores this type of language in order to find deeper meaning in the trinity.

One of the central aspects of this relationship between God and humanity is that God does not remain untouched in the relationship. Heyward contrasts her view of God with that of liberal Christianity, which she describes as offering a view of a benevolent deity who graciously gives to those in need but who remains untouched. The dynamic of relationality between God and humanity leads Heyward to develop a view of God that has certain commonalities with the God of process theology.[93] God is the one who "calls us in the ongoing process of creation itself."[94] Heyward offers a view of God "who reaches and is reached, touches and is touched, empowers and is empowered."[95] In the tradition of other liberation theologies, Heyward views God as not impartial to the victim, the sufferer, and the oppressed in any relational transaction. This God "is from the beginning, and will be forever, on the side of the suffering and the poor."[96] The suffering that we endure, in fact, is described as a reflection of God's own suffering. In addition, this God needs us just as we need God, for a relationship with a lover calls for mutuality. Like all lovers, God and humanity need each other to engage in the act of love.

Relational Christology

While no attempt will be made here to enter into a detailed analysis of Heyward's christology, I will make two observations. First, Heyward rejects traditional notions of the divinity of Jesus, on the grounds that traditional trinitarian language has fostered a kind of "Christolatry" that does little to promote God's love on earth. In particular, she sees as "necessarily destructive to most people in the world . . . the insistence that Jesus Christ is Lord and Savior of all."[97] Christianity has used Jesus' name in blasphemous ways by promoting, rationalizing, justifying, and blessing capitalism, racism, sexism/heterosexism, and anti-Semitism. In western Christian society, "Christian" values serve to keep the wealthy in power and to punish those who would challenge the status quo. Thus, like Delores Williams and others who challenge a christology that promotes notions of suffering servanthood, Heyward rejects christological teachings that result in the disempowerment of struggling peoples.

While Heyward rejects traditional, orthodox christology, she is careful to distinguish herself from those feminists who have little place for Jesus in their theologies. In fact, Heyward feels it is important not to lapse into a natural or universal religion without the "particular Christ."[98] For Heyward, the work of feminist theologians is not to point to a distant Christ of the past, but rather to the present human community in which Christ's spirit is present. She writes, "As I speak . . . of the human commitment to justice and compassion, I literally am speaking of Christ."[99]

A second significant observation about Heyward's christology is her reference to religious pluralism. Heyward rejects traditional christological claims that assert that Christians have a special relationship to God which others do not. This assumption Heyward rejects outright. In one of her essays, "The Spark Is God," Heyward speaks of a God transcending all, living and breathing in every human and living creature. The "spark of God" resides in all who are passionate about human well-being.[100] Her doctrine of election rejects any notions that Christianity can be seen as somehow better than any other religion, or that certain Christians are inherently more treasured in God's eyes than others. Heyward writes of God's elect as all of us.

> God chose us all, Christians and Jews and Moslems and wicca and other so-called pagan peoples of all races and nations; both genders, men and women who are single, married, lesbian, gayman, heterosexual, celibate, sexually active; in good health and in poor health. God continues to choose us all.[101]

Embodiment

Related to the theme of relationality is the theme of embodiment. In *Models of God*, McFague's constructive efforts to "remythologize" the relationship between God and the world, she is careful to include the nonhuman as well as human world. The first metaphor with which she experiments is the idea of the world as God's body. This new interpretation of the resurrection allows for the possibility of the restoration of a sacramental understanding of the world. Using a methodology that intentionally ponders the possibilities of new images, McFague asks,

> If the world is imagined as self-expressive of God, if it is a "sacrament"—the outward and visible presence or body—of God, if it is not an alien other over against God but expressive of God's very being, then, how would God respond to it and how should we?[102]

McFague is aware that the metaphor of the world as God's body, like the metaphor of God as friend, is not without its limitations. If classical theological God language is too abstract, removed, and dependent on a transcendent God, then this model seems to lean in the direction of concentrating too heavily on God's immanence. McFague prefers to err in this direction. The model of the world as God's body is also open to the criticism that it is pantheistic, a notion McFague refutes, claiming that God is not reduced to that which we speak of metaphorically. God is always more.[103]

Despite its limitations, this metaphor of the world as God's body, as a living sacrament, has much to offer. It is rooted in the biblical story that calls on humanity to be the people of God. It is seen in New Testament images of the Eucharist, in which the bread is given as Christ's body. It is recalled in the image of the resurrection, where the presence of God in Christ is promised to be among us. It is a metaphor that can offer a healthy alternative to the anti-body stance of much of Christian theology.

McFague's embodied language for God is particularly useful for women, who have been taught to dislike our bodies, often going to great lengths to reduce all or parts of them in size, mask them behind makeup, wrap them in uncomfortable clothing, or stuff them in ridiculous shoes, all for the benefit of the fashion gods. In speaking of the world as God's body, McFague offers women the possibility that we might learn to love our bodies, regardless of size or shape, simply because they are, literally, of God.

Perhaps most important, the metaphor of the world as God's body offers possibilities for reflection on the relationship between humanity and other living creatures, the ecological health of the planet, the consequences of nuclear and other forms of war, the use of natural resources, and technological development. It also holds up the possibilities for us to rethink our connection to others who are different from us, whether on account of geography, politics, race, gender, or sexual orientation. Within this image of the world as God's body is the possibility of appreciating differences, understanding the need for greater cooperation among nations, and hope for moving the world toward God's justice.

God Embodied in Sexuality

Heyward's theology offers another example of the theme of embodiment through her assertion that God is Lover.[104] Heyward takes very seriously the creative moment and God's participation in creation. Heyward then shows that creation, in part, involves sexuality. Speaking of the moment of creation, Heyward says that "In that cosmic moment pulsating in possibility, God breathed into space and, groaning in *passion* and pain and hope, gave birth to creation."[105] Sexuality provides the creative impetus, the power, and the yearning to draw near to another and to bring about the justice that is in the best interests of those who most need it.

While Heyward does not label it as such, she leaves the impression that it is almost sinful to be unaware of one's sexuality, for in one's sexuality one is drawn near to others: "To be out of touch with our sexuality is to be literally cut off—physically, emotionally, spiritually, politically—from our remarkable and potent capacity to co-create, co-redeem, and co-bless the world."[106] Furthermore, being out of touch with our sexuality cuts us off from our strength and from God's movement in the world. In looking at Heyward's argument, it is clear that her ideas of God as a God of sexuality and relation have implications for her notions of praxis and justice. God is Lover, and we, too, are called to be lovers, "making love," in Heyward's words, in the streets, the board room, the office, as well as in the bedroom. Just as God is creator, lover, and bridge builder, so too we are called to "transcendence" as lovers. This anthropology of transcendence is one of Heyward's gifts to her readers, in that she calls us to bridge difference, creating respect among those who may be of different gender, racial, ethnic, age, or class backgrounds.

While Heyward's frank talk of the sexuality of God may be surprising, it follows quite logically from her desire to have an "embodied" theology that takes seriously the human condition. Similar to Sallie McFague, who proclaims the world as God's body, Heyward argues that "our hands are God's hands in the world."[107] In a nearly literal sense, she believes that human hands and hearts are God's hands and God's heart acting in the world in the name of liberation. The opposite side of this argument is that human suffering is God's suffering. When humans hurt, God hurts. In her view, our suffering and our tears are also God's pain and tears. Not only does God experience pain and suffering when we do, but God also experiences joy when we rejoice. Thus, she is able to assert that "our sexualities, our expressions of sexuality, our lovemaking in this world, is God's own expressiveness, God's own lovemaking, in history."[108] We "are embodied bearers of the erotic/God with one another, as she crosses over among us."[109] Thus her reliance on the notion of God's transcendence appears once again in the relationship of erotic friendship as well as in nonerotic relationships of mutuality.

While some of her thinking on God, the body, and sexuality is influenced by Latin American liberation theologians' concern for human physical and material well-being, other aspects of her thought stem from her own personal experience as a lesbian Episcopal priest. Because she had to come to terms with the church's teachings on sexuality and homosexuality in the process of making a decision to make her own sexual orientation public, Heyward offers keen insights into the connections between body, God, and lesbian sexuality. She makes the claim that Christian homophobia is rooted in the church's failure to comprehend the "radical transcendence" of God as she who carries us beyond ourselves into relationality with others. Hence, we have not been able to experience the stirrings of sexuality, and of lesbian sexuality in particular, as the very stirrings of God.

Having established the groundwork that all sexuality is of God, and that the Creator God is a God of yearning toward the other, it is easy for Heyward to make the claim that lesbian sexuality is of God. Here she draws on her concept of God as I AM WHO I AM; we are created in God's image to be who we are. "Who she is" is lesbian in God.

God's Power among Us

In looking at the theme of God's power and empowerment in the thought of Sallie McFague, her understanding of parable as metaphor is central. In claiming Jesus as the parable of God, McFague connects epistemology with ethical decision making. Jesus' parables are a way to know God. They are not seen merely as interesting stories but rather as a form of communication that invites the hearer to respond to the call for justice making. Parables are concerned not primarily with what we know but with what we are "becoming in our lives," once again underscoring the processive nature of the journey toward knowing God.[110] The object of a parable, then, is that the hearer be moved to new insight *and* action. Here McFague's epistemology is reminiscent of Latin American liberation theologian Gustavo Gutiérrez, who insists that "to know God is to do justice."[111]

The notion of empowerment to do justice is embedded in McFague's epistemological assumptions about the nature of the parable. God's word in Jesus' parable empowers us to act. Through the parable we come to know God, which for McFague necessitates action for justice.

A second way in which Sallie McFague treats the theme of empowerment can be seen in her latest work, *The Body of God* (1993), which is subtitled "an ecological theology." Here she departs in an important way from her earlier work, which she had titled *Metaphorical Theology*. McFague's

interest in addressing the ecological disaster that she feels our planet is facing leads her to a preference for the model of the world as God's body. In
this model, God as spirit breathes life into the body of God, which is the
universe and all forms of creation. Her metaphor of God as spirit avoids
the androcentrism of earlier models by emphasizing that all creatures rely,
metaphorically, on the breath of God. Particularly important, she high-
lights the human responsibility of caring for the planet. McFague's notion
of the world as God's body is no mere metaphor, suggested because of its
cognitive appeal. McFague intends to suggest that in the very notion of the
world as God's body is a powerful, creative force that, if we pay attention,
can bring us to responsible action in caring for our world. This model
engenders hope for addressing the survival of the human, plant, and animal species, as well as the rest of the universe.

God as Power-in-Relation

Another important constructive contribution of white feminist theology to the theme of empowerment can be seen in Carter Heyward's treatment of God as power-in-relation. She is not interested in the God "who
batters like a ramrod through the priestly pages of Leviticus and on into the
misogynist diatribes of Jerome, Martin Luther, and John Paul II."[112] For
Heyward, God's power is present among us, drawing us into right relation
with each other. This call to right relation was made by Jesus.

> To be in Christ is to share this power of God which drives toward jus-
> tice, the moral act of love between people, black and white, Jew and
> Christian, rich and poor. To be in Christ is to live dangerously . . . to
> be in Christ is to live with passion . . . to be with Christ is to realize
> that God's relational *dunamis* is *the* authority under which all other
> authorities—laws, Scriptures, traditions, governments, religions,
> and institutions—rise and fall.[113]

The power that goes forth from Jesus is *dunamis*, which Heyward describes
as "raw, spontaneous, unmediated power."[114] This power is capable of righting wrongs, of speaking against traditions that benefit the privileged, and of
bringing about right relations among people. Hinting at her position on
religious pluralism, Heyward writes that the power of God does not belong
to any particular group. It is "never a 'possession' of Jesus, you, me, the
United States, the Christian church, or the Ayatollah Khomeini."[115] God's
power does not belong to Jesus or even to Christianity. In fact, for Heyward,
God's power is not something to be possessed but rather quite the opposite.
God's power is to be passed on.

There are several significant aspects of Heyward's understanding of God's power. First, God's power is not a characteristic defining Godself but rather Godself-in-relation. This power is, in Heyward's view, transcendent: reaching beyond Godself and beyond individuals into community.

Second, as mentioned above, when dealing with the issue of God's power, Heyward is careful to articulate an understanding that God's power belongs to all people rather than to just Christian people. In part because of her understanding of personal freedom and community responsibility, she calls for "a different way of perceiving who God is among us and what God is doing."[116] This "different way" is key to her views of religious pluralism. Contrary to what might be termed the "traditional way," in which God's power is perceived to be either uniquely or at least best displayed in the Christian faith, Heyward find's God's power at work in the universe in human and nonhuman entities. The ethic of justice, which is more important to Heyward than traditional creedal understandings, leads her beyond the limits of Christianity to an appreciation for the ways that God works in all religions. According to Heyward,

> the personal (*my* business) becomes transpersonal (*our* business); and the transpersonal and the personal universalism become *im*personal in the sense that god is Godself moving and growing throughout the universe, related no more to any one of us than to all others.[117]

A third aspect of Heyward's concept of God's power is that she makes a direct connection between the nature of God and humanity; loving, reaching out, respecting the earth and all creation are the prerogatives of *both* God and humanity. This view of God's power as that which empowers others to do justice is directly related to Heyward's methodological presupposition about the centrality of praxis. Theological reflection on God is done in the context of justice work. This "high" anthropology gives her the confidence to proclaim in her liturgical work that the power of God belongs to humanity.[118] God's power, then, leads us into justice making that is both cooperative and co-creative. It moves people to work together in solidarity. God's power here, rather than being described as the "raw *dunamis*" above, is that which leads us to be "vulnerable," "touched," and "open," words not typically evoked when we think of power.

Heyward uses the concept of incarnation to connect her view of God as the power that moves us into right relation and her ethical emphasis on praxis as the human response to being empowered by God. As co-creators with God, we "are participants in ongoing incarnation, bringing god to life in the world."[119] This view of God and humanity in partnership is one that Heyward fully accepts. Her understanding of the incarnation has nothing to do with abstract dogma, but rather with a new deciphering of the meaning of the incarnation. As Heyward writes,

> God is here/now. She is no absent deity, no God away in God's heaven, but rather the power of *actual* love among us. This is our God incarnate. Our God in flesh. Our God with us, among us, between us. God our sister. God our mother. God our father. God our brother. God our friend. God our lover.[120]

For Heyward, God's love is experienced in relation to others—family, friends, and lovers. God is the source of all relationality between created beings. Linguistically, it is important to note that Heyward employs an ambiguous semantic unit in this description of God. Without the copula "is," we do not have the clear statement, "God is our sister," or "God is our friend." Without the simile "like" or "as," we cannot assume that she intends the meaning, "God is like our sister," or "God is like our friend." One cannot help but notice the somewhat striking semantic skeleton of the descriptive phrases, "God our mother. God our father. God our brother. God our friend. God our lover." One is left to puzzle whether Heyward intends metaphor, or simile, or whether perhaps in some literal sense she means to say that God is actually *among us*, *in us*, and in our relationships.

Thus for Heyward, the circle is complete—God is the Empowering One; we are called both to be empowered and to empower others. To love God is to do justice, borrowing a refrain from Latin American liberation theology. There can be no separation of epistemology and praxis, faith and justice. What we know of God we know through our experience with humans who struggle. To be faithful and to love God is to act as an agent of empowerment into right relation. God's power is love. Our power is the same.

Characteristics in Common

Several characteristics link the theological explorations of white feminist women as they think about God. One characteristic of white feminist theology has been that it seeks to find new ways to speak of God. Language, metaphor, and symbol are all opened up for renaming. For Carter Heyward the importance of "the words with which we express our experiences of God (our theological imagery) cannot be overstated."[121] Here, she follows in the tradition of Mary Daly, and others, who have pointed to the necessity of women naming their experience and understandings. Language is not politically neutral, but rather serves as a tool of empowerment or oppression. For Heyward, language about God serves as a source of empowerment for women. In an effort to rename God, white feminist theology has rejected the removed, abstract, transcendent God of traditional theology and has indicated a preference for thinking of God's immanence. Daly began the effort by creating new images of God with the verbs "Sparking" and "Spinning," fanning the flames of women's revolution. Ruether has proposed the word "God/dess" to keep ever-present before us the idea that God is not male. McFague has a somewhat related interest in developing a variety of nonpatriarchal models for God. Somewhat differently, Heyward redefines the term "transcendence" in radically new ways to include immanence.

The development of new God language shows the methodological similarity in the work of these women as well, that is the experimental nature of the naming of God. Like McFague, Heyward argues for a tentativeness when speaking of God. The enigmatic God, after all, is a "surprise." Any attempt to rigidly define God will be met with God "defiant." McFague's God resists human attempts at static descriptions, for God is God Becoming. Each author has continued to experiment with new symbols.

A third commonality is concern about the connection between God and christology. Many of these women are concerned in different ways with the problem of how a male savior can be redemptive for women. Daly answers the question by claiming that women must go outside the Christian patriarchal tradition to find new being in sisterhood. Ruether rejects any notion of particularity for the maleness of Christ and emphasizes instead the humanity of Christ. McFague is interested in looking at alternate language to describe the incarnation of God. Heyward is interested primarily in finding the spirit of Jesus alive and well among justice-seeking people who work for right relation.

Fourth, the theme of relationality is fundamental for these white feminist theologians. Whereas McFague uses the metaphors of God as mother, lover, and friend and the metaphor of the world as God's body to illumine the relationality of God, Heyward moves toward an understanding of God as power-in-relation. Her definition of transcendence allows her to understand God as she who bridges. This bridging God reaches beyond herself to humanity and calls on humanity to draw near to each other in acts of justice.

Fifth, white feminist theology has a concern for embodied theology. McFague's notion of the world as God's body and her metaphor of God as lover is paralleled in Heyward's God of sexuality, the lover and beloved who draw near to each other. Both writers are interested in erasing all traces of dualistic thinking that place the body at odds with the spirit or the mind, particularly because women have been most often injured by this split.

Sixth, white feminist theology explores the themes of God's empowerment in women's lives. For McFague, Jesus as the parable of God empowers those who have ears to hear to "go and do likewise." Thus we are empowered to act out the justice called for in Jesus' teachings. In addition, McFague's understanding of the world as God's body offers women God's very own strength as a resource for bringing about justice. Heyward's treatment of the theme of empowerment is combined with her emphasis on relationality, for God is power-in-relation. God's power is our power to effect justice. As with McFague, for Heyward, the role of praxis is important, for they both insist that knowledge of God and doing God's will are inextricably related. While this theme of action and reflection is not as well developed in white feminist theology as in Latin American liberation theology, it is nonetheless an important concept. Here Heyward's concept of transcendence is particularly useful, for in taking up our call to be bridge builders among differing peoples, we reflect the bridge-building God. Based on her theology of radical transcendence, her understanding of God's power as empowerment of humanity for right relation, and her ethical priority of praxis, Heyward calls Christians into a community that can wrestle with its differences. Confronting difference and making a commitment to justice are central for Heyward:

> I am convinced that our future as people on this planet rests on our commitments to reach over the walls that divide us—white women and black women, Jewish women and Christian women, women and men—not by pretending that we do not live different lives and not by attempting to dilute or diminish the structures, practices, and beliefs peculiar to our people; not by seeking false peace, but rather by addressing one another, listening to one another, and committing ourselves—without "losing" ourselves—to a common task, the making of justice in the world.[122]

Heyward's notion of God's transcendence is a powerful tool for those interested in multicultural work, for the primary work of Heyward's God is to bring us together. This God is "She who crosses over among us. He who invites us to a meal from which no one is excluded. They who pull us beyond the boundaries of our own skins into solidarity with the whole creation."[123]

Before leaving this chapter, it is important to remember Audre Lorde's critique of Mary Daly, for in remembering this early critique we can be intentional about the need to take seriously issues of race in our conceptions of God. By offering white, European goddess images without suggesting the possibility of their African counterparts, Daly offered white women a mirror image in which to see themselves while claiming to represent all of "women's experience." Lorde's criticism is instructive to all white feminists doing theology:

> To imply ... that all women suffer the same oppression simply because we are women, is to lose sight of the many varied tools of patriarchy. It is to ignore how those tools are used by women without awareness against each other.[124]

Lorde then clarifies the specific tool to which she is referring, the patriarchal tool of racism:

> The oppression of women knows no ethnic nor racial boundaries, true, but that does not mean it is identical within those boundaries. Nor do the reservoirs of our ancient power know these boundaries, either. To deal with one without even alluding to the other is to distort our commonality as well as our difference. For then beyond sisterhood, is still racism.[125]

In looking at the constructive theology being developed by white feminists, it is clear that a consciousness of the imperative to deal with issues of racism has begun to grow. Many white feminist authors are cognizant of this need and make an effort to include the category of race along with other forms of oppression. One example is Carter Heyward's critique of Christian assumptions about the goodness of "light," which "shines above 'dark' (the 'tainted' and 'unholy,'), associated with darker skin pigment as well as with female sexuality and bleeding."[126] In passages such as these Heyward clearly calls for white feminists to wrestle with a biblical tradition that has had profound racist implications.

The work of Sharon Welch is another example of the efforts of white feminists to struggle with white privilege and racism. Her insistence that white women need to think of themselves as both oppressor and oppressed is helpful.[127] This dual identity serves as a reminder that privilege cannot be taken for granted. Unless we are always conscious that our lighter skin can grant or remove privilege in a racist world, our work will fail to be liberating.

Substantial work still needs to be done to develop constructive models for doing feminist theology that move us away from the reign of racism and toward the reign of God. Such critique of white feminist theology is not meant to discredit the work that Carter Heyward, Sharon Welch, Mary Hunt, Beverly Wildung Harrison, Ann Kirkus Wetherilt, Susan Thistlethwaite, and others are doing in solidarity with women of color. It is simply a reminder that the task of undoing the damage done by racism rooted in Christian theology should give us cause for concern for some time to come.

2

Hispanic and Latin American Women's Views of God

The Emergence of Hispanic and
Latin American Women's Theologies

IN TURNING to the thought of Hispanic women in the United States and Latin American women doing liberation theology, it may be informative to begin with a few broad characterizations of their work and with an explanation of how each of these is influenced by Peruvian Catholic theologian Gustavo Gutiérrez (1928–), one of the leading figures of Latin American liberation theology. Many women theologians recognize in Gutiérrez a willingness to attempt to understand the oppression of women. However, these women are much more likely than their male counterparts to recognize the depths of the patriarchal nature of church and society. Carmen Lora de Ames is an associate of Gutiérrez, editor of the journal *Páginas,* and project coordinator for the poor and working-class women's project sponsored by the Bartolomé de Las Casas Institute, an institute closely identified with Gutiérrez and liberation theology. As Ames notes, "The church must be understood within the context of a society that is obviously patriarchal; it is difficult to separate one from the other."[1]

The first broad characterization of the theologies of liberation undertaken by women theologians is that they seek to wrestle with the oppression of women inherent in Latin American and U.S. Hispanic societies. As Gutiérrez stresses the importance of the experience of the poor as a starting place for theology, it is logical for women doing theology to place their own experience at the center of theological reflection.

A second characterization of women's theologizing is that its creativity is born of struggle. According to Ames, "For women and for the poor in general, it is above all the experience of struggle that indicates their great creative capacity, and that continues to bring them out of oppression in order to attain liberation."[2] Gutiérrez's notion of the "irruption of the poor,"[3] or the poor becoming agents of their own destiny, informs the work of these women, as they attempt to demonstrate the particular ways that women respond creatively to the struggles of their lives. These creative solutions include everything from the development of cooperative farming techniques to soup kitchens to cooperative day care to the witness of the Mothers of the Disappeared in Chile. This creativity can also be seen in their theological reflections about God. Emphasizing creativity and rejecting a purely rationalistic approach to doing theology, Latin American women are free to use their intuition as well as reason in theological discourse.[4]

A third broad characterization of this theology includes the recognition that women *are* the poor. As Fryne Santisteban, of the Bartolomé de Las Casas Institute, has stated,

> Our approach focuses on women's class situation within the context of their community. It is important to understand these women's view of their oppression, because women frequently feel and express the daily situation of the poor more than men do.[5]

Implicit in this statement is the realization that male liberation theologians such as Gutiérrez initially focused on the category of "the poor" without fully understanding that, more often than not, it is women who are the poor and who suffer from the injustices of economic oppression. Particularly in his early work, Gutiérrez failed to recognize the explicit nature of women's economic oppression. Since then, he has come to appreciate the nature of women's oppression, and he has become a strong advocate in naming sexism as one central locus for liberation.

One final broad characterization of the work of Latin American women doing theology is their emphasis on the community of struggle. Argentinean theologian Nellie Ritchie, an ordained minister with a licentiate in theology who has served as superintendent of the Evangelical Methodist Church in Argentina, writes that the communitarian struggle is not one against men, but rather "on behalf of a true humankind: participatory, family-spirited, creative, and united in solidarity."[6] It was Gutiérrez, Leonardo Boff, and others who first spoke of the community of struggle, insisting on the priority of the people gathering together for theological reflection in ecclesial base communities and in other forums.[7] Women have continued in this tradition, often holding leadership positions in the ecclesial base communities. However, at the level of professional theologians, a distinction can be seen in the ways that theology is produced. Male theologians, such as Gutiérrez, Leonardo Boff, Juan Luis Segundo, and others, have come together in meetings such as those sponsored by CELAM, the Consejo Episcopal Latinoamericano (the Episcopal Council of Latin America). Particularly important were CELAM II (Medellín 1968) and CELAM III (Puebla 1979). Nonetheless, their work has remained largely an individualistic effort. Women theologians have taken the next step in trying to shape a truly communal theological reflection process, meeting when possible and drafting communal documents to address the needs of women.

It is important to note that women have long been active in the liberation movements of Latin America. Nevertheless, despite some twenty years of publishing Latin American liberation theology, women's voices are just beginning to be heard. Several factors are responsible for this void. First, the Latin American academy, like its counterpart in the rest of the world, has tended to hire and promote male theologians more often than women. Without access to the benefits of academia, such as funding for travel and conference presentations, it is much more difficult for women scholars to become known. In addition, the Roman Catholic church has been responsible for providing travel benefits to priests, while nuns have tended to be denied access to those financial resources that would make travel feasible. Even radical priests, including those exiled to Rome, such as Camilo Torres, have greater access to education than women religious. While in Rome or during periods of being "silenced," radical priests have had access to education and periods of sabbatical for writing and creative work. Third, the Latin American scholarly publishers have been slow to publish the works of women scholars, with the exception of the Costa Rican press Departamento Ecuménico de Investigaciones, which has been responsible for publishing the works of women. Finally, at least for U.S. audiences, our own monolingualism has contributed to our ignorance of much important untranslated work published in Spanish and Portuguese by Latin American women.

One would wish that the names of women writing Hispanic and Latin American liberation theologies were more familiar to U.S. audiences. These authors are important because they represent the key voices of women doing theology from U.S. Hispanic and Latin American perspectives, and they deserve a much wider hearing in the United States. Cuban-born Ada María Isasi-Díaz and Chicana activist Yolanda Tarango co-authored one of the first published efforts of Hispanic women in the United States doing liberation theology, *Hispanic Women: Prophetic Voice in the Church* (1988).[8] *Hispanic Women*, as well as Isasi-Díaz's later work *En La Lucha/In the Struggle: Elaborating a Mujerista Theology* (1993), are essential for understanding the contemporary situation among Hispanic women doing liberation theology in the United States.[9]

Of all the women writing theology in Latin America, Elsa Tamez is perhaps the best known in the United States. A Methodist from Mexico, Tamez represents a Protestant voice among the many Catholic women from Latin America doing liberation theology.[10] There are several others whose work will be considered more briefly. María Clara Lucchetti Bingemer is an important Brazilian lay Catholic theologian, professor of theology at the Pontifical Catholic University of Rio de Janeiro and at the Santa Ursula University.[11] Ivone Gebara, a Roman Catholic sister from Brazil and professor of philosophy and theology at the Theological Institute of Recife, has made important contributions, as has Ana María Bidegain, born in Uruguay and now a citizen of Colombia.[12]

Before beginning this treatment of the emergence of Hispanic and Latin American women's voices in liberation theology, some clarification of terms is in order. In a lecture on "Hispanic Women and the Church" at the Graduate Theological Union in Berkeley, California, Professor Gloria Loya outlined the difficulty of naming the Latina/Chicana/Hispanic women's community, by remarking that the word "Hispanic" is basically meaningless.[13] It is a term with which few women of Latin American descent identify. It is one imposed by the Anglo community and it is most often used by institutions. In her survey of some 170 "Hispanic" women in the San Francisco Bay area, only one referred to herself as Hispanic; almost none said they were Chicana or Mexican-American. Very few said they were North American or from the United States. Most women referred to themselves in terms of the country of birth of their parents. In studying the contributions of "Hispanic" women to a theology of liberation, the situation is even more complex. The context of those women writing from Latin America and those from within the United States is often quite different, a difference that has been characterized by Ada María Isasi-Díaz and Yolanda Tarango as a difference of physical survival in Latin America versus that of cultural survival in the United States.[14]

Ada María Isasi-Díaz, who previously described her work as "Hispanic women's liberation theology," now advocates the use of the term *mujerista* to describe the theological reflection of U.S. Hispanic women. This theology is described as follows:

> *Mujerista* theology articulates religious understandings of Hispanic women. It always uses a liberative lens, which requires placing oneself radically at the core of our own struggling pueblo. *Mujerista* theology brings together elements of feminist theology, Latin American liberation theology, and cultural theology—three perspectives that intertwine to form a whole.[15]

Until more satisfactory terms arise, I will follow the lead of Isasi-Díaz and Tarango in using the term "Hispanic" or "*mujerista*" when referring to women writing within the U.S. context and that of Elsa Tamez in using "Latin American" to refer to women writing out of a Mexican, Central American, or South American context.

As Mexican theologian Elsa Tamez points out in *Through Her Eyes*, and as Thomas and Marjorie "Margarita" Melville demonstrate in *Whose Heaven, Whose Earth?*, women have long been active in the liberation movements in Latin America.[16] Women have played critical roles in the literacy efforts spawned by the work of Brazilian educator Paulo Freire, in Catholic Action groups, in the teaching of youth about the problems of the poor, in their denunciation of ruthless governments, and in the ecclesial base communities. Ivone Gebara's essay on methodology, "Women Doing Theology in Latin America," outlines the ways that three types of women have been involved in doing theology in her context, which she defines as the northeast part of Brazil.[17] First, she names those poor women who do theology "from the simple fact of sharing life." This is not necessarily an activity of the erudite classes, for some of the women doing theology are illiterate. A second group of women doing theology are the women she terms "popular catechists," women who take on a "revolutionary role" in helping the people deal with contemporary issues. Third, Catholic sisters are engaged in bringing about radical changes in the ways that theology is done. A final category might include women trained as scholars or theologians in the traditional, technical sense. For Gebara, each of these groups of women can be understood as doing theology.

In *Hispanic Women: Prophetic Voice in the Church*, Isasi-Díaz and Tarango describe the context of theology in the life of U.S. Hispanic women. Because many Hispanic women have not felt empowered by the traditional church, they have tended to develop a spirituality that is independent of traditional church doctrine and practice. This has led to the development of a women's spirituality that is quite distinct from men's spirituality. It is clear in reading the divergent theologies of Latin American and Hispanic backgrounds that the role of women is central in both the teaching and nurturing of faith. Woman after woman describes how her mother and grandmother, rather than priest or church, have been the primary ones responsible for her faith. Christianity is spread through family and community at least as much, if not more, than through the institutional church. Beyond this observation lie several complex issues.

Although women comprise well over half of the membership of the Catholic church, the church has stubbornly refused to grant bona fide leadership opportunities to them. In response women have adopted two strategies. Some women simply do not attend church; instead they practice their faith in the home. This view is articulated by Adela, one of the women interviewed by Isasi Díaz and Tarango. "I do not go to mass. I practice my religion in my house, but going to mass, no. Nor do I send my children. . . . It is because the priests have hurt me so much that I do not believe them."[18] Lupe expresses a similar dislike for priests and a separation of her faith from the institutional church. She says, "Very early on I separated the religion of my home from what the priests said. The priests in my church were Spaniards, but what they said was not the real thing for me."[19] This attitude of separation from the church seems to be one way that women respond to a patriarchal and imperialistic institution that is irrelevant to their experience.

A different approach is taken in Central and South America by women who are actively involved in the base ecclesial communities. Rather than putting their energy into the institutional church, they devote their efforts to the base communities. In fact, women often take strong leadership in these communities. Even here, however, women continue to face discrimination and call for an end to *machismo* and for the beginning of a new society based on partnership between men and women.

Despite this important leadership role that women play, until recently their presence has largely been ignored in Latin America. In tracing the history of involvement of women in Latin American liberation theology, Ana María Bidegain writes of the painful invisibility of those women present in the movement, suggesting that women had to abandon their female identity, to "reason like men, act with the same combativeness . . . and live a man's spirituality. In a word, we had to become male, or at least present ourselves as asexual beings."[20] The use of feminist theory was similarly discouraged, as Bidegain notes. "Anyone embracing feminist theory . . . was put in her place with the allegation that feminism was an imperialist theory calculated to divide and weaken the popular sector."[21] Another factor contributing to the invisibility of Latin American women was that initially Latin American men were the authors being published on the subject of liberation theology. Though Gutiérrez is given credit for including "men and women" in his 1971 introduction to *Teología de la Liberación*, nowhere did he specifically address the concerns of women in his early work, a point he has since acknowledged and sought to redress.

During the 1980s and 1990s women have become recognized for their work doing liberation theology. Elsa Tamez, in fact, pinpoints the date of 1985 as the beginning of trained women theologians gathering to voice their concerns:

The starting point for reflection on Latin American liberation theology from a woman's perspective is a meeting held in Buenos Aires from October 30 to November 3, 1985. Twenty-seven women from nine Latin American countries met. We "bared ourselves" and set about the task of confronting and stopping the different "arrows" fired at us by our machistic society; and, we searched for ways to assist with the birth of the Christ child among us, among Latin Americans.[22]

The 1985 Latin American Conference on Theology from the Perspective of Women in Argentina and the 1986 Intercontinental Women's Conference in Mexico both recognized the contributions of women to the field. Today, a liberation theology from the perspective of women is being developed, lived, and recorded.

Methodological Considerations

Having briefly described the context out of which Latin American and Hispanic women's theologies have developed, it is appropriate to turn to the methodological considerations that inform their work. In the final statement of the 1985 Latin American Conference on Theology from the Perspective of Women, eight "strivings" of women's theological activity were identified. These strivings are important to understand the methodological presuppositions that govern the work of Latin American women theologians. According to the Buenos Aires document, women's theological activity strives to be "unifying, bringing together different human dimensions" such as strength and tenderness, happiness and tears. It strives to be communitarian and relational, and it strives to be contextual and concrete, with its starting point being "the geographical, social, cultural, and ecclesial reality of Latin America." It strives to be militant, taking part in the peoples' struggles for liberation. It strives to be marked by a sense of humor and joy, and it strives to be filled with a "spirituality of hope, whose starting place is our situation as women."[23] Further, it strives to be free and open, accepting of challenges. Last, it strives to be oriented "toward refashioning women's history." It is a theology striving to construct new images of God, of humanity, and of society.[24] Many of these characteristics can be observed in the writings of individual women.

U.S. Hispanic theologians Isasi-Díaz and Tarango describe the presuppositions that govern their work in terms of "commitments." They outline three clear commitments: "to do theology; to do theology from a specific perspective; to do theology from a specific perspective as a communal process."[25] First, Hispanic women, like Hispanic men, *do* theology. They do not simply think it or write it. They are involved in praxis and reflection and bringing about justice. Orthopraxis takes primacy over orthodoxy. Second, Hispanic women do theology from the concrete experience of their everyday lives. In the interviews conducted by Isasi-Díaz and Tarango, they ask women questions about how their experience of God impacts their daily lives. Isasi-Díaz devotes a chapter of *En La Lucha/In the Struggle* (1993) to a discussion of praxis and "lived-experience" in *mujerista* theology. There she writes, "Our lived-experiences have to be the building blocks of our self-understanding and of our morality if we are not to lose ourselves in the process. We have to depend on how we understand and live the events of our daily lives."[26] Because of this commitment to integrating theology, praxis, and "lived-experience," Hispanic women's theology notes the ways that the Catholic church has contributed to the oppression of women. The rituals, festivals, and songs of popular religion provide resources for theological reflection. The struggle for cultural survival is a central theme of *mujerista* theology.

In addition to doing theology from a standpoint of praxis and from the perspectives of poor women's "lived-experience," Hispanic women do theology as a community. Isasi-Díaz and Tarango use a community process of interviewing and/or group reflection. They attempt, where possible, to record verbatim the words of the women interviewed, and those women are consulted to be sure that their ideas have been presented correctly. They feel that theology should be communicated in language that can be understood by the people whose thought it reflects.

Taking as its starting point the experience of women, Isasi-Díaz and Tarango carefully set about describing who Hispanic women are. While their work concentrates primarily on the situation of women in the United States, their insistence on taking seriously the ethnic and racial heritage of Hispanic women is important for all women of the Americas. They note that Hispanic women are the product of "three very different cultures and histories: the Amerindian, the African, and the Spanish."[27] Caribbean women may be more influenced by African and Spanish cultures, while women from Mexico, Central, and South America may be more influenced by American Indian and Spanish cultures. Some women reflect the heritage of all three groups.

Hermeneutics

Feminist liberation theologians in Latin America and in the United States have noted one major difference between Latin American liberation theology and feminist theology. While Latin American liberation theology can unequivocally say that the God of the Bible is the God of the poor and oppressed, women cannot say that the God of the Bible is the God of women. Patriarchal and androcentric renderings of the text in its initial recording, redacting, and interpretation all provide problems for women seeking liberation. In dealing with these problems, various women adopt different attitudes toward scripture. Isasi-Díaz and Tarango find in their interviews of women of Cuban, Puerto Rican, and Mexican heritage that the Bible is not a central source for their faith.[28] At the other end of the spectrum, and perhaps because of the emergence of ecclesial base communities in Central and South America, Elsa Tamez and Brazilian Ivone Gebara see scripture as a very important source of Latin American women's theology.

For those women for whom scripture is central, it is important to examine the hermeneutical principles that inform their reading of scripture. Luz Beatriz Arellano indicates that in Nicaraguan women's spirituality it is important to reread the Bible from the viewpoint of women, "with women's eyes, with women's feelings, so as to rediscover or continually rediscover, from our own perspective, a new face of God, a more human and closer image of Jesus."[29] Arellano indicates that for her, God's face is ever changing. This processive view of the revelation of God's face is directly tied to a hermeneutics that places women's experience at the center. God's face can take on new forms, based on women's discoveries. This perspective includes two insights that are fundamental to women's liberation theology in Latin America. First, the hermeneutics is not purely rational. Arellano is concerned with women's feelings in discerning the new face of God. Second, this hermeneutics leads to a discovery of a Jesus who is closer than the Jesus presented in traditional christology.

The central problem for women who use scripture as a primary source for theology is bringing a woman's perspective to the reading of the text. This means rereading all of scripture through a woman's lens. It means addressing the problem of what to do with texts that are oppressive to women. It also involves the realization that women *are* the poor. Whereas Gutiérrez and other male theologians articulated a hermeneutics of reading scripture from the eyes of the poor, it was the women theologians who noted that in Latin America, as elsewhere in the world, most often it is the women and their children who are the poor.

María Pilar Aquino, originally from Mexico and now living in the United States, has pointed out that the option for the poor, a primary notion in the thought of male liberation theologians of Latin America, is an option for women.[30] Aquino points out that the Puebla Document of 1979 recognizes the double oppression of women as women and as poor. In order to emphasize the relationship between women and impoverishment, Aquino writes that "to the degree that the Latin American church insists upon meeting the needs, the aspirations, and the interests of the poor, it promotes the participation of women."[31] Likewise, Ivone Gebara regards as parallel notions the ideas of oppression and poverty in women's lives. Theological reflection is "based on an encounter with the experience of the oppression of women as an experience of the oppression of the poor."[32]

Ana María Bidegain also points to the importance of class analysis in the reading of scripture. She refers to the now well-documented fact that women, though comprising more than half the population and spending twice as much time at work as men, receive one-tenth of the world's income and possess less than one percent of the world's wealth. Bidegain is clear that women's impoverishment is due to sexism and is "complemented by racial oppression."[33] She sounds a clear note of correction to those Latin Americans who would criticize her analysis of women's poverty as a white North American feminist concern:

> Racial discrimination, sexism, and capitalist exploitation in Latin America constitute the triad that keeps women in subjection. Latin Americans who dismiss feminism as a "bourgeois issue" are altogether off the mark. On the contrary, one of the basic tasks incumbent on Christians is to struggle against all discrimination—social, racial, and sexual.[34]

Thus, from the perspective of paying close attention to class, race, and gender analysis, it is easy to understand how Bidegain comes to understand scripture in nontraditional ways. From the perspective of the poor woman, Jesus is understood as the one who "was never discriminatory." Mary, too, is important, for she is perceived as "the power and model of liberation."[35]

This attention to class analysis and the impoverishment of women is more carefully articulated by Gebara and Bidegain than it is in Tamez's early work. Tamez does not seem to take into account the particular issues of women's poverty when she states that "a reading from a woman's perspective has to go through this world of the poor,"[36] as though the world of the poor were somehow a distinct reality from women's lives. Despite the fact that Tamez does not clearly articulate the relationship between women and poverty in her early work, she does not ignore this in her later work. In fact, in her more recent work, she specifically lists women among the poor who are doubly oppressed. Among this group, which includes orphans and foreigners, are widows—women who are particularly vulnerable not only to poverty but also to sexual violation.[37] Other evidence of Tamez's concern for women's impoverishment can be seen in her article "The Power of the Naked," which gives to poor women a central place in the reflection of Latin American women doing theology. Here she writes that theology is being transformed by the incorporation of women's experience, "especially that of poor women."[38] In addition, her article "Amada Pineda: A Woman of Nicaragua" leaves no doubt that Tamez comes to take the poverty of women seriously. She writes,

Central and Latin American women cannot embark on a struggle for their rights if they do not first consider the lives of the majority of their sisters. . . . We believe that we must work for equality starting with women who are poor, since working from this perspective tends simultaneously to change economically oppressive structures as well as male chauvinistic structures.[39]

In searching for a hermeneutics that will help women interpret those passages in scripture that are oppressive to women, several approaches can be taken. Elsa Tamez argues that women are called to question such gospel texts. Claiming that women are created in the divine image, she asks women to call into question those passages that might tarnish the divine image in which women have been created.[40] In addition, she argues that "women are called . . . to deny the authority of those readings that harm them."[41] Her hermeneutics of "gaining distance and coming closer" helps her gain the necessary distance from oppressive texts so that they cannot harm her and also come closer to those texts that reflect the reality of Latin American women's experience.

Raquel Rodríguez is less certain about how to treat oppressive passages. She hesitates, saying

No tenemos todavía la última palabra. Hay mucho trabajo por hacer y debemos acercarnos a ellos con temor y temblor pero con responsabilidad y compromiso para no caer en una interpretación lígera sino fiel a nuestro compromiso con el Evangelio.

We don't yet have the last word. There is a lot of work to do and we must approach it with fear and trembling but also with responsibility and commitment so as not to find ourselves making a hasty interpretation but rather one that is faithful to our commitment to the gospel.[42]

In deciding how to approach scripture, both Tamez and Rodríguez make use of a hermeneutics of suspicion. Particularly in her biblical work, Tamez consistently asks questions about the situation of women in the text, about their absence, and about their silence. Tamez accomplishes this with her hermeneutics of "gaining distance," which allows her to separate her reading of scripture from a traditional male reading. Beatriz Melano Couch goes beyond a hermeneutics of suspicion to a hermeneutics of hope, described as a "hermeneutic of engagement."[43] This hermeneutics of hope seeks to avoid "the danger of reading into the text only our own conditioning, with the aim of freeing the text, letting the text speak with all its urgency, depth, and power."[44] Freed from ideological captivity, the text can then reframe our questions and our understandings in ways that will lead to liberation.

These are just some of the elements of the methodology and hermeneutics used by Latin American women in dealing with scripture and tradition. This methodology is only beginning to take shape as women move toward the center of the community of scholars doing liberation theology.

Conceptions of God

Having described some of the methodological presuppositions and hermeneutical principles that inform the work of Hispanic and Latin American women theologians, it is appropriate to turn specifically to their understandings of God. In looking at the concepts of God present in their theologies, a wide variety of metaphors and images takes shape. Some women relate to God in traditional male images. Others see God as both male and female. Still others see God as a force or spirit of strength in their lives. Mary and La Virgen de Guadalupe take on quasi-divine or divine characteristics in some women's theologies. Other women retain images of God from native American or African traditions.

Visions of God among U.S. Hispanic Women:
The Question of Gender

In *Hispanic Women: Prophetic Voice in the Church* (1988) Ada María Isasi-Díaz and Yolanda Tarango report on interviews with several groups of Hispanic women, asking them various questions about their theologies. Of the many questions they explore, the question of particular relevance concerns these women's perceptions of God, many of which are strikingly different from the traditional image of God as father.

One woman interviewed, Marta, speaks of God as spirit; "he is prettier and more supreme the less shape I give him." This image is interesting in that the word "pretty" is not an adjective traditionally used to describe either God or spirit. However, this image of God is followed by a traditionally masculine image of God as father, as can be seen reflected in her statement, "He is my father, my ultimate father."[45] Some women interviewed, then, do maintain rather traditional notions of God as father.

Another woman, Lupe, writes that "God is like a composite of the qualities I admire in other people." She also sees God as a presence in time of suffering. "It seems to me that God is more where there is pain."[46] Both of these images are gender neutral. Lupe's image of God is quite broad, for God represents all that she admires in others. Her God is not unlike the God of process thinkers who see God as a God of compassion who responds to suffering. In fact, for Lupe, God's own being responds directly to human suffering by somehow becoming "more" where there is pain. A second way of imaging God, then, is in very human, though nongendered, terms.

In the interviews, a woman named Inez explains that initially she thought of God as punisher. She writes, "I used to see him as a tall man, white, with a long, white beard." In part, she says that she got this image from her grandfather. Yet her grandparents "talked more about the Virgin of Mt. Carmel" than about God. "God was not important for them." Despite her initial response that she thought of God as a male punisher, she later says that God "is like a sentimiento [deep feeling], a force that makes me move, which pushes me in difficult moments." Then she changes images. "But if they would ask me to draw God, I would draw my grandmother smiling." She later writes, "I pray alot to my grandmother."[47] This image of God as grandmother appears in the theologies of many Latin American women.

In the theological reflection of Inez we see a complex set of images of God. She pictures a traditional male God with a beard and white hair, yet this God is not central to her theology. Much more central is the notion of God as a "sentimiento," a deep feeling that strengthens her in times of struggle. The face of this God takes on the face of her grandmother, just as for her grandparents, the face of the Virgin of Mt. Carmel was more important than more traditional notions of God.

Interviewees María and Olivia see God in both male and female terms. María writes that "God became that love of a mother and a father that I never had."[48] The language Olivia uses to describe her concept of God is of mixed gender: "I see God as a man—because that is the way God is pictured."[49] The cultural influences of patriarchal art have highly influenced her image of God. Nonetheless, she writes, "To symbolize him I would draw a mother with her child. You know how when a child hurts his hand and the mother kisses the little hand, the child feels all better? That is the way I feel when I talk with him."[50]

Adela answers the question "How would you describe God to someone who has never heard about God?" with a simple response. "I would look for a garden of only red roses and I would show it to him, and I would tell him that for me red roses mean very much . . . with them I can show my love . . . a rose; a rose that signifies love."[51] In another response, she indicates that God takes care of her; "he has given me everything."[52] For Adela, traditional images of God are not central to her conceptions of God. Instead, the image conjured when she thinks of God is a rose, a red rose, which to her symbolizes love.

These are just a few examples intended to demonstrate some of the richness of imagery provided by the group interviews of Isasi-Díaz and Tarango. It is clear that God is perceived in much more than purely masculine terms by these women. In fact, God is perceived as female as often as God is perceived as male. At other times, God is seen in images of mixed gender. Finally, nongendered images of God such as a red rose or a spiritual force are also recounted by these Hispanic women in the United States.

The Embodiment of God in the Lives of the Oppressed

In Latin American liberation theology, God's embodiment in the world is revealed in the lives of the oppressed. God hungers, God knows pain, and God suffers in the concrete, lived experience of God's people. A wide variety of images and metaphors for God depict this understanding that God appears in the faces of the poor and the marginalized.

In looking at the work of Latin American women doing theology, I begin with the work of Elsa Tamez, whose work is well known in the United States. Tamez begins with the premise that God is on the side of the oppressed. The words Tamez chooses are important, for here she distinguishes herself from Gutiérrez, who earlier had articulated the phrase that God is on the side "of the poor." In choosing the phrase "the oppressed" or "the subjugated," as Tamez does elsewhere, she is careful to indicate that women are among the oppressed or subjugated. As an example of this understanding of God, she cites the popular Mass of the Nicaraguan Farmers, which reads as follows:

> Christ, Christ Jesus,
> be one with us.
> Lord, Lord my God,
> be one with us.
> Christ, Christ Jesus,
> take sides
> not with the *oppressor class*
> that squeezes dry and devours
> the community,
> but with the *oppressed*,
> with my people
> thirsting for peace.[53]

This use of the Farmer's Mass as an example of a God on the side of the oppressed is important. First, it indicates that Tamez makes use of the liturgy of popular religion as a source for her theologizing about God. Second, this passage is important because it demonstrates the ways in which God and Christ or Christ Jesus function synonymously at times. Tamez states that "this experience of *God* . . . finds expression today in the religious life of oppressed peoples."[54] The Mass of the Nicaraguan Farmers and the Kyrie chant, in particular, are used as examples of this conception of God. However, the text of the chant speaks alternately of Christ, Christ Jesus, Lord, my God. In this case, these terms for God function synonymously, without distinction between God, Christ, Jesus, and Lord. The text expresses in simple language the fact that God favors the oppressed. The emphasis of the text is practical, with ethical ramifications for Christian praxis.

The God of Liberation

A second aspect of the way that Tamez speaks of the embodiment of God draws on the biblical narrative. The Exodus tradition as well as Psalm 74:22 and Psalm 72:12–14 are cited as examples of a God who is concerned with liberation from oppression.[55] Tamez paints a picture of a compassionate God responding to the oppression of the Hebrew people with a desire to bring them into a physical, concrete liberation as well as spiritual liberation. "The oppression the Hebrews suffered in body extended as well to the innermost parts of their being. It touched their inner-selves, the transcendental part of their being, their dignity, their persons."[56] The God who sides with the oppressed, then, is a compassionate God concerned with the physical well-being of God's people as one aspect of their spiritual well-being. God hears the cries of God's people under the forced labor of the taskmasters, knows their sufferings, and responds.

This God knows that oppressors come in many forms, not only in the form of Egyptian slaveholders. When the Jewish people reject God and inflict injustice, God is equally concerned for the weak and poor who suffer injustice. Here Tamez employs a feminist and class analysis, noting that God is on the side of the poor and the women who suffer at the hands of other Jews who oppress them. The poor, the needy, and the hungry are all objects of God's favor. In fact, notes Tamez, some texts equate acts of oppression against the poor with acts of oppression against God.[57]

According to Tamez, God is concerned for the oppressed because their inner spiritual condition is related to material oppression. The physical conditions of forced labor, hunger, and violation, including rape of women, result in a degree of dehumanization that is unacceptable to God. "The oppressed suffer oppression in their bodies and in their interior selves. The result is a high degree of dehumanization and depersonalization. It is necessary to 'revive the spirit of the humble.'"[58]

In developing the theme of God being on the side of the oppressed, Tamez explores the economic ramifications of this proposal. The God of the oppressed is against all hoarding of economic resources, because such hoarding results in the impoverishment of others. Key here is the word "impoverishment," rather than poverty. In the use of the word "impoverishment," Tamez rejects the notion that poverty is simply part of the condition of humanity. Instead, she wants to demonstrate that at the root of poverty is the fact that oppressors hoard economic resources, which *causes* the impoverishment of God's people. Tamez relates the sin of impoverishment to idolatry, declaring those nations who worship wealth over God to be "pagan." Here Tamez agrees with Raul Vidales's connection of oppression with idolatry, a sin that is used as much as a critique against the so-called pagan nations as it is used as a critique of the oppressor classes in Israel itself, those who began to build Israel not on the model of liberation but rather on the master/slave model.[59] The God who brings about liberation from oppression for the people of Israel is the same God who brings liberation to those who are later oppressed by the oppressors within Israel.

To Know God Is to Do Justice

In Tamez's theology, God's embodiment in the world is revealed as God takes the side of those who suffer and are oppressed. If one is to know God, one can find God in the faces of babies crying, young men working, and old women laughing. God is never pleased with poverty and suffering; therefore, God's embodiment in the world is also revealed in the mandate for liberation. Here Tamez employs an epistemological twist akin to Gutiérrez. For both Gutiérrez and Tamez, to know God is to do justice. Tamez's version of this understanding is that "Turning to God calls for both love and knowledge. But knowledge of God does not mean an intellectual grasp of the fact that God exists and an understanding of God's attributes. To know God means to do justice to the poor."[60] Tamez refuses any absolute distinction between mind and body, thought and action, theology and ethics. For Tamez, as for many other Latin American liberation theologians, the one who knows God is actively engaged in bringing about the reign of liberation. For this reason, Tamez finds central to her theology the passage from James 2:14–17, which describes faith without works as dead.[61] One aspect of the embodiment of God in the human struggle for liberation is this emphasis on praxis. For Tamez and other Latin American liberation theologians, the descriptive task of elaborating the nature of God's activity requires that one also be about the task of doing justice. That is what knowing God means.

God's Availability to All Persons

A third aspect of Tamez's reflection on God's embodiment in the world is that she believes that God's will for the oppressed is broadly inclusive of all persons, regardless of their national or religious background. She writes, "It is important to note that God hears and defends the cause of all the oppressed and not just of those who are oppressed in Israel."[62] While this theme is not highly developed in Tamez's early thought, it is clear that she expresses an openness to understanding God's favor as being extended to people of all religious traditions. "Clearly, then, the vision of some of the biblical writers goes beyond Israel. It extends to all of the human race God's preferential love for the exploited peoples of the world."[63] This view of God as one who is concerned for all oppressed peoples is evident in Tamez's treatment of the Letter of James. Tamez specifically notes that the Letter of James does not mention whether the oppressed are Christian or not. What is important is that "God, the giver of life, hears them."[64]

To summarize, for Tamez there are at least three important items one must mention in speaking of the embodiment of God in the world. First, God is on the side of the oppressed, a category that includes many women in Latin America. Second, those who know God must do justice. There can be no separation of theology, ethics, and praxis. Finally, God's will is not limited to Christians alone; God wills liberation for all oppressed persons.

An Embodied Trinity

In looking at the work of other Latin American women who focus on the embodiment of God in women's lives, María Clara Bingemer and Ivone Gebara offer important insights. In her essay "Possible Openings for a Feminist Trinitarian Theology" Bingemer provides an analysis of the trinity, critiquing its traditional male language and hoping to uncover some of the forgotten feminine aspects of trinitarian God language.[65] She retrieves such images for God as *rachamim*, the Hebrew word often translated as "mercy," which is related etymologically to the term "womb." She also discusses the Hebrew word *ruach*, grammatically feminine, and translates it as God's "breath" or "spirit." The Hebrew *hochmah* and Greek *sophia*, words translated as "wisdom," both grammatically feminine, are used to describe the nature of God. The Hebrew word *shekinah* is also feminine and is used to describe the glory of God. Based on her analysis of these biblical words having feminine connotations and on her historical work uncovering their use to describe God in the writings of early church historians and theologians, Bingemer suggests that we find ways to think of trinity in new terms that go beyond those that are male in gender. Her emphasis on biblical images for God that come, literally, of woman's body is not new to the feminist theological arena. However, her work reminds us that it is important to remember those aspects of church tradition that can help us in the development of embodied theologies that take women's bodies seriously.

Ivone Gebara addresses the necessity for thinking of the trinity in radically different ways. She stresses the concrete experience out of which Latin American women engage in theological reflection about God. She writes that

> There is something quite special in the way that women do theology. The elements of everyday life are intertwined with their speaking about God. . . . When women's experience is expressed in a church whose tradition is machistic, the other side of human experience returns to theological discourse: the side of the person who gives birth, nurses, nourishes . . .[66]

Women bring to the theological enterprise the concrete experience of their bodies; however, this concrete experience is not limited to birthing and mothering. In addition to referring to women's embodied loving through giving birth, she likewise honors those Madres de Plaza de Mayo in Argentina who have literally put their bodies on the line in their resistance to injustice. Like María Clara Bingemer, Gebara writes of the need to create new images of God. She offers a trinity quite different from traditional notions when she speaks of the need for "the image of a God committed to the liberation of the poor, of a Mary closer to women's problems, of a Jesus who is less remote and whose words are understandable in our own situation."[67] Here the God of the poor, a Mary who stands close by, and a Jesus whose words are relevant to the contemporary situation form three aspects of the trinity that inform the ways Gebara understands God's activities in the world. This emphasis on theology being done from concrete, everyday experience is characteristic of the embodied liberation theology being done by women throughout Latin America.

The Relational God

Brazilian Roman Catholic laywoman Ana María Tepedino describes another important conception of God: God is ultimately relational.[68] According to Tepedino, women experience God "in their own manner, as the One who really protects the weak and is the defender of those who have less life." She believes, as does Peruvian Consuela de Prado, that since women carry children in their wombs, they experience God differently, in a "relational" manner that "goes beyond conceptual coldness." Her experi-

ence of life embraces "strength and tenderness, happiness and tears, intuition and reason."[69]

For Tepedino, women express the "tender (hesed) side of God, the
maternal womb (rahamim), concern for those children who suffer the
most."[70] Citing Clement of Alexandria, she speaks of God having a tenderness that "makes Him a Mother. The father becomes feminine through loving. We see the greatest proof of this in the Son who proceeds from God's
very bosom."[71] As can be seen in the previous examples, Tepedino tends to
view God in ways traditionally viewed as feminine, arguing that women's
essential nature causes them to experience God differently, relationally.

Another variant on the theme of God's relationality can be seen in
Tamez's notion of the processive revelation of God in the activity of liberating the oppressed. Tamez proposes a model of revelation that ultimately
relies on a relationship between God and humanity. In fact, in Tamez's
understanding, in order for revelation to occur, this relationship is required.

It is important to see how Tamez understands what she terms the "cor-
relative" situations of oppression and liberation.[72] For Tamez, the task of
liberation involves a twofold interplay between God and God's people. The
act is not one accomplished by Yahweh alone:

> In situations of oppression the oppressed and Yahweh meet and join
> forces. The one cries out (sa'aq) and the Other listens and heeds
> (shama'); then the one learns that the Other has listened and heeded
> the cry (Exod. 4:31). Both listen to one another, and both struggle as
> though they were a single person, because the enemies of the
> oppressed are also the enemies of God (Judg. 5:31).[73]

One concrete example of the relationship between God and humanity
can be seen in Tamez's treatment of the story of Hagar and Ishmael. She
notes that Hagar, the slave, is the only woman of the Old Testament to experience a theophany. It is Hagar who describes God as "the one who sees."
This God not only sees but hears her cries and the cries of her son. Tamez
notes,

> Before giving her water God gives her courage, spirit, and hope. God
> has heard the cry of Ishmael: he is called Ishmael, because God is,
> and always will be, ready to hear the cries of the son of a slave.
> Ishmael signifies in Hebrew "God hears."[74]

Elsewhere Tamez speaks of the interplay between God and humanity in
relationship to God's silence. In her essay "Letter to Job," Tamez gives
account of God's silence in the face of Job's pleas by noting that

without the silence of God we can't become men and women. . . . God remains silent so that men and women may speak, protest, and struggle. God remains silent so that we may become really ourselves. When God is silent and men and women cry, God cries in solidarity with them, but God doesn't intervene, God waits for the shouts of protest. Then God begins to speak again, but in dialogue with us.[75]

Tamez is clear that there is no liberation once and for all. For her, "liberation is a process."[76] This process of liberation "implies a tenacious and unceasing struggle."[77] The struggle of liberation is effected in the interplay between God and God's people joining forces to struggle against oppression, crying out against poverty, unemployment, hunger, and death, and in God's response as God hears these cries protesting injustice. This process involves a relationship between God and God's people that is personal, communal, and collaborative. This God, just and liberating, calls the people into acts of solidarity with the oppressed and into the concrete realization of love. God, the manifestation of justice, righteousness, mercy, and truth, calls the people to act in righteous, just, merciful, and honest ways.

Sources of Empowerment: The Spirit of God, Jesus, and Mary

Latin American and U.S. Hispanic women understand God's empowerment in terms of the Spirit of God active in women's lives, the notion of Jesus as liberator, and by new images that portray Mary as a source of strength and empowerment.

God's Spirit Empowering

One theologian exploring the role of the Spirit is Luz Beatriz Arellano, who asserts that the presence of the Spirit calls women to conversion, which she defines as "the establishment of more just structures for the benefit of the poor."[78] The presence of the Spirit calls for the formation of a new woman and a new man. This new woman and new man, empowered by God's spirit, work together to build a new society, a realm of justice and equality on earth. This view of the role of women and men working together in partnership is directly tied to women's new understandings of themselves in relation to God, the Virgin of Guadalupe, and Mary. In opposition to the previous church teaching, which might lead a pious woman to expend her energy praying a novena or calling on the Lord, liberation theology offers women a new view of themselves as agents of change in society—women who, empowered by the Spirit of God, are unafraid to challenge governments, the military, and multinational corporations that exploit them. In Arellano's terms, this new woman, reading the Bible in terms of her own situation, becomes a committed woman with a new responsibility within history.[79]

Directly related to this new definition of women's responsibility, the presence of the Spirit creates a willingness to take on revolutionary acts, which often in a Latin American context results in martyrdom. Such women as Nicaraguan Mary Barreda, killed by the contras for her work in the coffee harvest, are led by the Spirit to work for justice. Through the Spirit, Barreda was led to dedicate her revolutionary act of love to the Nicaraguan people, in hope that it might bring about "health care, cloth-ing, shelter, roads, education, food, etc."[80] The Spirit of love that leads these women to act for justice is revealed in John 15:13, which states, "There is no greater love than this; to lay down one's life for one's friends." Many women in Latin America perceive the Spirit to be the source of courage and resis-tance in the face of much oppression:

> Women, wives, widows, sisters, and mothers raise the cry on every front in defense of human rights . . . mothers transcend the limits of fear and take on a warlike struggle to find the son or daughter who has disappeared through the forces of destruction and death.[81]

The God of Life: Celebration in the Midst of Struggle

The themes of the embodiment of God in the lives of the oppressed, the relationality of God and human efforts for liberation, and the empower-ment and resistance offered by the Spirit of God come together in a com-mon assertion heard in Latin American women's theologies, namely that God is the God of Life. Luz Beatriz Arellano and María Teresa Porcile, among others, assert that in the context of much death in Latin America, God indeed is the God of Life. A Roman Catholic sister from Nicaragua, Arellano speaks of a "new experience of God" that can be discovered in the "suffering, oppressed, and outcast countenance of our poorest brothers and sisters." Present in history in the face of those who suffer, this God is not the God "we had been taught" but rather is "the God of life, closer to us, as one who journeys with us through history."

Arellano's contribution to an understanding of God includes her obser-vation that it was women who made the specific discovery of God as a God of life, a central theme that was later echoed by male liberation theolo-gians. Arellano writes, "I recall that it was women who most insisted on discovering God as God of life." She believes that women were better able to make this discovery because of their calling to motherhood since moth-erhood "is a calling to life and peace." In turn, women "themselves become stronger and more conscious as defenders and bearers of life."[82] The biblical basis for this theological understanding of God as the God of Life comes from the passage, "I came so that they might have life and have it in abundance" (Jn 10:10).

As part of her assertion that God is the God of Life, Arellano discovers the feminine elements in God, which she describes as

> care and concern for children, even those who are not their own, defense of life, love, affection, and empathy for suffering. Such characteristics—more feminine, if you will—of a God found to be closer to us and more tender-hearted, led to a rediscovery of God as mother, not just as father, not just as protector, but as one who is immensely concerned for the poor and for the least, for those who have been left unattended.[83]

Both Tepedino and Arellano use an essentialist understanding of women's nature—one that has been critiqued by feminist theorists who want to encourage *both* men and women to be caretakers of each other, of children, and the planet. Tepedino and Arellano's point is relevant, however, because at least in terms of role socialization, it is largely the women of Latin America, and elsewhere, who are responsible for bearing children and who provide nurturing for each generation.

Another theologian who writes of the God of Life is Alida Verhoeven. In her article "The Concept of God: A Feminine Perspective," Verhoeven suggests the need for clear and concrete language in theological reflection.[84] She calls for dynamic language about God to reflect the idea that "the Presence of Creative-Recreative Spiritual Force, the source of Life and Love, is like an ongoing movement, an ebb and flow that moves in growing waves that wash over everything."[85] The God of Life she envisions is both creative and recreative; for her, God is a "Spiritual Force." She even likens the creative force of God to that of a great ocean wave.

The insight that God is the God, not of death, but of Life, is one of the unique contributions of Latin American women to liberation theology. In the midst of enormous suffering and death, life is celebrated. María Teresa Porcile, a Roman Catholic theologian from Uruguay, locates the biblical basis for this understanding of God in Exodus 5:1, where Moses and Aaron confront the Pharaoh, saying,

> Así dice el Señor, el Dios de Israel: Deja salir a mi pueblo para que me celebre una fiesta en el desierto.[86]

> Thus says the Lord, the God of Israel, "Let my people go, so that they may celebrate a festival to me in the wilderness."[87]

God did not tell Moses to tell the Pharoah to let the Jews go so that they could sleep or rest or even plan their route to the Promised Land. Instead, unexpectedly, God told Moses to prepare for a fiesta or party. This deep-rooted understanding of the need for celebration in the midst of suffering leads Porcile to write, "La fiesta es el secreto de la fuerza del pueblo que sufre." (Celebration is the secret to the strength of those who suffer.)[88]

María Pilar Aquino, like Arellano, Verhoeven, and Porcile, insists that in the midst of much suffering, God is a God of Life who provides women with cause for hope and celebration:

> Though the grass-roots woman cannot identify the actual state of society as "good", she remains capable of celebration. Life is affirmed, but not life as the powerful say that it is. The woman as dominated sufferer is not the reality, because that reality has been invaded by a new process in which women take the initiative. They create projects. They enliven celebrations. They multiply communities. Life and hope are affirmed against death.[89]

The ability to celebrate life in the midst of hardship is a key insight that would enrich the theologies of many outside the Latin American context. The view of God as a God of Life serves as a source of hope and celebration in Latin American women's liberation. The God of Life is not simply a God who calls people to celebrate to escape their misery. The God who calls women to work unceasingly for justice in often very difficult circumstances is a God who understands the human need for joy and laughter.

Jesus the Liberator

Without going into a detailed christological investigation, it is important nonetheless to raise several critical issues regarding the view of Jesus represented in Latin American women's thinking, because for some women, there is a direct connection between their conceptions of God and Jesus. In fact, in some women's minds, there appears to be little distinction made between the persons of the trinity. This point of view can be seen in the thought of Luz Beatriz Arellano. "Jesus is identified as God, man and woman, standing in firm solidarity with the struggle. This is a God who is sensitive to suffering, a God who goes along with the people incarnate in history."[90]

In looking at the ways in which Latin American and Hispanic women understand the role of Jesus, it is first clear that some women hold to traditional ideas, taught by the church, of Jesus as the son of God. Second, some women do not relate to Jesus in significant ways at all; their prayers most often go to Mary. These women tend to practice a private spirituality within the home and family setting and are often alienated from the institutional church. This point of view is represented by Adela, one of the women interviewed by Isasi-Díaz and Tarango. She says, "I cannot say if he [Jesus] is God. I do not pray to Jesus."[91] Other Hispanic women reflect similar views. According to Isasi-Díaz and Tarango, these women "either do not believe that Jesus was divine, or they do not consider him or his divinity something relevant in their lives."[92] This is the type of theologizing that leads Isasi-Díaz and Tarango to the conclusion that for Hispanic women, "christological questions are peripheral."[93]

A third attitude toward Jesus is represented by those women working out a new understanding of Jesus' role in the lives of the oppressed. Many women theologians active in the ecclesial base communities in Central and South America often speak of Jesus as liberator. Argentinean theologian Nellie Ritchie, an ordained Methodist minister, uses this image of Jesus as liberator in her article on "Women and Christology."[94] Arellano calls for a new image of Jesus as "a Jesus who is brother and sister, in solidarity on the journey toward liberation, the people's journey and their own journey; a Jesus who is a compañero [colleague, fellow revolutionary] in building the new society."[95] This Jesus is God in history, standing firmly in solidarity with the struggle. Here we see the vision of Jesus as the God/man who is divine liberator, immanent in the lives of the people, acting to bring about justice. This immanent view of the divine can be seen in María Pilar Aquino's understanding of the lives of men and women as the sacrament of Christ. Here Aquino speaks of a new society, "in which men and women drink together of the wine of rights and are the sacrament of Christ in history."[96]

Elsa Tamez similarly develops the image of Jesus in the faces of the marginalized poor and oppressed:

> Priests, pastors and believers have discovered the hidden face of the crucified Jesus in the faces of the unemployed, in the faces of the hungry and those suffering from disease, in the death of the innocent, in the suffering of the tortured, in the eyes of the mother whose child is missing, in the burden of the prisoner, in the weathered faces of the indigenous person, in the tired face of the black person and the woman worker.[97]

Here Tamez takes absolutely seriously the notion that God in Jesus is present in the lives of "the least of these," those suffering and oppressed persons of the earth. Tamez rejects those theologies that have encouraged the poor to accept their plight as suffering victims. Instead, she offers a contrary vision, namely that the resurrected Jesus is present in the hands of fighters, masons, farming peasants, and all the suffering poor working to build a new society. This understanding of Jesus as the active force in people's struggle for liberation is what Tamez describes as "a new mode of perceiving God."[98]

The New Mary

Another important aspect of Hispanic and Latin American women's understanding of God's empowerment concerns the relationship between God and Mary, who at times takes on divine or quasidivine status. This status may be derived from the layers of goddess imagery present in the memories of indigenous women despite five hundred years of colonization, or it may have developed in resistance to the passive image of Mary handed down through church tradition. At least in the minds of some women, the Mary of liberation theology is a source of God's empowerment in women's lives. María Pilar Aquino offers a clear analysis of the symbolic function of a "resisting" Mary:

> There exists in Latin American history a long trajectory of practices and a symbolic world that has helped the subjugated woman persist as capable of dreaming and creating. . . . All contain elements of criticism and resistance to oppression. All indicate dreams of a new and different society, either before or after death.[99]

The example Aquino offers is that of Our Lady of Guadalupe, whom she describes as being expressly linked "to the processes of independence and a struggle for the land, a struggle always on the side of the poor." She describes the activities of Mary as a "timid rebellion, a silent rejection of the status quo."[100] This depiction of Mary's resistance as both "timid" and "silent" is in contrast to the portrayal of a much more forceful and boisterous Mary in the thought of other theologians.

For other authors, the connection between Mary and empowerment for women is much less ambiguous. Far from being the traditional, passive Mary passed down through church tradition, the new Mary is seen as liberator of her people.

> We lift our gaze toward Mary, the mother of Jesus, and we contemplate her as the new woman, the liberated woman, prophetess of the God of the poor, who in anticipation sang of the liberating exploits of God on behalf of the poor, who surrendered her womb and her whole life to the realization of God's liberating plan in history. In her, Nicaraguan women see the model for their own commitment to history and their new spirituality.[101]

Clearly in this instance Mary is not perceived as a divine being. Instead, she is named as "the new woman" and "the prophetess of God" and becomes a role model for the new woman of Nicaragua.

As a further example of the new way that Mary is seen as a liberator, Arellano provides the words to a song written by Carlos Mejia Godoy, a poet and composer.[102] Careful analysis of this view of Mary reveals key aspects of Latin American women's spirituality. First, the new image of Mary shows that she knows the suffering of the people and the hardship of their labor. She is no fair-skinned Mary of the oppressor; she is dark, the black and brown colors of her people:

> Mary virgin bird,
> Joyful virgin bird,
> you with the aching feathers,
> you with the thorns and roses.
> Little bird in the cotton fields,
> bird in the coffee groves,
> brown-skinned virgin bird,
> black bird in the canefield

This Mary knows suffering; she wears "aching" feathers. She is clothed with roses but also with thorns. This Mary knows the toil of labor. She can be seen in both cotton fields and coffee groves. She also knows the suffering of racism, for she is of brown and black skin. In addition, the new Mary knows long days and nights. She is:

> Mary, bird out in the sun,
> selling fried food on the corner,
> little bird up all night,
> little bird on militia duty

Here Mary is also symbolic of the revolutionary impulse. She takes up arms in defense of her people. Yet hers is no cold defense; it is a defense born of the pain of sorrow, the sorrow that a mother knows when her child is tortured.

> Mary, bird and mother
> of my tortured brother

Yet what Mary wants, ultimately, is not war, but peace. In spite of her experience with the pain of life, she remains the "virgin bird" whose flight is not to be stained with bloodshed, but kept for peace:

>   Virgin bird, when you fly,
>   don't let your flight be stained,
>   little bird of peace

Mary wants to feed her children. Just as birds are responsible for pollinating the plants and sowing seed, Mary is connected with all the mothers of the earth who feed their children. She is related to the Corn Mother of indigenous peoples. Here, Arellano makes use of a theological resource with clear ties to the Corn Mother goddess. Unlike the Mary first illustrated above, here Mary is clearly symbolic of the divine. She is Provider:

>   Virgin bird, seed,
>   Mary of the corn that has been resown
>   Virgin bird of maize

Because she loves her children, this revolutionary Mary is unafraid to do what must be done to protect her children:

>   brash little birdie,
>   border-guarding bird
>   birdie Nicaragua,
>   bird of Revolution,
>   freedom-loving birdie,
>   little bird without borders,
>   necessary bird,
>   little guerrilla bird

Most of all, this new liberator Mary is source of hope for the people. She is wise with the maturity of her womb. She knows both the bitter and the sweet of life. And she will not be conquered:

>   Birdie with a mature womb,
>   bitter and sweet beak;
>   there won't be cages in the future,
>   little bird of insurrection.
>   The hope of your wings,
>   will penetrate all the pain,
>   birdie Guatemala,
>   birdie El Salvador.

In the final verse of this poem, Godoy uses a double entendre to indicate that the birdie is "El Salvador" or "the savior." This clearly refers to the nation, El Salvador, as the restorer of hope to the people and, at the same time, it claims for Mary, Virgin Birdie, the role of Savior, a title normally reserved for Jesus. In looking carefully at Godoy's understanding of Mary, and Arellano's endorsement of this understanding as a viable resource for women's theological understanding of the divine, we have here the picture of a Mary who is a source of strength and hope, the goddess of the ancient Corn Mother traditions, the Savior of her people.

This vision of Mary and the Virgin as a source of strength and resistance is related to two different views of God: the first is the God of Life; the second is the God of the Poor. In and through Mary and the Virgin, who for some women is a source of divine strength and power, the God of the Poor and the God of Life take on the everyday appearance of the peasant woman. This accessible God/dess provides hope and strength in the midst of suffering.

A Many-Layered Theology: Indigenous Voices

In developing an understanding of the God of Life, Latin American theologians have begun to take seriously the wide variety of religious practices which have developed as a result of the multicultural, interracial history of the continent. Because of indigenous and African spiritual influences in Central and South America, Christian spirituality takes on many layers in that context. These layers reveal something of women's conceptions of the sacred from this part of the hemisphere. With the essay "The Power of the Naked," first published in Spanish in 1986, Elsa Tamez begins to develop an understanding of God that takes into account the colonization of the Americas, an event that accounts for the many layers of spirituality that are celebrated. Here, Tamez moves beyond traditional Christian categories, pondering the relationship between the religious beliefs of indigenous peoples and the Christian beliefs that often overlay those beliefs. Because of the history of colonization in Latin America, Catholicism has largely replaced indigenous religious belief systems, at least on the surface. Yet what Tamez and others have noted is that, to a large extent, there exists encoded in ritual and myth a memory of indigenous beliefs that are available to the people as a source of strength and resistance.

Quetzalcoatl and the Christian God

In her 1986 article, Tamez explores the myth of the Toltecan god of life, Quetzalcoatl, as a resource for women, and she begins to articulate her understanding of the relationship between Quetzalcoatl and the Christian God of the Bible. Tamez compares the birth of Ce Acatl Topiltzin, the

famous high priest of the indigenous Mexican Toltecan culture, who even-
tually became known by the name of the god he served, Quetzalcoatl, to the
current situation of women doing liberation theology in Latin America.
She describes the birth of Quetzalcoatl as a result of the union of the Toltec
chief Mixcoatl and the non-Toltecan woman warrior Chimalman.[103] When
Chimalman met Mixcoatl, she dropped her shield and stood before him
naked. Mixcoatl, upset by the actions of Chimalman, began firing arrows at
her, which she easily ducked or caught in her hand. According to legend,
Chimalman fled, and when Mixcoatl could not find her, he began mistreat-
ing the women of Cuernavaca. Chimalman, upon hearing of Mixcoatl's
actions, went to find him and once again dropped her weapons and stood
naked in his presence. Mixcoatl's attempts to shoot her were unsuccessful,
and he "became one with her," with their union resulting in the conception
of Quetzalcoatl.[104] According to Mexican legend, when Quetzalcoatl became high priest, he helped to spread the culture of the Toltecs, including
their belief in the god Quetzalcoatl, as well as their knowledge of agriculture, writing, creating and using a calendar, and medicine.

Tamez then compares the efforts of Latin American women doing theology to the actions of Chimalman. Latin American women doing theology are engaged in naming the "attacks" of Mixcoatl. "The arrows he fires
at women are commonly known as discrimination, subjection, oppression,
and violence; his sharpest and strongest arrows are directed at poor
women."[105] Chimalman provides a model for Latin American women theologians. "Chimalman did not attack the warrior, she left her arrows on
the floor, instead she invited him also to undress, that is, to know himself
and to meet her as an equal."[106] Tamez is careful to indicate that Latin
American women are interested not in attacking male theologians, but in
working with all men toward partnership in a just society. According to
her analysis, the interaction between Chimalman and Mixcoatl offers the
possibility that "the two of them, woman and man, on an equal basis, in
justice, peace, love, and pleasure, might produce a new culture with the
blessing of the living god: Quetzalcoatl."[107]

In looking at the legend of Quetzalcoatl, Tamez first intends to demonstrate that the model of Quetzalcoatl shows the possibility for equality and
justice between men and women. The possibility for justice in society
exists because it lives within the very being of the Toltec god of life,
Quetzalcoatl. In using this example from indigenous religious belief,
Tamez is trying to design a new model for God in contemporary Christian
culture, a model that takes seriously the experience of women in calling for
an end to machismo and other forms of oppression against women.

Second, Tamez demonstrates a new method for understanding the interplay between indigenous religious belief and Christian thinking. Here there

is no hint of superiority of Christian belief—no suggestion that indigenous traditions play second fiddle to Christian notions of faith. Quite the opposite: Toltecan mythology is used to articulate the Christian concept of justice. In a radical move, Tamez rejects traditional Christian missiology that attempts to subvert indigenous belief and replace it with the Christian understanding of the Spanish conquistadors. Instead, she insists on collaboration between Quetzalcoatl and the Christian God: "The god of the indigenous Mexican culture is the one who . . . enters into coalition with the God of the Bible."[108] This god Quetzalcoatl is described as

> the god of life who, according to legend, creates men and women with his own blood. . . . He is a friend who teaches his creatures how to sow . . . corn, to work jade, and to build their homes. He voluntarily dies alongside the others so that men, women, older people, and children might move and breathe. Furthermore, he is a god who rejects human sacrifice and battles with other gods and priests who feed on human blood.[109]

The parallels between Quetzalcoatl and the God of the Bible then become obvious. Tamez clearly paints a picture of the God of the Bible and Quetzalcoatl as partners in the struggle against injustice. Then, in a somewhat ambiguous move, Tamez speaks of Jesus and Quetzalcoatl, without clearly indicating whether she has moved from referring to the God of the Bible and the god Quetzalcoatl or to the son of God, Jesus, and the priest of Quetzalcoatl, who came to be known by the name of the god he served. "Jesus and Quetzalcoatl, born in exile, persecuted by their enemies, concerned about humankind, enter into an alliance to fight those foreign gods who make slaves of men and women."[110] The reader is left with the somewhat ambiguous impression that for Tamez, the distinction between God and Jesus, and between Quetzalcoatl the god and Quetzalcoatl the priest are less important than the understanding that these represent the same entity—the struggle of justice over injustice and oppression.

Tamez acknowledges her own struggle over this issue: were it not for indigenous peoples claiming their rights to their indigenous Gods, she might not have thought about the issue of the relationship, figuratively speaking, between Quetzalcoatl and Jesus. Two events in particular drew Tamez's attention to the issue of religious pluralism in Latin America. The first was the second ecumenical consultation of the indigenous peoples, which met in Quito, Ecuador, in July 1986. The second was the declaration from the spiritual leaders of the indigenous peoples of Abya Alya (the Cuna indigenous term for Latin America, meaning "mature land"), which was developed at a meeting in La Paz, Bolivia, in June 1992. At issue for Tamez is her desire to hear "the other." She wants to hear those indigenous voices that claim both their gods and the Christian God and to find a way to incorporate this understanding in her own theology:

> The experience of God within these communities will not allow a response to this challenge that comes out of a western, analytic, rather dichotomous rationalism. . . . To reduce this spirituality to the classification of a "syncretistic practice" that needs to be overcome is to ignore "the other."[111]

In putting ourselves in the place of the indigenous or the poor, as Tamez advocates, our thinking radically changes. In doing so, we come to understand Tamez's willingness to wrestle with the possibility of understanding both Quetzalcoatl and the God of the Bible as the same God of Life. For this reason, Tamez is able to report that when she hears "in a Christian worship service words from the Popol Vuh or other sacred traditions, [she feels] that God is speaking."[112] Tamez clearly feels that it is possible to conceive of both indigenous and Christian representations of the divine working in alliance to fight forces of oppression.

Pachamama: Mother Earth

A second attempt to understand the influence of indigenous traditions on Latin American women's conception of the divine can be found in the work of Aurora Lapiedra, who describes Pachamama, the God of women who live high in the Andes mountains of South America, as "Madre Tierra . . . deidad feminina especializada en la agricultura" (Mother Earth . . . the feminine deity of agriculture).[113] It is she who gives life, food, and balance to relationships between humanity and the earth. The spirit of Pachamama permeates all of creation:

> la vida lo invade todo; la coca, el maíz viven, los cerros y los valles, la nieve y el agua . . . viven; la fuente de la vida radica en la tierra por lo que a su espíritu se le llama "Pachamama" "madre tierra".

> Life invades everything; the coca, the corn, the mountains and the valleys, the snow and the water . . . are alive; the fountain of life springs from the earth and its spirit is called "Pachamama," "Mother Earth."[114]

Pachamama gives life to "la coca" and to "el maíz." The hills and valleys, the snow and even the water live because the spirit of Pachamama infuses them with life.

The spirituality of these Andean women is intricately tied to this view of Pachamama. Lapiedra describes this spirituality as a lived harmony between the natural world, the agricultural world, and the human family. It is, second, a relational spirituality of concord and reciprocity. Third, it is a spirituality based in the "everydayness" of life, with little separation between notions of the sacred and the secular. Fourth, sharing is a central aspect of this spirituality, and it is the woman who sees that it happens. Fifth, this spirituality affirms that God is a God of Life. Finally, it is an embodied spirituality that values fertility as an expression of harmony.[115] The following example of a poem to Pachamama combines these central elements of Andean women's conception of Pachamama:

> Pachamama que alimentas a todo hombre
> dáme mucho fruto
> para todos tus trabajadores
> para tu paloma que vuela por lo alto
> para tu gusano que se arrastra en el suelo.

> Pachamama, you who feed everyone,
> give me abundant nurturing
> for all your working people
> for the dove that flies on high
> for the worm that crawls on the ground.[116]

Pachamama gives food, nutrition, and life to every human being in the spirit of abundance, "much fruit."

Lapiedra's study of Andean women's spirituality shows clear examples of the ways that Christian women from the mountain regions of Latin America understand God, a God quite different from the God portrayed by priests in the liturgical language of the institutional church. Yet these women identify themselves as Christian. Both Tamez and Lapiedra are involved in the work of thinking constructively about how to deal with the many layers of religious images that form women's conceptions of the sacred. Similar efforts are taking place in the United States.

Native American and African Voices
in North American and Caribbean Traditions

In the work of Norma Alarcon and Gloria Evangelina Anzaldúa, we discover two Hispanic women working in a U.S. context who have contributed important insights to the emerging consciousness of God/dess among Hispanic women.[117] Like the women of Latin America, they are concerned with the many layers of Hispanic women's spirituality. Both have described Native American roots in the image of Tonantsi(n), who is the Native American forerunner of the Catholic Virgin of Guadalupe.[118] For many Hispanic women of mixed racial heritage, identifying the indigenous images behind the legend of Guadalupe gives strength and hope for cultural survival.

Among Hispanic and Latin American women who are exploring new terrain in claiming their spiritual roots is Mirta Quintanales, an immigrant to the United States from Cuba, who describes herself as a Latina lesbian feminist. She too speaks of the ways in which her theology is shaped by images of the divine from differing cultural contexts. In her article "I Paid Very Hard for My Immigrant Ignorance," Quintanales demonstrates the ways that Hispanic women's conceptions of God are shaped by the richness of several cultural traditions, referring particularly to the mixing of African and Christian traditions. Here she confesses that she secretly prays "to Yemaya, Chango, Oshun, and the Virgen de Guadalupe," making reference to African god/desses as well as to the Christian Virgin.[119]

This section has illustrated some of the profound and varying insights of Hispanic and Latin American women doing theological reflection on the nature of the biblical God, the Spirit, Jesus, Mary, local understandings of the Virgin, and indigenous and African images for the divine. What is clear is that Hispanic and Latin American women pray to the God/dess, Virgin, or saint with whom they most significantly identify. At times this symbol is male or gender neutral; at other times it is female. While some women offer prayers to God, to Jesus the Liberator, or to Mary, who carries the hopes of the people on her wings, other women pray to Pachamama/Madre Tierra, Abuela, Yemaya, Chango, Oshun, and to Guadalupe. The sense of the sacred experienced by these women comes in part from ancient Native American and African sources that can be seen in the language they use to speak of God. Centuries of cultural exploitation have not robbed these women of the memory of God's many names. She is the one who is present with them in the midst of pain and struggle and also the one who gives birth to acts of courage and gives cause for celebration.

Contributions

Hispanic and Latin American women have made many significant contributions toward the development of constructive thinking about God. First, Hispanic and Latin American women employ a class analysis, which results in a view of God as the God of the Oppressed, who takes sides with the poor and suffering, and with women and their children. Second, a wide variety of images of God are available for further exploration. Tamez and others speak of the God of the Oppressed. She also, along with Tepedino, is concerned with the relationality of God. Liberation occurs as humanity cries out to God and God hears. Together in relation, God and humanity work toward liberation. Other images contribute toward an embodied theology that seeks to end dualistic splits between sacred and secular and between body and spirit. God is the God of Life. God is concerned, literally, with people's bodies, that they not be emaciated and starving, that they be whole. This embodied theology views the Spirit of God and Mary as resources for resistance to poverty and oppression. María Pilar Aquino and Luz Beatriz Arellano speak of the empowering God, who strengthens women as they put their bodies on the line in the name of Life, standing up to the oppression of the death squads and other forces of evil. This God of the Oppressed, the God of Life, is a relational, embodied, empowering God. A third strength of *mujerista* and Latin American women's theological reflection on God comes from its willingness to take seriously the multilayered religious history of Hispanic and Latin American peoples, giving credence to pre-Christian images of the divine as valid resources for theological reflection. Finally, Tamez and others, in speaking of God, are beginning to address issues of religious pluralism. While this discussion began in the context of dialogue with indigenous peoples, Tamez is willing to consider addressing the relationship of the Christian God to the understandings of the divine held sacred by other religious peoples. This discussion promises to be fruitful in the future.

One significant critique has developed internally within *mujerista* and Latin American women's theologizing. Realizing that male Latin American liberation theology had failed to take seriously women's experience, women began to write from their own perspectives to address the sexism of Hispanic and Latin American theologies and societies. Women theologians then pointed out that male Latin American liberation theology had initially failed to address adequately issues of racism and ethnic privilege. As Isasi-Díaz notes, this is particularly troublesome because "Brazil has the second largest black population in the world, while countries such as Peru, Bolivia, and Ecuador have a high percentage of Amerindians."[120] Women, too, discovered that their own theologizing was in need of a more adequate analysis of issues of race and ethnic prejudice. This question is beginning to be addressed in concrete ways, as evidenced by the work of Tamez, Isasi-Díaz, Lapiedra, and others. Just as we in the United States must work to deconstruct the propaganda that has taught us that ours is a classless society, so those working for liberation have much work to do to counter the myth that has particularly been prevalent in South America that theirs is not a racist society.

A second concern stems from the use of essentialist notions of "woman" that undergird some Latin American conceptions of God as feminine. As noted in this chapter, some Latin American theologians believe women to be capable of a type of nurturing or *hesed* that is reflective of the compassion of God. I noted earlier that it may be true that in Latin American culture women are assigned the role of nurturer; however, I find more productive the notion that both men and women are capable of living out the praxis of compassion in their lives, nurturing future generations in nonsexist ways. Perhaps this critique could be incorporated into Latin American women's theologizing about the partnership of men and women for the new humanity.

One final comment will be made about the theological observations of *mujerista* and Latin American women doing liberation theology. Because this process of theological reflection is relatively new, it is considered in process. It is a theology that resists definitive characterization because it is new and unfolding. It also resists static description because the context of Latin America and the situation of Hispanic women in the United States is also in flux. As Luz Beatriz Arellano has observed, "It is impossible to come to a definitive conclusion about the new women's spirituality. Nicaragua is changing."[121] This attitude, that much is changing for Hispanic and Latin American women, allows for a certain tentativeness, creativity, and freedom in developing new language for God.

3

Womanist Theological Reflections on God

The Emergence of Womanist Theology

WOMANIST THEOLOGY emerges out of the experience of Black women in the United States. Born of the need to create a space for African-American women to reflect theologically and ethically on concerns relevant to them, it is distinct from Black male theology, white feminist theology, and so-called third-world theologies of liberation. Womanist theology developed out of two painful realities. One of those realities was that Black male theology had tended to render invisible the experience of Black women. In response, in 1982 Jacquelyn Grant issued the following challenge to Black male theologians:

> Black theology cannot continue to treat Black women as if they were invisible creatures who are on the outside looking into the Black experience, the Black church, and the Black theological enterprise. It will have to deal with women as integral parts of the whole community.[1]

A second painful reality was that "feminist theology" had likewise largely ignored the realities of Black women's lives, as revealed in Audre Lorde's 1979 letter to Mary Daly, and Delores Williams's 1985 critique of Rosemary Radford Ruether, discussed in chapter 1. The critiques of Lorde and Williams point to a major difference in the theological starting place for womanist and white feminist theologies. Whereas white feminist theology had largely placed sexism at the center of theological reflection, womanist theology does not allow the categories of sexism, classism, and racism to be separated, since each of these categories intersects in the lives of many African-American women. Womanist theology, instead, wants to address the experience of African-American women without relinquishing their relatedness to African-American men or to women of other racial and ethnic backgrounds. Womanist theology insists on the interconnectedness of the human race.

The work of theologian and ethicist Katie Geneva Cannon is central to the development of womanist theology. Her description of a womanist liberation theological ethic will be cited at length. In the words of Cannon,

> A womanist liberation theological ethic places Black women at the center of human social relations and ecclesiastical institutions. It critiques the images and paradigms that the Black Church uses to promote or exclude women. A womanist theo-ethical critique serves as a model for understanding the silences, limitations, and possibilities of Black women's moral agency, by identifying Afro-Christian cultural patterns and forms, perspectives, doctrines, and values that are unique and peculiar to the Black Church community, in order to assess the dialectical tensions in Black women's past social relations as well as our current participation in the Black Church. A Black womanist liberation Christian ethic is a critique of all human domination in light of Black women's experience, a faith praxis that unmasks whatever threatens the well-being of the poorest woman of color.[2]

One of the first-generation scholars and foremothers of womanist theology, Cannon provides an important critique of the concepts of God shaped by both the dominant culture and the Black church, offering new constructions of God from a womanist perspective.

Delores Williams's 1993 *Sisters in the Wilderness: The Challenge of Womanist God-Talk* characterizes womanist theology as follows:

> Womanist theology attempts to help black women see, affirm and have confidence in the importance of their experience and faith for determining the character of the Christian religion in the African-American community. Womanist theology challenges all oppressive forces impeding black women's struggle for survival and for the development of a positive, productive quality of life conducive to women's and the family's freedom and well-being. Womanist theology opposes all oppression based on race, sex, class, sexual preference, physical disability, and caste.[3]

Womanist theology, then, is a theology of liberation centered in the experience of Black women in the United States. However, womanist theology also places itself in solidarity with all women who suffer oppression: it takes the courageous position of opposing racism, sexism, classism, and homophobia. It likewise names oppression based on physical disability, and it names the sin of oppression of caste, heretofore an untouchable item for discussion in the United States, where every man, according to melting-pot mythology, is able to lift himself up by the bootstraps.

In addition to addressing these various forms of discrimination, womanist theology clearly links itself with "the folk," with poor African-Americans, and with Black church tradition. Womanist theology attempts to establish itself as a legitimate relation of the academy while at the same time communicating in the language of "the folk." This stretch to legitimize "folksense" while rejecting the academic "nonsense" of traditional (read white, Eurocentric, male) theology, feminist nonliberationist (read racist, classist) theology and Black (read male, sexist) theology of liberation causes strained relations among these discourses. If Williams is correct, that womanist theology is "related,"[4] in an organic way, to the family of Black liberation theology and to feminist theology, then this family is one that at times has felt the strain[5] of its relationships. Family members in the predominantly white academy are challenged to take seriously the experience of Black women. Family members in the Black church are challenged to hear the message of Black women calling for an end to sexism, classism, homophobia, and other forms of oppression.

What does it mean to be a womanist? Alice Walker's *In Search of Our Mothers' Gardens* defines "womanist" in four distinct ways.[6] First "womanist" is "From *womanish*." This means a black feminist or a feminist of color acting grown-up, being responsible and in charge.

Second, a "womanist" is "a woman who loves other women, sexually and/or nonsexually." In this section of the definition, Walker indicates that womanists are committed to "survival and wholeness of entire people, male *and* female."

The third aspect of womanism as defined by Walker includes a love of life, music, dance, and the Spirit. Womanists are committed to "the folk" without sacrificing their own sense of self.

Finally, in a sentence that describes the distinction between white feminists and womanists, Walker declares that "Womanist is to feminist as purple to lavender." Here she emphasizes the notion that womanists have their own unique style, values, and commitments while at the same time having some relationship to white feminists.

This definition of "womanist" offered by Walker has deeply influenced the theology being written by African-American women in the United States. Delores Williams's reflections on Walker's complete discussion of womanism (summarized above) may be helpful. First, womanist consciousness is informed by the guidance and counsel that mothers offer their daughters, as suggested in Walker's examples of the mother-daughter wisdom offered about skin color. The ethical and moral counsel of the mother-

daughter exchange can serve as an important resource for womanist theological reflection. Second, noting the problem of tensions around skin
color, with "some men's preference for light-skinned women,"[7] Williams
notes that womanist consciousness is anticolorist. It critiques the many
ways in which society values light over dark, including the ways that theology has contributed to this message. Third, womanist consciousness names
poor Black folk as the locus of its values. Poor Black folk, notes Williams,
practice a kind of creative economic sharing that has enabled their survival
and that has value for contemporary society. Fourth, womanist consciousness values women as leaders in the African-American community. Walker
alludes to the example of Harriet Tubman as a type of leader who has acted
as an agent for change. Fifth, womanist consciousness demonstrates a concern for survival and for the building and maintenance of community. In
Williams's words, "The goal of this community building is, of course, to
establish a positive quality of life—economic, spiritual, educational—for
black women, men, and children."[8] Sixth, womanist consciousness is concerned about the whole human community. Walker's insistence that womanists are not separatists, according to Williams's interpretation, means that
Christian womanist theologians must be concerned for the entire Christian
community and the larger human community. Seventh, womanists are
reminded to love themselves "regardless"; womanists are not intended to
bear more than their share of the burden for justice and must be concerned
for their own well-being. Eighth, Williams wants to affirm womanist connection to feminism but with the caution of Walker's statement, "Womanist
is to feminist as purple to lavender." Affirming both commonality and difference allows womanist consciousness to set its own agenda and pursue its
own direction. Ninth, womanists do not promote divisions based on
homophobia, "colorism," or class hierarchy. Walker's womanist loves other
women, sexually and/or nonsexually. She values all shades of skin color. She
also loves "the folk," and works in solidarity with poor Black folk.

One final characteristic that Williams ascribes to Walker's term is that a
womanist values mothering and nurturing. Noting Walker's emphasis on
Black mothers relating to their children, Williams is careful to note that
women who mother and nurture are not necessarily bearers of children,
citing Harriet Tubman as an example of one who nurtured many Black
people in the struggle for liberation. Whether one might take issue with the
terms "mothering" or "nurturing" to describe the actions of Tubman, it is
clear that Williams's intent is to demonstrate womanist concern for others
who may or may not be biologically related. These ten characteristics,
claims Williams, are intrinsic to womanist struggle for selfhood and for
survival and quality of life among her people. Another womanist scholar
offers the following summary of what it means to be a womanist:

To summarize, the womanist is a black feminist who is audacious, willful and serious; loves and prefers women, but also may love men; is committed to the survival and wholeness of entire people, and is universalist, capable, all loving, and deep.[9]

Method

Delores Williams offers a clear and concise treatment of womanist methodology. Based on Walker's definition of the word "womanist," Delores Williams describes four essential principles that inform womanist methodology. First, Christian womanist theological methodology is intentionally multidialogical, placing itself in community with others beyond the African-American women's community. This commitment to dialogue with "many diverse social, political, and religious communities"[10] is necessitated by the genocide of many cultural groups and the "omnicidal" threat of nuclear war. While engaging in dialogue with others, however, womanist speech and action will focus on "the slow genocide of poor black women, children, and men by exploitative systems denying them productive jobs, education, health care, and living space."[11]

Second, womanist methodology is informed by a liturgical intent, which means that womanist theology will be both accountable and challenging to the Black church. Womanist theology uses the prayers, sermons, and songs of the Black church as sources for theological reflection. However, when those sources perpetuate the oppressions of sexism, homophobia, or classism, they are challenged by womanist critique.

Third, womanist methodology is informed by a didactic intent, offering new ethical, spiritual, and moral insights to church and to society. At the same time, womanist theology should itself be schooled by the stories of Black folk wisdom, such as Brer Rabbit literature, and by Black women's moral wisdom as conveyed in their literature.

Fourth, womanist theology is committed to both reason and to Black women's experience as related in their imagery and metaphoric statements. This final category, allowing Black women's language to construct new theological imagery for the church, may offer challenges to Christian moral teachings about such topics as love and humility. These four principles of womanist methodology, together with the presupposition that womanist theology is to be an instrument for social change and not merely for theological assertion, serve as guiding principles for early womanist theology.[12]

Another important methodological principle that informs the writing of womanist scholars is their rejection of a bifurcation between the sacred and mundane aspects of life, for God appears in the holy love expressed in the everyday chores of fixing supper and tending sick children just as clearly as

God shows up in church on Sunday. This principle is in operation in the work of Katie Geneva Cannon. While Cannon does not specifically treat Black women's views of God as a separate theme in her work, *Black Womanist Ethics*, she nonetheless reveals understandings that are important for womanist reflection on God.

In understanding this concept of God in African-American women's lives, Delores Williams may be helpful as she describes the use of God-talk in her own work:

> God-talk in this book assumes, as most black scholars do, that black consciousness does not make a dichotomy between the sacred and the secular. Therefore, even when the language about black women's lives in this book does not mention the word *God*, it is still god-talk in the sacred-secular sense.[13]

Similarly, one can discover much about Cannon's views of God in places where the word "God" is not necessarily mentioned.

One final methodological consideration to be noted concerns the language for God and Jesus. In this chapter, usual trinitarian distinctions between language about God and about Jesus will be suspended, following the suggestion of those, such as Jacquelyn Grant, who argue that in the Black church, little distinction is made between God and Jesus. Grant asserts that the names are used interchangeably and that there is often no distinction made between the persons of the trinity. In speaking of the names Jesus, God, and Holy Spirit, she agrees with Harold Carter, who writes, "All of these proper names for God were used interchangeably in prayer language. Thus, Jesus was the one who speaks the world into creation. He was the power behind the church."[14] Asserting that Jesus *is* God for Black women, Grant writes, "For Christian Black women in the past, Jesus was their central frame of reference. They identified with Jesus because they believed that Jesus identified with them."[15] It is important, therefore, to pay attention to christological concerns when describing womanist conceptions of God.

Sources for Theological Reflection

One of the most creative aspects of womanist theology is the development of new sources for theological reflection that stem from African-American life and culture and African-American women's lives in particular. Not only scripture and church tradition, but also slave narratives, biographies of African-American women, and the musical tradition of African-American spirituals, as well as contemporary theologies of liberation serve as source materials for theological reflection.

In *Black Womanist Ethics*, Katie Geneva Cannon argues that the African-American woman's literary tradition is a critical source for theological reflection, in part because it exists as a record of the spiritual understanding of African-American women at a time when they were not taken seriously as academic theologians. In attempting to understand the larger theme of Cannon's views of the ways God acts in Black women's lives, it is important to note her choice of both the life and work of Zora Neale Hurston as sources for theological reflection. Implicit in claiming the life of Hurston is the notion that somehow Hurston's very being serves as a model for God's action in the life of an African-American woman, for in Hurston's life story, Cannon finds active the dignity which God bestows on each human being. Cannon is interested in this concept of dignity, which is evident in the life story of Hurston and in the characters constructed in her novels and other literary works. Because this chapter relies heavily on Cannon's use of Hurston as a source for theological reflection, we will look briefly at the biography of Zora Neale Hurston.

Zora Neale Hurston (1901?–1960)[16] was the most prolific Black woman writer in the United States from 1920 to 1950. Her mother, Lucy Ann Potts (1865–1904), was a former schoolteacher and provider of wisdom to Hurston. Though she died when Hurston was only nine years of age, she left her counsel that her daughter should "jump at de sun. . . . We might not land on the sun, but at least we would get off the ground."[17] In other words, Hurston learned early on in life lessons of self-worth and dignity as her mother encouraged her to express herself in ways she felt important. Hurston's father, John Hurston (1861–1917), was a carpenter and Baptist preacher. In the earliest days of her youth, Hurston heard the rhythmic cadences of Baptist preaching that would later serve as source material in her work to record the folk culture of poor Black people in the South. At the age of nine, Hurston was sent away to live with older siblings attending boarding school in Jacksonville, Florida. Because of a lack of finances and a poor relationship with her father and stepmother, she lived on her own at age fourteen, working as a receptionist, wardrobe girl, manicurist, waitress, servant, and nursemaid. She enrolled in Howard Preparatory School in 1918 and received the Associate Arts degree in 1920. She earned a scholarship to Barnard College, from which she earned her B.A. degree. One of her Barnard professors, impressed with her work, introduced her to famous anthropologist Franz Boas, with whom she worked as an apprentice as she began her life's work of collecting, preserving, and presenting the folk traditions of Black life.

Hurston completed four novels, *Jonah's Gourd Vine* (1934), *Their Eyes Were Watching God* (1937), *Moses, Man of the Mountain* (1942), and *Seraph on the Suwanee* (1948). She also completed two books of folklore, *Mules and Men* (1935) and *Tell My Horse* (1938), as well as an autobiography, *Dust*

Tracks on a Road (1942). Committed to a new genre of literature, Hurston rejected a scholarly anthropological approach to recording Black folk culture in the South and instead attempted to write in the language of "the folk," using the colorful style of storytelling and imagination as a way of portraying the wisdom of that culture.

In Cannon's selection of Hurston as a resource for womanist theologizing, Cannon clearly has chosen a figure whose work comes from the same appreciation of Black folk culture as Alice Walker outlines in her definition of the term "womanist." In her autobiographical *Dust Tracks on the Road*, Hurston describes the struggle she encountered as she moved between the world of her roots—poor, rural Black culture—and the world of academia. Her first effort to collect anthropological data in the South was a disaster:

> My first six months were disappointing. I found out later that it was not because I had no talents for research, but because I did not have the right approach. The glamour of Barnard College was still upon me. I dwelt in marble halls. I knew where the material was all right. But I went about asking, in carefully accented Barnardese, "Pardon me, but do you know any folk-tales or folk songs?" The men and women who had whole treasures of material just seeping through their pores looked at me and shook their heads. No, they had never heard of anything like that around there.[18]

Hurston learned that in order to hear the stories of "the folk," she had to be one of them, sitting on porch steps and rocking away hours in porch swings or rocking chairs, telling her own tales with the best of them. As bell hooks describes Hurston,

> In Eatonville, Hurston was a subject in the community speaking with, and to, other subjects with mutual pleasure and exchange. Implicit in this approach was the deconstruction of the subject/object relationship that characterized the anthropological work she had studied.[19]

In devising a new methodology for doing scholarship, Hurston made clear that her commitment, ultimately, was not to the academy but to "the folk." As Cannon notes,

> The primary impetus for all her writings was to capture the density of simple values inherent in the provincialism of blacks who work on railroads, live in sawmill camps, toil in phosphate mines, earning their keep as common laborers.[20]

One example of the way in which Hurston captures the simplicity of folk life can be seen in a brief passage from one of her articles, "John Reading Goes to Sea":

> No one in their community had ever been farther than Jacksonville. Few, indeed had ever been there. Their own gardens, general store, and occasional trips to the county seat—seven miles away—sufficed for all their needs. Life was simple indeed with these folks.[21]

This methodological principle, that one must be part of the community in order to tell the stories of Black women's lives, their misery, their children, their resistance, and their God, is one close to the heart of womanist theologizing. Hurston, then, serves as an example of how to go about the task of constructing God-talk.

While Cannon gives much attention to historical research to surface African-American women whose names and theological viewpoints have been lost to history, she is also open to using the writings of African-American males and others with liberation perspectives as resources for womanist reflection. In addition to the literary traditions of slave narratives and the writings of Zora Neale Hurston, she uses aspects of the theologies of Howard Thurman and Martin Luther King, Jr. , emphasizing in particular the *imago dei* concepts in each. Thurman's mystical emphasis on community and King's emphasis on justice are both important to her thinking. Using the notion that each Black woman is made in the image of God, Cannon offers a constructive womanist ethic for survival and for changing unjust conditions. She calls on Black women to move toward "the common ground of relatedness," alluding to Thurman's mystical sense of divine/human connectedness.[22] She writes that "the mystical ground of dignity and the need for love and community in struggle really must be made explicit in our contemporary times."[23]

Hermeneutical Considerations

Jacquelyn Grant argues for the centrality of Black women's experience as key to womanist theological reflection, rooting Black women's experience in the biblical tradition. She writes,

> The source for Black women's understanding of God has been twofold: first, God's revelation directly to them, and secondly, God's revelation as witnessed in the Bible and as read and heard in the context of their experience. The understanding of God as creator, sus-

tainer, comforter, and liberator took on life as they agonized over their pain, and celebrated the hope that as God delivered the Israelites, they would be delivered as well.[24]

The hermeneutical principle for womanist theology offered by Grant is that "the Bible must be read and interpreted in the light of Black women's own experience of oppression and God's revelation within that context."[25] Grant places importance on the biblical witness, with emphasis on Jesus' question to those around him, "Who do you say that I am?" (Mark 8:29). For Grant, it is important to ask the question, "Who do womanists say that Jesus Christ is?"[26]

Delores Williams also intentionally struggles with developing new hermeneutics for interpreting scripture and church tradition, both of which have been used to oppress African-American women. Williams's hermeneutics differ concretely from those of Jacquelyn Grant, as well as from those of James Cone and other male Black liberation theologians, who lift up the exodus theme and its God of Liberation as the governing motifs of the Bible. By pointing to the story of Hagar, the slave whose story, claims Williams, was not one of liberation but of survival, Williams offers a counter-motif to that of Black male liberation theology. Hagar's story, insists Williams, was one of human ingenuity for survival. Hagar was not liberated; she merely struggled to beat the odds to survive. Her story of survival is one that has been passed on through the Black church and deserves to be named as a resource for womanist understanding of God.

In addition to offering the story of Hagar as a model for womanist understanding of the ways God acts in Black women's lives—ways that are not always liberating—Williams wrestles directly with other nonliberating aspects of scripture and church tradition. Among these, she lists Amos 9:7, in which the term "Cushites," dark-skinned Ethiopians, is used pejoratively and the story of Ham in Genesis 9:20–27, in which Noah cursed the land of Canaan, decreeing it to be "a slave of slaves," a verse used in the pulpit as a defense of the institution of chattel slavery of Blacks in the U.S. Similarly in the New Testament, Paul's advice to slaves to obey their masters, in essence, condones the institution of slavery. Discovering this nonliberative thread of biblical tradition, Williams comments: "The fact remains: slavery in the Bible is a natural and unprotested institution in the social and economic life of ancient society—except on occasion when the Jews are themselves enslaved."[27]

Pointing to the problem that non-Jews who are slaves are not included in the election of the exodus theme, Williams devises a new biblical hermeneutic, identification and ascertainment, for dealing with these nonliberating aspects of the tradition. She wants to speak of both "a God who liberates (the God of the enslaved Hebrews) and a God who does

not liberate (the God of the non-Hebrew female slave Hagar)."[28] Her
hermeneutic is intended first to help theologians discover the subjective
aspects of their own experience that they share with biblical events and
characters. This introspection helps theologians to identify hidden oppressions, such as the exclusion of the biblical Hagar from the exodus motif. It
is also intended to help theologians understand the ways that contemporary Hagars, the most marginalized of Black women, are excluded from the
liberation motif of Black (male) liberation theology. In addition to this
personal or subjective introspection, the theologian is asked to pose similar questions to the faith community to which he or she belongs. This
communal inquiry is intended to reveal further assumptions and biases
coded in sermons or songs that do not do justice to African-American
women. Finally, Williams asks that

> theologians engage the objective mode of inquiry that ascertains
> *both* the biblical events, characters and circumstances with whom
> the biblical writers have identified *and* those with whom the biblical
> writers have not identified, that is those who are victims of those
> with whom the biblical writers have identified.[29]

This process of identification and ascertainment is intended to provide the
necessary perspective for theologians to be critical of the biblical text when
it is oppressive and to be critical of those methods of interpretation that fail
to take into account the situations of those, such as Hagar, whom God does
not liberate.

This reading of scripture through the eyes of Hagar, and the positing of a
"God who does not liberate" alongside a "God who liberates" is critical for
Williams. Recognizing that scripture and church tradition may not always
be liberative, Williams wants to add other sources for womanist theological
reflection. These "woman-inclusive correctives"[30] may come from either
non-Christian or non-Jewish sources, including African sources, particularly those of West Africa during the slave period.

The category of experience is placed on equal par with the use of the
Bible as a source for womanist theology. However, Williams is critical of the
term "Black experience" as it has been used in the theologies of Cone and
others, for it has largely ignored the experience of Black women. Instead,
she proposes the category of "wilderness experience" as a more inclusive
category that includes women, men, and families. She prefers "wilderness
experience" to "Black experience," in part, because this term is inclusive of
the biblical Hagar's survival experience in the wilderness. It also speaks to
that aspect of the exodus story in which the ex-slaves complained of the
work necessary in the struggle for freedom. In addition, Williams prefers
this term because "the biblical wilderness tradition also emphasizes sur-

vival, quality of life formation with God's direction and the work of building a peoplehood and a community."[31] In Williams's hermeneutics, the
story of Hagar and her "God who does not liberate" are crucial to her
understanding of the role of womanist theology as the story of survival of
Black women and of all those for whom they are concerned.

Womanist Conceptions of God

In turning to the conceptions of God being outlined in womanist theology, several themes become apparent. Jacquelyn Grant describes the relationality of God in terms of encounter with Jesus as a central feature of
womanist theology. Delores Williams's insistence that God is not always a
God of liberation offers further insight into womanist understandings of the
relationship between God and African-American women. Williams offers
the metaphor of encounter with Jesus in the wilderness because she feels that
the wilderness describes womanist struggle for survival. The relationality of
God is further explored in Katie Geneva Cannon's emphasis on a personal,
direct relationship with Jesus—one often learned in the context of family
and home—as another aspect of womanist theology and spirituality.

A second theme I explore in this section returns to the necessity of survival. Here I look at the connection between womanist understandings of
the omnipotence of God and the struggle to resist evil. The question on
some basic level is "Who's in charge?" Is the all-powerful God ultimately in
charge, and, if so, why did God allow the evils of slavery? How does God
empower African-Americans to resist the evils of oppression?

A third theme I explore is that of the embodiment of God in African-
American women's lives. In this section I will rely on Katie Geneva
Cannon's use of Zora Neale Hurston as source for theological reflection as
she focuses on the ways that God acts in African-American women's lives to
give them a sense of dignity, of courage, and of grace.

The Relationality of God: Encounter with Jesus

Jacquelyn Grant introduces the motif of encounter with Jesus as key to
womanist survival in *White Women's Christ and Black Women's Jesus:
Feminist Christology and Womanist Response* (1989). Grant discovers in the
slave narratives and other literary records that God is seen as one who is
available for encounter. She finds this encounter described in the words of
an old slave woman, who prays, "Come to we, dear Massa Jesus."[32] This
Jesus who comes encounters all that the old woman has to offer—her tears
and her love. This Jesus comes to help and comfort when high and mighty
white folk will not bother. This Jesus, greater than even Mr. Lincoln, is not
ashamed to care for her.

Grant also uses the example of Sojourner Truth. When asked by a preacher if she used biblical texts as the source of her preaching, Sojourner Truth is reported to have answered, "When I preaches, I has jest one text to preach from, an' I always preaches from this one. My text is, when I found Jesus."[33] Texts such as these lead Grant to speak of "the time that she [Sojourner Truth] met Jesus" and of her "encounter with Jesus."[34] This language is characteristic of Grant's description of the personal, experiential character of Black women's relationship with God.

The Wilderness

Delores Williams further develops the theme of encounter with God in Jesus in her description of divine/human relationship in the wilderness, which she places at the center of womanist spirituality. In part, Williams chooses the metaphor of the wilderness because she feels it is descriptive of the personal experience that many African-American women have with God.

For Williams the metaphor of the wilderness signals the place of divine/human encounter, an understanding gleaned from her analysis of African-American spirituals. The wilderness represents in Black folk religion the "sacred-space-meeting-Jesus,"[35] the place where Hagar learns to survive. In one spiritual, it is the place where "I wait up-on de Lord, My God" and the place you go "if you want to find Jesus . . ." or if "you want to get religion" or "if you spec' to be converted." The wilderness is the place where "Jesus a waitin' to meet you." As one refrain notes, "If you want to find Jesus, go in de wilderness."[36] In this sacred encounter the divine is spoken of alternately as "de Lord," "my God," and "Jesus," with little or no distinction made between these names for the divine. In the wilderness, one has the opportunity to meet the Lord/God/Jesus and be changed.

Williams notes five elements of this transformative divine/human encounter in the wilderness, as reflected in the spiritual songs of the antebellum period.[37] First, the religious experience was structured as a period of physical isolation of the slave from the environment of slavery. One "goes to" the wilderness on a solitary journey. Second, a relationship is established between Jesus and the slave. Third, Jesus heals what is most in need of healing. Fourth, a transformation occurs as the slave is converted. Finally, the slave returns changed in some way.

The highly experiential, transformative nature of the wilderness journey can be noted in a second spiritual analyzed by Williams. In this spiritual, the refrain "How did you feel when you came out de wilderness?" is repeated throughout.[38] In order to ascertain whether or not the transformation had occurred, ethical questions are asked: "Did you love your brother when you came out de wilderness . . . Did you love your sister when you came out de wilderness?" The true test of transformation is revealed in the implied answer to the question, "Tell me, brudder and sister, did you meet Jesus in de wilderness?" The wilderness signifies a positive experience, though not necessarily an easy one, where slaves struggled to find Jesus and to be healed in significant ways. In choosing "wilderness" as a key metaphor for representing African-American women's experience of survival and of their encounter with the divine, Williams emphasizes the importance of religious experience in womanist theologizing about God.

Meeting God at Home

A third dimension of the relationality of God through personal encounter with Jesus can be found in Cannon's autobiographical statements about her own spirituality and the spirituality of her family. These reflections revolve around the centrality of prayer, the importance of personal experience of God, and the experience of God in relationship to loved ones. Cannon speaks of God in several ways. She writes of God as "the Creator who sustains me morning by morning, day by day."[39] In addition to understanding God as a personal source of sustenance, she finds God present in various rituals, often centered around family. Family prayer is a "sacred corporate event."[40] Claiming that she does not know "all the rituals and symbols that make God present,"[41] Cannon writes that "gospel music is essential."[42] There is a direct connection between experience of God and music. This comment is followed with a statement about the presence of God in relationship. Cannon writes, "I also notice something when I'm playing with my nieces and nephews. . . . And I experience God when I'm with them."[43] This glimpse of Cannon's personal experience of God as a source of sustenance, and as one who is experienced in the words and rhythms of Black music, as well as one who is experienced as family, points back to a spirituality that has been nurtured at home.

As Cannon describes her mother's faith, she once again links the importance of prayer with a personal relationship with God:

> Believing that a direct personal relationship with God exists, my mother always concludes her stories with a long prayer of intercession, praise, and thanksgiving. Kneeling beside the couch, she prays for the needs of both the immediate and the extended family. She celebrates God's goodness, majesty, and mercy. She frequently enunciates thanks for the gifts of the earth and for all the blessings received. After a period of silence, my mother then provides time for

every family member to bear witness to the immediate power of Jesus as "heart fixer and mind regulator."[44]

Looking at this passage, one notes that not only does Cannon's mother have a personal relationship with God, but that every family member is invited to speak of the power of Jesus in their lives. In another passage, Cannon speaks of her father, Esau Cannon, testifying to his own personal experience with God "under the unction and guidance of the Holy Spirit."[45] Thus, personal relationship with God and/or Jesus forms one basic tenet of her family's faith heritage.

Prayer, along with stories and music, communicates the nature of that faith. For Cannon's mother, prayer involves intercession, praise, and thanksgiving. The God portrayed here is one with whom one can communicate. Presumably this God hears one's prayers for oneself and for others in need. Cannon's mother celebrates the goodness, majesty, and mercy of God. She thanks God for "the gifts of the earth," for creation and for food and for all God's blessings. What is of particular interest is that Cannon describes this family time of prayer, storytelling, witnessing, and singing as a ritual practiced in the midst of thunderstorms, when they would unplug the electrical appliances and gather together to wait out the storm. In other words, Cannon's family practice is to assert the goodness of God in the midst of a storm, to be thankful as the winds rage, and to praise God as thunder roars.

God's Power unto Survival:
On the Omnipotence of God and Womanist Resistance to Evil

Like Williams, Cannon is interested in the theme of survival in African-American women's lives. Cannon's *Black Womanist Ethics* investigates this theme of survival, describing the moral situation of Black women in this country since slavery, in an attempt to demonstrate the theological and ethical understandings that have guided the praxis of Black women in the struggle for their own survival and the survival of their communities. Cannon demonstrates that an important source for womanist theological and ethical reflection is the literary tradition of Black women. In looking at the moral situation of Black women since slavery and the values reflected in their literary tradition, Cannon hopes to provide a framework for a constructive approach to womanist ethics.

Cannon is interested in exploring slave narratives as a resource for theological reflection, in part, because she believes they convey important values to the African-American community that have enabled its survival. In the historical section of *Black Womanist Ethics*, Cannon illustrates some of the ways that Black slaves viewed God. Here she describes what she terms the "double-edged sword" of the antebellum Black church—it helped slaves to accommodate to the horrors of slavery when their best hope was merely to survive, and it also served as a source of strength for resisting the tyranny of slavery.

> Confidence in the sovereignty of God, in an omnipotent, omni-present, and omniscient God, helped slaves accommodate to the sys-tem of chattel slavery. With justice denied, hopes thwarted and dreams shattered, Black Christians believed that it was God who gave them emotional poise and balance in the midst of their oppression.[46]

When all else around them seemed hopeless, Black slaves could turn to God, singing, praying, and shouting their troubles away. At the same time, the Black religious experience provided slaves with a religion that enabled them to resist slavery and to work for freedom. Cannon writes that it was "unwavering faith in God"[47] that provided Blacks with both the patience and perseverance to engage in struggle and resistance. Slave narratives depict belief in a sovereign, omnipotent, omnipresent, omniscient God whose justice will win out despite all indications to the contrary. The spirituals depict a God who provides slaves with a will to freedom and the strength to resist the institution of slavery. These slave narratives and other literary sources provide Cannon with a wealth of material that demonstrates the ability of Black people to persevere and survive in the worst of circumstances.

In addition to finding literary sources which support womanist survival ethics, Cannon also critically examines the writings of one author whose literary themes she views as "Christian apologies for slavery."[48] Phillis Wheatley (1753?–1784) was the first African-American woman to publish a book of poetry, which was entitled *Poems on Various Subjects, Religious and Moral.* Cannon cites one of Wheatley's poems to demonstrate the extent to which some Black women "imitated the felicity of thought and the literary style of the patron slaveowners."[49]

> 'Twas mercy brought me from my Pagan land,
> Taught my benighted soul to understand
> That there's a god, that there's a Saviour too:
> Once I redemption neither sought nor knew.
> Some view our sable race with scornful eye;
> "Their colour is a diabolic dye."
> Remember, Christians, Negroes, black as Cain,
> May be refined, and join the angelic train.[50]

The process Cannon uses here, of looking critically at traditions in Black church life to discern those that are liberating and those that are nonliberating, is an example of what Williams has come to term the "identification-ascertainment" hermeneutic.

In contrast to the view expressed in Wheatley's "On Being Brought from Africa to America," cited above, Cannon finds just the opposite view in spiritual songs. She writes that "slaveholders spoke of slavery being 'God ordained,' while slaves sang a song of resistance:

> O Freedom! O Freedom!
> O Freedom, I love thee!
> And before I be a slave,
> I'll be buried in my grave,
> And go home to my Lord and be free."[51]

Jacquelyn Grant, who also uses African-American literary tradition as a source for her reflection, treats the theme of God's omnipotence and womanist resistance to evil by stressing the relationship of African-American women with Jesus. Using the slave narratives, she identifies the power of God in Jesus as "one who empowers the weak."[52] Jesus knows the struggles of Black women because he has struggled too, and he lends Black women the strength to carry on. God in Christ is a source of empowerment. This identification of Christ with Black women enabled Jarena Lee to preach, enabled Sojourner Truth to fight for freedom from the oppression of slavery, and gave her reason to believe that women could possibly save the world. Jesus, the source of empowerment, dignity, and love to Black women enabled Sojourner Truth to exclaim, "Lord, I can love even de white folks!"[53] Grant cautions the reader that this love was neither sentimental nor passive, but rather "a tough, active love"[54] born of her own sense of self-worth.

The Embodiment of God in African-American Women's Lives

The theme of God's embodiment in the lives of African-American women can be illustrated in Cannon's treatment of black women's moral agency. As mentioned earlier, it is important to note that while Cannon may not speak specifically of the attributes of God, she assumes the sacredness of all life and of African-American women's lives in particular. In *Black Womanist Ethics* she surfaces three primary qualities that describe the lives of African-American women, qualities that are of God. These qualities, in part, have been necessitated by historical oppression and resistance to evil in the survival strategies of African-Americans living under slavery and in a racist society. Cannon names these "invisible dignity," "quiet grace," and "unshouted courage." She discovers these three key concepts of Black women's moral agency in the life and work of Zora Neale Hurston.

Human Dignity as the Embodiment of God

Cannon notes that throughout her life and work, Hurston insists on the dignity or, as Cannon says, the "human beingness" of people of color.[55] This understanding stems from a belief in the *imago dei* concept that God created all people in God's image. Insisting on the dignity of Black people, Hurston cites the folk wisdom that says, "God made people duck by duck."[56] Hurston rejects the prevailing notion that Black people were somehow inferior, and she also rejects any internalized view of the tragedy of Black life, writing instead in her 1928 essay "How It Feels to Be Colored Me" that she does not bemoan her situation in life:

> But I am not tragically colored. There is no great sorrow damned up in my soul, nor lurking behind my eyes. I do not mind at all. I do not belong to the sobbing school of negrohood who hold that nature somehow has given them a lowdown dirty deal and whose feelings are hurt about it. . . . No, I do not weep at the world. I am too busy sharpening my oyster knife.[57]

This sense of human dignity is reflected both in her autobiographical writings and in her efforts to capture the wisdom of southern Black folklore.

One could surmise from her life and work that Hurston's own sense of dignity and courage were rooted in her view of her essential equality with Black men and with white people. It was important for her to preserve in her literary works examples of the oral tradition of poor Black folk which demonstrate this deeply felt sense of God-given dignity. One of the more famous sermons she recounts, "The Wounds of Jesus,"[58] provides a necessary corrective to the racist mythology of the period that treated Blacks as inferior to whites. In this sermon, the preacher begins by reciting the story of the creation of the world. In this story, God declares that God is ready to "make man" [sic] and asks the question "Who shall I make him [sic] after?" The sun, moon, and stars, portrayed anthropomorphically, each ask to be the one in whose image humanity is created. To these requests, God responds, "NO! I'll make man [sic] in my own image, ha!" The creation narrative preserved in Hurston's work serves the purpose of ensuring the Black community that God creates all people in God's image. Despite whatever message of subjugation one might hear all week long, on Sunday morning the message was that God chose to create each person in God's own image, a sure sign of the individual worth of each human being.

One can also find evidence that Hurston believed in the essential equal-ity of men and women in her account of the sermon "Behold de Rib!" in *Mules and Men*. The preacher tells the story of creation and then specifically confronts the sexism prevalent in society:

> Behold de rib!
> Brothers, if God
> Had taken dat bone out of man's head
> He would have meant for woman to rule, hah
> If he had taken a bone out of his foot,
> He would have meant for us to dominize and rule.
> He could have made her out of back-bone
> And then she would have been behind us.
> But, no, God Amighty, he took de bone out of his side
> So dat places de woman beside us;
> Hah! God knowed his own mind.
> Behold de rib!
> And now I leave dis thought wid you,
> Let us all go marchin' up to de gates of Glory . . .
> Male and female like God made us
> Side by side[59]

In illustrating "invisible dignity" in the lives of Black women, Cannon emphasizes the concept of *imago dei*. The sermons "Wounds of Jesus" and "Behold de Rib!" illustrate the idea that God is a God of equality, intention-ally creating humanity in God's image, male and female as equals meant to walk "side by side." The concept of human dignity in these writings cannot be overemphasized in understanding how Cannon perceives God to be working in the lives of women and men in the Black community.

Hurston's personal religious commitment remains ambiguous, since she never stated that she accepted the belief systems she so ardently sought to preserve in her collection of Black folk culture. Nonetheless, it is clear that Hurston believed that these stories, sermons, prayers, and portrayals of Black folk life were important aspects of Black culture that deserved greater attention. For Cannon, they serve as important sources for contemporary womanist theological reflection.

Grace and Courage as the Embodiment of God

In continuing the discussion of the ways in which God is embodied in the lives of African-American women, Cannon offers a second feature of Black women's moral agency, which she terms "quiet grace." Asserting that

Black women have never had the option of either becoming immobilized by the terrors of slavery and racist society or of complaining too loudly, Cannon ascribes the term "quiet grace" to the quality of hushed resistance found in the lives of Black women. If one were to ask Cannon what this has to do with her view of God, probably Cannon would posit that "quiet grace" *is* God acting in the lives of Black women for their survival and for the survival of the Black community. Made in God's image, poor Black women move with all the stealth, craftiness, and wisdom of the God Who Knows the Truth in order to effect survival.

Cannon points to the character Nanny Crawford in Hurston's *Their Eyes Were Watching God* as one such example of a strong Black woman whose survival wisdom can empower later generations of Black women. First, Nanny passes on mother wisdom to her granddaughter Janie. In this passage, Nanny describes the wretched situation of the Black woman:

> Honey, de white man is de ruler of everything as fur as Ah been able tuh find out. Maybe it's some place way off in de ocean where de black man is in power, but we don't know nothin' but what we see, so, de white man throw down de load and tell de nigger man tuh pick it up because he have to, but he don't tote it. He hand it to his womenfolks. De nigger woman is de mule uh de world so fur as Ah can see.[60]

Nanny is not content with this view of the world, however. And so she follows this commentary with her rejection of this role for Black women, saying, "Ah been praying fuh it tuh be different wid you. Lawd, Lawd, Lawd!"[61] In Hurston's portrayal Nanny Crawford's God hears her protests against Black women being treated as "de mule uh de world." Implicit is Nanny's view that God is someone to whom one can pray when one wants to protest unjust oppression. Nanny does not settle for what she is given; instead, she implores God to change injustice into justice.

Nanny Crawford's view of God also reveals her belief in God as protector, someone who keeps watch over her in the face of the injustices of slavery. Having been beaten because her child resembles the white slave-owner who exploited her, and fearing for her child's life, Nanny runs away and hides in a swamp. Bleeding from the lashes of a whip and afraid of the sounds and the animals of the swamp at night, she nonetheless declares, "But nothin' never hurt me 'cause de Lawd knowed how it was."[62] "De Lawd" provides Nanny with a source of strength and courage that allows her to prevail. "De Lawd" protects her because "de Lawd" understands her predicament. "De Lawd" knows her suffering and her pain and wills her survival.

A second example of "quiet grace" can be seen as Janie Crawford comes to the end of a thirty-year search for personal and spiritual freedom. Tea Cake Woods, her third husband, is the source of much happiness for her. However, the tragedy of her own quest is that she is forced to kill him in self-defense when he becomes violent toward her. In a dialogue with her friend Pheoby, Janie reveals the wisdom of her spiritual search for her sense of self as a woman:

> It's uh known fact, Pheoby, you got to *go* there tuh *know* there. Yo' papa and yo' mama and nobody else can't tell yuh and show yuh. Two things everybody's got tuh do fuh theyselves. They got tuh go tuh God, and they got tuh find out about livin' fuh theyselves.[63]

Here Hurston establishes a new genre of protagonist for Black women who refuse to accept their oppression and instead find acceptance in the sanctity of their very selves.[64] As Janie Crawford comes to a sense of her self, she asserts that God is the one you go to while, at the same time, you are seeking your own answers. God does not provide all the answers; they must be found through human seeking and surviving. In citing Janie Crawford as an example of "quiet grace," Cannon too reveals her understanding that as women "go tuh God," and as they "find out about livin' fuh theyselves," hope is born.

Not entirely unrelated to Cannon's notion of "quiet grace" is her notion of "unshouted courage," a third concept of Black women's moral agency demonstrated in the work of Hurston. This is how Cannon defines it:

> Unshouted courage is the quality of steadfastness, akin to fortitude, in the face of formidable oppression. The communal attitude is far more than "grin and bear it." Rather, it involves the ability to "hold on to life" against major oppositions. It is the incentive to facilitate change, to chip away the oppressive structures, bit by bit, to celebrate and rename their experiences in empowering ways. "Unshouted courage" as a virtue is the often unacknowledged inner conviction that keeps one's appetite whet for freedom.[65]

Cannon understands the virtue of "unshouted courage" to be a result of "the forced responsibility of Black women."[66] This courage enables Black women to meet the difficulties of their lives "with fortitude and resistance."[67] God is the one who gives Black women their source of strength and courage to prevail against all odds, a formula requiring cooperation between God and humanity. For Cannon, this occurs as Black women affirm their own personhood and seek the survival of their community in the face of slavery, lynching, and all forms of racial oppression.

Jesus the Black Woman

As noted previously, Grant and Heyward argue that often in spiritual songs, slave narratives, and in the prayers and sermons of the Black church, little distinction is made between God and Jesus. Because of this correlation between the terms for God and Jesus in the life of the Black church, womanist thoughts about christology and atonement are directly relevant to their discussion of God-talk.

In her 1982 article, Grant focused attention in particular on the issue of christology, calling for Black theologians to rethink "the meaning of the total Jesus Christ Event"[68] through the experience of oppressed Black women. Her work, *White Women's Christ and Black Women's Jesus,* takes up this very challenge. This work makes clear the distinction between the christological questions of many white and Black women. Whereas white women have questioned the possibility of a male savior, Black women have maintained that Jesus is central to their liberation struggle. Grant critiques white feminist theological attempts to provide a constructive feminist christology by pointing to the racism inherent in much of white feminist thought. Grant criticizes the work of Rosemary Radford Ruether, Letty Russell, and others for failing to adequately treat the issue of racism in developing a feminist christology. Grant therefore rejects Russell's model of Jesus as archetypal servant, Ruether's model of Jesus as sister, and Carter Heyward's model of Jesus as brother, asserting that none of these models takes seriously Black women's experience.

Grant makes use of slave narratives and Black women's literature as resources for her womanist theological reflections on Jesus. In looking to these sources, she discovers that asserting that Jesus is God meant that "white people were not God."[69] Just as the biblical expression "Jesus is Lord" implied that Caesar was not, so the understanding that Jesus is God implies that white people are not God. Grant recalls that among slave women, it was common to refer to "Massa Jesus" as "de one great Massa," with the implication being that the white "massas" were far from God.[70]

In addition to looking to the slave narratives as source material for theological reflection, Grant looks also to Black theologians. Here she finds the essential affirmation that Jesus as God incarnate represents freedom. This political messiah means freedom "from the sociopsychological, psychocultural, economic and political oppression of Black people."[71] This Jesus is concerned with freeing Black people from all forms of oppression. Using the insights from James Cone, J. Deotis Roberts, and others, Grant observes that "the identification is so real that Jesus Christ in fact becomes

Black."[72] This God in Jesus, identified with "the least of these," becomes identified with Black people. Grant cites Cone's observation that "the least in America are literally and symbolically present in Black people."[73] Having established that God in Jesus, who identifies with "the least," is present in Black people, Grant then makes the assertion that since Black women suffer the triple oppressions of racism, classism, and sexism, Black women most appropriately represent "the least" in U.S. society. She writes, "To locate the Christ in Black people is a radical and necessary step, but an understanding of Black women's reality challenges us to go further. Christ among the least must also mean Christ in the community of Black women."[74] Grant writes, "For me, it means today, this Christ, found in the experiences of Black women, is a Black woman."[75]

In her most radical statement, that Christ is a Black woman, Grant demonstrates her belief that "the significance of Christ is not his maleness, but his humanity."[76] For Grant, the humanity of Christ identifying with "the least of these" is best expressed in the lives of Black women. Thus she offers a challenge to both Black theology and to white feminist theology to rethink christology.

God in Jesus: On the Blood of the Cross

Delores Williams takes up this challenge to rethink christology. In an article entitled "Black Women's Surrogacy Experience and the Christian Notion of Redemption," Williams continues the christological discussion from a womanist perspective. In this article, she offers a striking womanist critique of atonement theories that view Christ as surrogate sufferer for humanity. Williams begins with a historical analysis of the role that Black women have played as involuntary and voluntary surrogates. The "mammy" role forced on them by the institution of slavocracy demanded that they be available to the sexual whims of the white slavemasters and that they provide surrogate motherhood to white families, while often having their own children torn from them and sold into slavery. In the period after slavery, voluntary surrogacy replaced involuntary surrogacy. Because of societal racism and sexism, often the only employment a Black woman could find was as a domestic. The pattern of sexual exploitation continued in the era after slavery, with Black women domestics subject to violation by white male employers. In addition, these domestics served as mammies to white families, providing nurturing to their children. Working long hours in order to survive, these women often saw little of their own children.

Given this historic background, Williams questions the Christian doctrine of atonement that sees Jesus as the God who comes to suffer among us. Williams writes,

More often than not the theology in mainline Christian churches, including black ones, teaches believers that sinful humankind has been redeemed because Jesus died on the cross in the place of humans, thereby taking human sin upon himself. In this sense Jesus represents the ultimate surrogate figure standing in the place of someone else: sinful humankind.[77]

Seeing Jesus as "the ultimate surrogate figure" leads Williams to question whether it is appropriate or even possible for Black women to relate to this traditional understanding of redemption. She writes,

It is therefore altogether fitting and proper for black women to ask whether the image of a surrogate-God has salvific power for black women, or whether this image of redemption supports and reinforces the exploitation that has accompanied their experience with surrogacy.[78]

For Williams, the answer is clearly that the surrogacy image of Jesus cannot speak of redemption to Black women. The task of the Black female theologian is

to use the language and sociopolitical thought of black women's world to show them that their salvation does not depend upon any form of surrogacy made sacred by human understanding of God.[79]

In her 1993 work, *Sisters in the Wilderness*, Williams raises the question again:

Can there be salvific power for black women in Christian images of oppression (for example, Jesus on the cross) meant to teach something about redemption?[80]

This time her answer is even more poignant. Here she claims that the task of the womanist theologian is

to show black women their salvation does not depend upon any form of surrogacy made sacred by traditional and orthodox understandings of Jesus' life and death. Rather, their salvation is assured by Jesus' life of resistance and by the survival strategies he used to help people survive.[81]

In other words Williams rejects outright both "traditional" and "orthodox" theories of atonement. She uses the synoptic gospels as a resource for rethinking the ways that redemption comes to Black women. In looking to the synoptics, Williams focuses on the teachings of Jesus about the Kingdom of God, his healing ministry, his concern for proclaiming a word of life to the downtrodden, and on his strategies for resisting oppression. Her focus is not on the cross but on the resurrection. If the contemporary theologian is to take seriously Black women's historic experience of surrogacy, "The theologian must show that redemption of humans can have nothing to do with any kind of surrogate role Jesus was reputed to have played in a bloody act that supposedly gained victory over sin and/or evil."[82] In attempting to construct a womanist view of redemption, it is important for Williams to demonstrate that God did not intend for Black women to be forced into voluntary or involuntary surrogacy roles. She flatly rejects the theology of the cross that places suffering at the center of redemption, announcing, "There is nothing of God in the blood of the cross. . . . Jesus did not come to be a surrogate. Jesus came for life."[83]

Following Grant's christological insistence that Jesus' presence among "the least of these" means that Jesus is present in the lives of poor Black women, Williams challenges Black women to think not of the suffering and death of Jesus as source of redemption but rather of his teaching, healing, and resistance as instructive for redemption. The example of Williams's treatment of the central concept of Christian redemption is included to illustrate the depth of rethinking of Christian theology that is necessary from a womanist perspective. Symbols as basic to Christian ritual and belief as the cross are being called into question as womanists such as Williams reflect on the meaning of God and Jesus in their lives.

The Role of the Spirit

As we observed in Latin American women's theologizing, contemporary liberation theologians are wrestling with the intermingling of indigenous and Christian representations of the sacred. The memories of the gods and goddesses that hallowed the lives of indigenous peoples before the introduction of Christianity surface in contemporary liberation theologies as resources for resistance to injustice. Womanist theology is similarly involved in an effort to understand the religious traditions of Africa that continue to give spirit to African-American Christianity. Womanist theologians have begun to discuss the relationship between the Holy Spirit of Christianity and the spirit(s) of African-based traditions. One point of contention has surfaced in the debate over whether the term womanist, which was originally defined by Alice Walker, should be used to describe African-American *Christian* women's theology. Cheryl J. Sanders has noted that "there are no references to God or Christ in [Alice Walker's] definition of womanist. For whatever reason, christology seems not to be directly relevant to the womanist concept."[84] Sanders notes that Walker embraces the notion that Black women "love the *Spirit*" without delineating any theological or christological content to that aspect of her definition. Therefore, Sanders has raised the question about the suitability of the use of the term "womanist" to describe Black Christian women's theological and ethical endeavors that affirm their connection to the Black church.

Emilie M. Townes offers a different interpretation of Walker's spirituality:

> To suggest Walker lacks a concentration on the sacred is, I believe, to miss the crux of her spirituality. Walker clearly spells out her conception of the divine, the Spirit, in the dialogue between Celie and Shug in *The Color Purple.* This view is implicit in her definition of womanist.[85]

Townes quotes the passage in which Shug explains her understanding of God to Celie:

> God is inside of you and inside of everybody else. You come into the world with God. But only them that search for it inside find it. And sometimes it just manifest itself even when you not looking, or don't know what you looking for.[86]

Townes, along with Delores Williams, asserts that one important area for further exploration in womanist theology is pneumatology—understanding the role of the Spirit. While Townes argues that African-American religious traditions have not emphasized a radically immanent concept of God, she connects the African-American experience of "walking with Jesus" with Walker's idea that "God is inside of you."

> This radically immanent concept of the divine is not readily found within the Afro-American religious experience. There is however a strong tradition of a personal Jesus who walks with us and shares our burdens and knows our sorrows. Walker's understanding of the Spirit challenges the Afro-American religious community to do what Delores Williams suggests—to create a well-developed theology of the Spirit. . . . Rather than finding Walker's understanding of the sacred marginal, I perceive her understanding of the Spirit as woven intricately into the very fabric of existence itself.[87]

In these few lines Townes points to one of the challenges facing womanist theology, as well as other forms of women's theologies, namely the development of a more articulate understanding of pneumatology in women's conceptions of the sacred. The roles of the Spirit, the spirit, the Holy Spirit, and the human spirit need to be clarified, not only in womanist theology but in all constructive liberationist efforts to understand and live God.

Contributions

There are many important links in the thought of Williams, Cannon, and Grant that show how womanist scholars are contributing to contemporary constructive theological efforts. First, womanist theology attempts to speak of God from the eyes of the poor Black woman. A commitment to the local Black church and to the community of Black men and women informs womanist understanding of God. Second, as Williams has noted, womanist theologians do not operate from a "two spheres" mindset, separating the sacred and the secular. Therefore, it is possible to speak of the sacred by talking of the experience of African-American women, without necessarily mentioning the word "God." Third, the category of experience is highly important in womanist conceptions of God. Williams's "wilderness experience" is the place of encounter between Black women and Jesus. Cannon similarly speaks of the importance of a personal relationship with Jesus in her family spiritual traditions, as does Grant in her christological investigations.

In addition to these consistencies in womanist theological efforts to understand God, each of these theologians emphasizes additional items for consideration. Williams's emphasis on survival in the wilderness and her distinction between a "God who liberates" and a "God who does not liberate" points to an important question. How does Williams understand "liberation"? How does her understanding of this term differ from that of other liberation theologians? This question will be addressed in the section dealing with commonalities and differences between feminist, *mujerista* and Latin American feminist, and womanist conceptions of God.

Cannon's reflections on Zora Neale Hurston and on her family spiritual heritage reveal other important womanist understandings of God. Primary among these is the *imago dei* principle, which insists that even the poorest Black woman is made in the image of God. Her sense of dignity and self-worth stems from her relationship to God the Creator and is not dependent upon others' estimation of her. Other images of God active in the spiritual understandings of the Hurston characters highlighted by Cannon include notions of God as protector, God as The One Who Knows the Truth, and God as source of courage. One additional set of images can be seen in Cannon's family heritage, which provides her with the images of the God who sustains us "day by day" and of the God Who Is Present in the Midst of the Storm. These images of God provide a rich resource for reflection and deserve further attention in the development of constructive womanist conceptions of God.

The views of God implicit in womanist theology maintain a delicate balance between traditional understandings of God's transcendence and God's immanence. This balance may be attributable to the historical context in which Black women have lived. Cannon speaks of both God's omniscience and omnipotence. In the face of white lies about the inferiority of Blacks, it is important to remember that there is a God Who Knows the Truth, an omniscient God who can distinguish between the lies of those who oppress and the truth of those who are victimized by oppression. This leads to a secondary insistence that Black women know, intuitively, as God knows. There is an aspect of God's truth that resides in the mind and actions of Black women struggling for freedom. Nanny Crawford illustrates this principle when she says that in spite of being beaten, nothing hurt her, because "de Lawd knowed how it was." The Lord knew that the slaveowner had beaten her because her child resembled him, and the Lord knew the truth of how that resemblance had come to be. Rape and sexual exploitation of slave women were commonplace. So the Lord knew, and Nanny knew. Thus, the transcendence of God is balanced with the immanence of God.

A similar analogy can be made about the omnipotence of God. In the face of those who seem to be all-powerful, whether slaveowners or slum landlords, it is good to remember that there is a God whose power is greater. Recognizing the finite nature of the power of slaveowners and slum landlords gives Black women their own power to resist, a power born of God. Nanny Crawford demonstrates this wisdom in her analysis of Black-white and male-female power dynamics. The white man passes the back-breaking work to the Black man, who then passes it to the Black woman. Being able to understand this power dynamic gives Nanny the power to resist—to pray that it might not be that way for Janie. Again, there is a delicate balance in play between understandings of God's transcendence and God's immanence in the examples that Cannon underscores as exemplary of the virtues of "invisible dignity," "quiet grace," and "unshouted courage."

In summary, African-American women reflecting on the ways that God works in the world offer fresh insights for theological reflection that are crucial to the Black community and to others who are willing to hear. They offer rich material for discussion and amplification as women from differing cultural perspectives construct new understandings of God.

4

Women's Theologies in Dialogue
Issues of Difference and Commonality

THE EMERGENCE of women's theologies of liberation has been marked by serious tension among women of different cultural backgrounds. Audre Lorde's critique of Mary Daly and Delores Williams's similar critique of Rosemary Radford Ruether serve as telling reminders of these tensions. Not only differences in race, but also in class, ethnicity, sexual orientation, and social context have caused women to develop their own culturally identified, separate strands of theology. A session of the Women and Religion Section of the 1991 American Academy of Religion entitled "Appropriation and Reciprocity in Womanist/*Mujerista*/Feminist Work"[1] marked the beginning of a constructive new era in which women from differing cultural backgrounds attempted to find a basis and ground rules for discussion and dialogue. The women theologians present thought they could benefit from learning about one another's efforts to construct new ways to think about God. It is my conviction that God is alive in this process as women of different racial, ethnic, cultural, and class identities work on their own projects and also work together in mutuality. Listening carefully to each other's words, hearing God calling across the boundaries of difference, we have the opportunity to enter into a new phase of constructive theology that respects difference and calls us to the common task of reknowing, renaming, and renewing the world. Outside the field of religious studies, feminist theorists have been engaged in important work relating to issues of particularity and difference in women's experience. This work is helpful to feminist, *mujerista,* and womanist theologians interested in multicultural dialogue and theological reflection. The work of Chela Sandoval is helpful, for she points to a juncture in our praxis wherein women of color and white feminists might work together.

Sandoval provides an important theoretical and methodological option for theologians interested in liberating praxis to bring about necessary social change. Given the importance of praxis to white feminist, *mujerista*, Latin American, and womanist theologizing, Sandoval's theory and method will be presented in depth. Her theoretical and methodological work has been characterized as follows:

> Chela Sandoval, from a consideration of specific historical moments in the formation of the new political voice called women of color, has theorized a hopeful model of political identity called "oppositional consciousness," born of the skills for reading webs of power by those refused stable membership in the social categories of race, sex, or class.[2]

The development of Sandoval's thought can be traced to a 1982 report on a conference of the National Women's Studies Association that dealt with the theme of racism. In her report, Sandoval critiques the methods and assumptions of the conference and presents possibilities for constructive efforts among women of color and others for dealing with difference as a positive strategy for social change. Her chronology of the white women's movement underscores the critique made by Audre Lorde and others:

> The contemporary women's movement was constructed with the best of intentions. But underlying contradictions began to emerge as U.S. feminists of color denounced the racism and classism inherent in a "unified women's movement" which could only be "unified" within the perimeters of white women's values.[3]

In response to this masking of real difference, women of color began to call the "women's movement" by a new name, "the white women's movement."[4]

To counteract the racism of the white women's movement, women of color began to develop strategies of resistance, including theories of particularity and difference. In addition, women of color began to work together in a united front as one means of confronting racism. In detailing the emergence of solidarity among women of color, Sandoval writes that women of color did not want to repeat what they saw as the primary mistake of the white women's movement:

> The previous (white) women's movement had attempted to create an empowered sisterhood through erasing our differences as women of color under the "unifying" category of "women," a category which has given its particular meanings in opposition to the category

"men." The privileging of this binary opposition, however, made invisible important differences within each of these categories. Thus racism was unthinkingly perpetuated in the name of liberation.[5]

In order to avoid this mistake, Sandoval describes a process whereby women of color learn to manage their differences by viewing them as a resource available to the group to confront racism and effect social change. Sandoval's vision of U.S. third-world feminism as a means to oppose oppressive power structures and ideologies involves shifting strategies, loyalties, and tactics, depending on the nature of the problem being addressed. She describes her theory and method of oppositional consciousness as follows:

> U.S. third world feminists must recognize that our learned sensitivity to the mobile webs of power is a skill that, once developed, can become a sophisticated form of oppositional consciousness. This is a form of oppositional consciousness which creates the opportunity for flexible, dynamic and tactical responses; it is another critical theory for political action which allows us no *single* conceptualization of our position in society. Rather, it focuses us instead upon the process of the circulation of power, on the skill of reading its moves, and on the recognition that a new morality and effective opposition resides in a self-conscious flexibility of identity and of political action which is capable, above all else, of tactically intervening in the moves of power in the name of egalitarian social relations.[6]

Sandoval understands oppositional consciousness as an intentional resistance to powers of domination and subjection that govern our society. According to Sandoval, the ability to analyze power structures and determine appropriate means of confronting them is a skill particularly highly developed among U.S. third-world feminists who have had to learn means of survival under oppressive conditions. Sandoval understands the realities of contemporary society as "complex, mobile webs of power" that must be confronted by a variety of tactics requiring sophisticated analysis and sensitivity. She also names one of the goals of oppositional consciousness, namely the development of a "new morality" that resists oppressive power structures "in the name of egalitarian social relations."

While Sandoval is writing primarily for women of color, she calls on both women of color and white women to recognize her model for change. "What is necessary is that the new model for political action and consciousness proposed here, and represented by U.S. third world feminism, be recognized by both white feminists and women of color alike."[7] Not only does

Sandoval offer a possible method whereby women might work together for justice, she also carves out a "juncture," a "location" wherein others might join in this effort:

> The juncture I am proposing . . . is extreme. It is a location wherein the praxis of U.S. third world feminism links with the aims of white feminism, studies of race, ethnicity, and marginality, and with post-modern theories of culture as they crosscut and join together in new relationships through a shared comprehension of an emerging theory and method of oppositional consciousness.[8]

Applying Sandoval's method to women's theological endeavors results in several challenges. The first is to provide a critical understanding of racism in the academy and among women. The second is to analyze issues of particularity and commonness of purpose. A third challenge is to analyze the "webs of power" that govern theological production and education. A fourth challenge is to develop multiple strategies and tactics for doing cross-cultural theological work. A fifth challenge is to engage in oppositional praxis that crosses cultural boundaries. In chapter 5, Sandoval's suggestions will be helpful in seriously considering these issues in the development of a constructive proposal for theologizing about God. Before turning to this effort, however, it is important to look at those real differences that mark the theologies of white feminists, *mujerista* and Latin American women, and womanists.

I should note at the outset that some of my observations are general in nature. Of course, it is impossible to characterize all white, Hispanic, or Black women in North America or all women in Latin America according to any particular schema without sacrificing some degree of particularity. Obviously there are many differences in the social contexts out of which different women write in Latin America. Some women are more closely allied with the academy; others work more closely with women in the base communities. Similarly, some women in North America are more involved in praxis than are others. Despite the variances within groups, which must be assumed, some broad commonalities can be identified.

Distinctives of White Feminist Liberationist Theology

Three distinctive elements of white feminist theology will be noted here. First, in chapter 1, I argued that the early period of white feminist theology owed some of its origins to white male theology, particularly to Paul Tillich's suggestion of the need to examine the trinity and to devise new symbols that are not exclusively male in nature, a project taken up in the work of Mary

Daly and others. Another aspect of those origins is that Tillich's was a theology of the academy. While his method of correlation was intended to position questions of culture relevant to that period alongside answers that spoke to people's ultimate concerns, his theology did not develop, as did that of Walter Rauschenbusch or even Reinhold Niebuhr, out of an experience with poor people on the streets of New York or Detroit.[9]

Carter Heyward is well aware of this problem, as can be seen in her critique of Tillich and of liberal theology in general:

> The liberal deity, in some anthropomorphic sense, may "love" us; but it is likely to tax our understandings of what actual loving involves. A God above God (or an essential God-Man) remains eternally unaffected by the clamor and clutter of human struggle.... God is simply above the fray.[10]

While white feminist theology sought to separate itself from traditional theology, it did not totally escape the legacy of its predecessors, resulting in at least one type of white feminist theology being rooted, not so much in praxis—as Latin American liberation theology claims all theology should be—but rather in the academy. Consequently, some white feminist theology has tended to be highly theoretical. It is written in the language of the academy and is somewhat distanced from mainstream church women, rather than being securely grounded in praxis, at least to the degree, for example, of the theology of some women working in the context of Latin American ecclesial base communities. It has also tended to gloss over issues of class and race.

I do not want to overstate the case or suggest that white feminist theology has developed without regard to praxis or social justice concerns. On the contrary, some white feminist theology has been directly involved with civil rights issues, with making the church a more just institution, and with the real life struggles of battered, sexually abused, and poor women. In this regard, the contributions of Nelle Morton, Anne McGrew Bennett, Letty Russell, and Beverly Wildung Harrison have been mentioned. Others whose names could be listed would include Mary Lee Daugherty's work with the women of Appalachia at the Appalachian Ministries Education Resource Center in Berea, Kentucky; Marie Marshall Fortune's work with the Center for the Prevention of Sexual and Domestic Violence in Seattle, Washington; or Mary Hunt's work with Women's Alliance for Theology, Ethics, and Ritual (WATER) in the Washington, D.C. , area. Many more white women, lay and ordained, have been led by their faith perspectives to work for justice in the World Council of Churches, the National Council of Churches, at the national judiciary level of their denominations, as well as in local antiracism workshops, elementary schools, Sunday schools, concert halls, soup kitchens, and in the kitchens of their own homes. The names of Joan Brown Campbell, Kathy Jan Johnson, Judy Mintier, Loey Powell, and Carole Etzler Eagleheart deserve to be remembered for their work in these contexts. Much more work needs to be done to document the history of the contributions of these white feminists as a critical part of the development of a white feminist theology of liberation in this country.

Having clearly indicated that not all white feminist theology has been of the "ivory tower" variety, sheltered from the concerns of those marginalized in society, I believe it is also important to acknowledge that some types of white feminist theologizing have been linked at the hip with the academy, limited by its protocols for objectivity, and influenced by both the content and methods of the field. My intent here is to suggest that, while Heyward was correct in criticizing Tillich for his "God above God," early white feminist theology, in particular, may be open to the critique that it posited a "Goddess above the (male) God," whose relevance to homeless, poor, marginalized, or disenfranchised people was not always clear.

A second distinctive of white feminist theology is that its starting point is white women's experience of sexism. Therefore, much of the work done by white feminist theologians has sought to develop nonsexist and nonpatriarchal images of God. This interest resulted in Mary Daly's choice of title for her work, *Beyond God the Father* (1973), in important recovery work done by Phyllis Trible in analyzing the God of Genesis 2 and 3, and in Elisabeth Schüssler Fiorenza's emphasis on "Sophia" as Jesus' preferred way of referring to God.[11] It also resulted in the publication of various texts designed for liturgical use, such as Casey Miller and Kate Swift's *Words and Women* (1977) and Sharon and Thomas Neufer Emswiler's *Women and Worship* (1974), and in Leonard Swidler's thorough cataloging of female images of God in *Biblical Affirmations of Woman* (1979).[12] This starting place is significantly different from that of Latin American women, for example, whose theology developed out of a concern for the poor and for whom class analysis, in general, is much more central to their work than it is to the work of white North American women.

A third distinctive of North American white feminist theology is Carter Heyward's and Mary E. Hunt's willingness to address lesbian concerns in their theologies. While this willingness is not unique, given that such womanist theologians as Delores Williams and Toinette Eugene have also described homophobia as one form of oppression, Heyward, in particular, has developed a distinctive lesbian theology. Heyward is quite open about her sexuality and her need to speak as a lesbian feminist theologian:

It is critical that we who can (we who have access to publishers, for example) simply speak the words, "I am a lesbian. I am feminist." The words I speak—whether about grocery shopping, Anglican spirituality, sex, or Christ—are lesbian feminist words because I speak them.[13]

The stance she takes, which argues that lesbian women are among the oppressed, "the least of these," may be a result of the influence of Latin American liberation theology. It is not a far step in moving from understanding God as the God of liberation for poor women to understanding God as the God of liberation for lesbian women. Heyward's interest in focusing on the yearning of God as a sexual aspect of the creative impulse provides rich material for cross-cultural discourse. Just as for some people, James Cone's assertion that God is Black and Jacquelyn Grant's notion that Jesus is a Black woman may open the door to new theological revelation, it may be equally valuable to develop images of God that include the notion that God is gay or that Jesus, present in "the least of these," makes her home in the community of poor lesbian women.

Distinctives of Mujerista
and Latin American Women's Theologies

In looking at the distinctives of U.S. Hispanic and Latin American women's theologies, two significant and related elements surface. First, because of their grounding in class analysis, Hispanic women's liberation theology and Latin American feminist theology have been interested in recovering images of God as the God of the poor and oppressed. At least in its early phases, the gender of God has not been their primary concern. A second interest, surfacing the forgotten indigenous and African images of God, however, has brought to light a history of female images for God that have survived in the memory of folk religion despite the efforts of the church to "Christianize" the Latin American and Caribbean peoples and to erase those memories. It is important to see how these two separate movements took place.

Class analysis of poverty serves as the starting point for Latin American liberation theology and for Hispanic and Latin American women's reflection on their experiences of God. This is particularly true for Latin American women, where a literal struggle for physical survival has been at stake. As Ada María Isasi-Díaz and Yolanda Tarango note, one of the distinctions between third-world contexts outside the United States and the context for U.S. Hispanics is that third-world peoples are often struggling for physical survival whereas "remnant groups" such as U.S. Hispanic women are more often struggling for cultural survival.[14] This focus on economic oppression and other forms of domination results in part from the influence of Gutiérrez and other theologians who make use of Marxian economic analysis and who have been influenced by the work of Paulo Freire and his efforts to effect a "conscientization" of the poor.

Since issues of class are largely the starting point for their reflection, Latin American women often refer to the God of the Poor, the God of the Oppressed, and the God of Liberation. For example, Elsa Tamez concentrated one of her early works on cataloging the many uses of the word "oppression" in the Bible, seeking to know more of the ways that the God of the Oppressed acts in women's lives.[15] This notion of God, developed in the context of a primary concern for the poor, is quite distinct from the early efforts of U.S. white feminists, who were involved in recovering and creating female images for God. In fact, in 1986, Tamez writes that the issue of inclusive language for God is not one that has been central to the thought of Latin American women, whom she feels may be more inclined to view the process of liberation as needing a change in macho attitudes and behavior as well as in language. While Tamez is aware of the problem of exclusive God language, she does not give priority to its discussion. In 1987 she analyzed the situation for Latin American women:

> In both Catholic and Protestant popular Christian communities it has occurred to no one to speak of Goddess, or to refer to the God of the Bible as mother. . . . And generally speaking this is still alien to Latin American feminist Christian women, or at least we do not consider it an important issue—yet.[16]

While Tamez does not wish to make the issue of a female God/dess central to her inquiry, she indicates that she has an interest in the God language suggested by Dorothee Soelle, which is "to call God Water, Light, Path, Bread, Life."[17] Thus, Tamez indicates a preference for using God language that is neither masculine nor feminine, preferring instead gender-neutral God language.

A second distinctive of the theologies advanced by Hispanic women in the United States and Latin American women is a willingness to embrace indigenous traditions. From this effort female images for God have emerged. Tamez illustrates this point in 1982 when she begins her article "Mujer y Varon Llamados a La Vida" with the following paragraph:

> Compañeras y hermanas,
> Corre una gran noticia para la humanidad latinoamericana y del Caribe: Iztaccihuatl movió una pierna, abrió los ojos y lanzó un grito. Iztaccihuatl, la mujer dormida, se está despertando.

Comrades and sisters,
good news is spreading for all Latin American and Carribean people:
Iztaccihuatl has moved her leg, has opened her eyes, and has cried
out loud. Iztaccihuatl, the sleeping woman, is awakening.[18]

Iztaccihuatl, which in the Aztec Nahuatl language means "the sleeping
woman," is the name given to one of the volcanic mountains outside of
Mexico City. Iztaccihuatl is accompanied by her admirer Popocatepetl,
another volcanic mountain, both of whom are shrouded in snow. The
indigenous folklore surrounding these two mountains provides Tamez with
a source for theological reflection as she proclaims, "Iztaccihuatl se está lev-
antando a la vida, para dar vida." (Iztaccihuatl is awakening in order to give
life.)[19] Symbolically equating the "sleeping woman's" awakening power
with the power of women coming into their own, Tamez calls on women to
use their life-affirming gifts in the face of the suffering and death that surrounds them. Iztaccihuatl, awakening in order to give life, also evokes the
image of the biblical God of Life essential to Latin American liberation theology. This is but one example of the ways in which Latin American and
Hispanic theologians are wrestling with the mixing of traditional indigenous beliefs and those brought to the continent by Christian missionaries
and others.

The title of a paper Tamez presented to the 1991 American Academy of
Religion, "Quetzalcoatl Challenges the Christian Bible,"[20] indicates that in
the ensuing decade of her work, Tamez has begun to wrestle even more with
the implications of indigenous and Christian beliefs. In this paper, she lists
three categories of religious response that were articulated as part of the
preparation for the 1992 quincentenary observance. The first group, active
in ecclesial base communities and in Protestant Bible study groups, rereads
scripture with new eyes, from the underside of history. This reading of
scripture from the eyes of the poor has resulted in an insistence that God is
the God of the Poor and the God of Life. The second group, composed of
non-Christian individuals, looks back to indigenous and African religions.
Tamez describes a third group who practice what she terms "an Indigenous
Christianity," in which Jesus Christ is known as savior and the spiritual and
ritual legacy of their ancestors is also honored. Readings from both the
Bible and other sacred books such as the Popol Vuh are sometimes read in
the same liturgy.[21]

A similar growing awareness and respect for indigenous traditions can
be seen in the works of other theologians in Latin America. We have already
noted the work of Aurora Lapiedra, who attempts to capture the significance of Pachamama in the belief system of women of the Andes. There,
among women who call themselves Christian, Pachamama is known as
"Madre de la tierra" and "Madre de la vida":

La Pachamama, Madre de la tierra, Madre de la vida, es una deidad feminina (con frecuencia por sus características se la identifica con la Virgen María) que tiene como peculiar la característica de la cotidianidad, actua en todo momento y penetra todos los elementos de la vida diaria. Está en la casa, en la chacra, siempre nos escucha lo que decimos.

La Pachamama, Mother Earth, Mother of life is a feminine deity (because of her characteristics, she is frequently identified with the Virgin Mary). She acts in each moment in every aspect of our daily lives. She is in our homes, in our farm fields, and she always listens to us.[22]

This contribution to theological reflection emphasizes the nearness of God to the everyday realities of women's lives in the gathering of food, the feeding of the family, and the making of rituals to honor the sacredness of life. Pachamama, ever present in the background and overhearing all that is said, is concerned about the welfare of her people.[23]

As has been suggested here, the spirituality of indigenous peoples, including their belief in indigenous Gods such as Pachamama, occupies a place of growing importance in the conceptions of God being advanced by Latin American women doing liberation theology. As a result, these understandings of God are being communicated in the catechisms of base ecclesial communities and in the work of such theologians as Gutiérrez. Hispanic women in the United States reveal a similar interest.

Isasi-Díaz and Tarango speak of a need to respect the indigenous and African religious traditions that are intrinsic to Hispanic women's spirituality. These traditions offer "needed correctives to some of the religious understandings of 'official' Christianity."[24] Among the influences from African culture, Isasi-Díaz and Tarango list "Our Lady of Regla," a title for Mary identified with Yemaya, Goddess of the Sea, in the African Lucumi religion which was brought to Cuba by slaves. Isasi-Díaz and Tarango also list the Cuban Saint Barbara, who is often identified with Chango, the Yoruban God of Thunder. With regard to Our Lady of Guadalupe of Mexican heritage, they ask, "Is she the Mother of Jesus? Or is she Tonantzin, the Aztec goddess, Mother of the Gods?"[25]

Isasi-Díaz and Tarango directly address the potential criticism that this form of women's belief is not Christian. Their claim is that Hispanic women's liberation theology is Christian because those women practicing this form of belief identify themselves as Christian, with the majority seeing themselves as Catholic. While some people may find it difficult to imagine how two or three traditions reflecting beliefs in different Gods can be incorporated into a faith structure, Isasi-Díaz and Tarango maintain that it is not difficult:

> How does Hispanic Women's liberation theology deal with these two religious strands? It deals with them the same way Hispanic Women do. It takes from each of them what is life giving, what is important for the struggle for survival, and leaves aside what is not relevant or is harmful.[26]

This last sentence indicates the connection between Hispanic and Latin American women's concerns for poor women and their concerns for the religious traditions of women of indigenous and African descent. The poor woman, whose God of Life is proclaimed in Tamez's early work, is also the woman of the Andes who offers prayers to Pachamama, the God of Life whose spirit infuses all. In the intersection of gender, racial, ethnic, and class concerns, a new, if very old, image of God emerges in the theologies of academics as well as in the poetry of the peasants and in the catechisms of the base ecclesial communities. This understanding of God in the eyes of poor women has the potential to serve as a source of radical transformation of Latin American and U.S. Hispanic societies.

Distinctives of Womanist Theology

If the starting point for theological reflection in white feminist theology is an analysis of sexism, and the starting point for U.S. Hispanic and Latin American women is an analysis of class, the point of departure for womanist scholars is a refusal to separate the categories of racism and sexism, and to a lesser extent, classism. Womanist theology, growing from a lack of feeling at home with either white feminists or Black male theologians, insists that gender, race, and class analysis be done simultaneously.

This triple oppression of Black women as a source of theological reflection appears in the work of Delores Williams. Her investigation into this experience of suffering and resistance among Black women who were slaves and who have worked as domestic servants has led Williams to radical new theological statements about God, in which she rejects traditional understandings of God's participation in the crucifixion and resurrection of Christ. Her rejection of traditional atonement theories and of any understanding of Jesus' role as a suffering surrogate is a serious challenge to both the theological academy and the Black church to rethink the relationship between God and Christ.

A second distinctive marking womanist theology is its commitment to historical scholarship. Because womanist theology makes use of Black

women's lives as source for theological reflection and because Black wom-
en's lives and thought are invisible in much of traditional theological scholarship, womanist scholars have been actively involved in identifying lost
sources. Womanist scholars are discovering a wealth of material that serves
as a corrective to sources derived from scripture, church tradition, and
much of theological scholarship. Katie Geneva Cannon's research into the
life and work of Zora Neale Hurston is one such example of probing historical material, in this case a forgotten literary figure, to discover the theological views inherent in her writing. By probing the theological imagination
of the characters of Hurston's fiction to understand their views of God,
Cannon has made available to the Black church and to theological scholarship images of God that might otherwise have remained lost.

In addition to Cannon's and Williams's historical recovery work, other
examples include Karen Baker-Fletcher's investigation into the life of Anna
Julia Cooper, which provides womanists with a late-nineteenth- and early-
twentieth-century role model who saw clearly the evils of racism, sexism,
and classism and denounced these from a faith perspective. Emilie M.
Townes's research into the life of Ida B. Wells-Barnett, who exposed the
horrors of lynching in the South, provides source material for womanist
reflection on God's justice.[27] These scholars are involved in an important
recovery of Black women's experience as a source for theological reflection
on God. Theirs is also a methodology that could be used by other marginalized groups in developing liberatory source materials to augment scripture
and church tradition.

A third distinctive of womanist theological reflection on God is the manner in which womanist scholars have begun asking questions about the commonalities and possible distinctions between the Spirit of God of Christian
faith and the spirit of African traditional religious beliefs.[28] According to
some womanist methodology, these African sources also serve as valid
resources for theological reflection. In debating whether Alice Walker's definition of womanism is inherently Christian or whether it refers to a much
more broadly defined notion of African-American women's spirituality,
womanist theologians reflect the larger concerns of the African-American
community about the need to retain the history and practice of important
African traditions. Because of questions about the role of the spirit in
African-American women's lives, Williams and Townes have called for the
development of a womanist theology of the spirit.[29]

One final distinctive to be mentioned is Delores Williams's argument
that God is not always a God of liberation. Most liberation and feminist
theology has perceived God as a God of Liberation, taking the side of the
poor and oppressed, opposing all unjust structures of society. Williams has
asserted, instead, that for Hagar and for many Black women, it is important
to posit a "God who liberates" and a "God who does not liberate," noting

that non-Jewish slave women were not included in the exodus motif of liberation. She emphasizes that it was not the liberating God who was present to Hagar, but rather a God who "becomes the element of necessity in the emergence of black women's survival and quality of life strategies."[30] In asserting that Hagar's God "does not liberate," Williams rejects Elsa Tamez's interpretation of the God of Hagar as a liberating God.

While I treat Williams's idea that God does not liberate as a separate distinctive of womanist theology, in looking closely at the arguments made by Williams and Tamez, it may be that their positions are not as distant as it might seem at first. Tamez writes, "To speak of liberation . . . is to speak of the struggle of an oppressed people in quest of their rights and spurred on by the hope that the victory will be real because their God is at their side in the struggle."[31] In another instance, she notes, "Liberation (i.e. the action of liberating) implies a tenacious and unceasing struggle."[32] In each passage, Tamez makes reference to the word "struggle" or "la lucha," which in a Latin American context may very well connote the effort for survival of which Williams speaks. Tamez also notes that the struggle is "unceasing," for Latin American liberation theology assumes that liberation is an ongoing process. Concerning her views about the relationship between the participation of God and of humans in liberation, Tamez speaks of "a fusion of God and his people. The people struggle by the power and strength of God, because God is a liberator."[33] The biblical source that Tamez uses to support her position is from Psalm 68:20, 35:

> Our God is a God of salvation; and to God, the Lord, belongs escape from death. The God of Israel . . . gives power and strength to his people. (RSV)

Here Tamez depicts God, not as the one who effects liberation alone, but as the source of the strength and power that enable God's people to "escape from death." In addition, in describing the situation of Job, Tamez writes that sometimes God is silent, waiting for humanity to cry out in protest. This God is not interventionist; neither is this God unmoved by the suffering of the people. While Williams and Tamez may not agree on the question of whether God liberates, it is clear that both women understand the ongoing nature of the struggle for justice and liberation, and both women conceive of this process as one requiring the participation of both God and humanity.

Searching for Common Ground

Before moving toward a comparison of white feminist, *mujerista* and Latin American feminist, and womanist conceptions of God, one final point should be made about distinctives and about difference. The goal of this book is to theologize across the boundaries of difference; it is *not* to erase difference or to presume that boundaries do not exist between differing cultural groups. As Gustavo Gutiérrez has said, "There is no theology that does not have its own accent in speaking about God."[34] Rather, the goal is to find ways to speak with each other that value different conceptions of God and celebrate our common ways of thinking and speaking and praying together to the Sacred whom we call by varying names.

New Methods

There are many commonalities among white feminist, *mujerista* and Latin American feminist, and womanist theologians who explicitly state that they are doing liberation theology. These theologies draw on the methodologies of Latin American liberation theology and Black theology in the United States in several ways. First, they offer a new method of doing theology that rejects neutral, objective scholarship and instead posits a commitment to the poor and oppressed. As noted earlier, Ada María Isasi-Díaz developed an ethnographic interview process in the development of her *mujerista* theology because of her commitment to giving voice to grassroots Hispanic women.[35] Zora Neale Hurston's methodology for gathering the folk wisdom of poor southern Black folk, in which she traded in her carefully accented "Barnardese" for a conversational style of swapping tales on country porches, represents a second model for doing research that is both responsive and accountable to "the folk," a technique instructive to liberation theologians.

A second feature of the new methods being developed in liberation theologies is a connection between theological method, epistemology, and praxis. This connection follows Gustavo Gutiérrez's notion that "to know God is to do justice."[36] While Gutiérrez, Heyward, and Isasi-Díaz may have slightly different notions of theology as a process of praxis and reflection, they all agree that both components are necessary. In each case, liberation theologians insist that it is impossible to know or to love God abstractly, and one certainly cannot come to know or love God by writing theological treatises. One can only know and love God in the context of concrete, committed praxis with the poor and oppressed, many of whom are women.

One way in which this praxis is being acted on—though perhaps not discussed—is in the refusal of many Protestant ordained women trained as theologians and ethicists to give up their ordained status in order to be seen as respectable in the community of scholars. It is no accident that many leading women Protestant liberationist scholars are "Reverend Doctor" by title. These women challenge the academy with the notion that praxis might actually be called ministry; at the same time, they challenge the church by responsibly teaching new ways of thinking about God and human responsibility. Their commitment to the church is an intentional effort to bridge the gap betweeen doing theology and praxis by this form of ministry. Taking their academic training to the local church, to revivals, or to convention halls is a way of demonstrating their commitment to "the folk." Many lay women of all denominations, trained as scholars, make similar efforts to influence church structures while being in relationship to local church people. Others take their praxis to the streets, volunteering time in grassroots organizations, serving on nonprofit boards of directors in community organizations, and becoming involved in local politics. Each of these means of connecting theology and praxis is valuable in developing new methods for doing liberationist theology.

In addition to this methodological commonality among women doing theology in differing cultural contexts, I would like to suggest further points of contact between these theologies. The assumption that I first brought to this project was that one might be able to posit that white feminists, *mujeristas*, Latin American women, and womanist scholars all speak of God as one who is relational, one who is immanent in women's lives, and who empowers women. (In examining the differing theologies presented, it now makes more sense to broaden the second category of immanence to speak of the embodiment of God.)

The Relationality of God

The relationality of God is a theme consistently present in the theologies of white feminists, *mujeristas*, Latin American women, and womanists. In the theology of Sallie McFague, her models of God as friend, mother, and lover are thoroughly relational. For Carter Heyward, relationality takes the form of God yearning toward humanity, drawing us closer to God and to each other. Her notion of God's transcendence as bridge further echoes this theme.

Among U.S. Hispanic and Latin American women, one form of God's relationality with humanity is illustrated in various women's understandings of God as mother, as Corn Mother, as Pachamama, and as a smiling grandmother. Other images are masculine in nature, revealing understandings of God as Father and God as revolutionary brother in the struggle for liberation. These highly personalistic views of God/dess form one type of understanding of God's relationality with humanity.

Another conception of God as relational is expressed in such writers as María Clara Luchetti Bingemer, who speaks of God's desire. For her, the Spirit of God, "divine desire poured out over history and over humanity," is the source of liberating desire among the people, which emerges "almost like a shout, as a power propelling them to struggle."[37] This term "desire," with all its sexual connotations, is similar to Heyward's "yearning." Last, Elsa Tamez's conception of God as the God of the Oppressed is a relational God who enters into the process of liberation with God's people. This process requires the cooperation of both God and humanity.

Within womanist scholarship, the theme of relationality is evident in the experience of encounter with Jesus in the wilderness, in a highly personal, individual relationship with Jesus, and in Katie Geneva Cannon's portrayals of God as the One Who Knows the Truth, the one who protected Black slave women in the midst of their oppression, and the God Who Is Present in the Midst of the Storm. Jacquelyn Grant's work focusing on christology demonstrates how God in Jesus is present in "the least of these," in the lives of poor Black women. Delores Williams, too, speaks of relationality in God, of a God who is present in the very lives of Black women struggling for survival. It is clear that if white feminist, *mujerista* and Latin American women, and womanist scholars wish to pursue the topic of God and relationality, each would have much to contribute to the discussion.

An Embodied God

A second commonality is that each of these theologies presents an embodied spirituality. In part, this effort stems from a rejection of the abstract theologizing of the past that excluded women's lives. Theological reflection is built on the concrete, everyday experience of women in each of these theologies. God, too, is seen as embodied, with real concern for the material, physical welfare of women and their families.

In white feminist theology, McFague's notion of the world as God's body comes to mind as she reflects on the concrete, dangerous realities of living in a nuclear and ecological age. Obviously, her point is that if the world is God's body, we will take care of God, of the earth, and of each other. Heyward's God can easily be imagined in the lives of those who are birthing children, in the faces of children, in the struggles of a gay man living with AIDS, in the last moments of life of one waiting on death row, and in the affection of lovers holding hands on the street.

Among Latin American women, an embodied theology proclaims that God is the God of Life. This assertion is made in the face of actual death—caused by the impoverishment of a continent, by hunger, and by death-dealing military governments. In the face of the "disappearance" of loved ones who have been kidnapped and murdered by death squads, Latin American mothers have called on the memories of their children, crying out their names and proclaiming, "¡Presente!" The God of Latin America is not simply a God who cries out against the injustice of war and hunger; this God is active in the lives of all who work in ecclesial base communities and in other coalitions to build schools, farming cooperatives, and health-care facilities.

Hispanic women in the United States interviewed by Isasi-Díaz and Tarango describe God as a deep *sentimiento* (feeling) that provides them with strength in times of trouble. God is depicted as a woman kissing the wounded hand of a child. God lives in the prayers passed down from generation to generation of mothers and daughters and in the preparation of food and flowers for community celebrations, such as the Festival of Guadalupe and the Day of the Dead. God lives in the tired bodies of farm-workers who toil in the fields all day, and God lives in the hopes and dreams of all who work for the cultural survival of their people.

Womanist theologians reject any separation of the sacred from the secular, understanding God's presence in women's lives, even when the name of God remains unspoken. Cannon's work focuses on naming aspects of Black women's moral agency that have enabled their survival: invisible dignity, unshouted courage, and quiet grace. Williams's form of embodied theology looks at the real oppressions of rape and beatings in the lives of slave women and at sexual exploitation in the lives of women who work as domestic servants in white households. In light of this experience of oppression of Black women's bodies, Williams rejects any possibility that God's body in Jesus' crucifixion was intended as a surrogate sufferer. God's embodiment in African-American women's lives often takes the shape of fighting racism in its many guises: discrimination in employment; inadequate schools and housing; crime in the streets; environmental hazards and carcinogenic substances spewing from smoke stacks in Black neighborhoods; and unhealthy working conditions in textile mills, factories, petrochemical plants, and other workplaces that largely employ people of color.

In their own ways, each of these theologies seeks to establish God's real presence among us. God is embodied in the prophets God has chosen to speak out against injustice among those who claim to be the people of God. Among these contemporary prophets are Latin American, Hispanic, African-American and white women who call for change. God is also embodied in the very lives of those who have never set foot in the academy, but whose lives are dedicated to work for change in our communities. Both concepts, the relationality of God and the embodiment of God, provide the basis for future discussion as women expand their conceptions of God through multicultural dialogue.

A God Who Empowers

A third commonality between these theologies can be identified as empowerment. In white feminist theology, this theme can be seen in the early work of Mary Daly, who speaks of women having the "courage to leave" patriarchal injustice. This theme of empowerment is also prevalent in the work of Carter Heyward, who defines God's power as power-in-relation, a shared power with humanity for the cause of justice. In Hispanic and Latin American women's theologies, the theme of empowerment is seen most clearly in the resistance to evil. The God of Life insists that in the midst of endless war and oppression, the people will rise. In the figure of Mary Virgin bird, as Godoy's poem refers to her, a revolutionary God is willing to take on militia duty, if necessary, to guard her people. In womanist theology, once again, the power of God is treated in relation to resisting evil. In the face of racial oppression, womanist theology affirms that ultimately God will prevail. God's justice will prevail, in part, because God has bestowed courage in the very soul of Black women who have been forced to devise strategies for survival in the face of great injustice.

Challenges Posed by Women's Theologies

Women's Experience as Source for Theological Reflection

White feminist, *mujerista* and Latina American feminist, and womanist theologies challenge traditional theological assumptions and also ask critical questions of each other. What are some of the criticisms raised by these theologies? What are some of the future challenges and unresolved issues facing women doing theology? Where do we go from here?

One of the major criticisms of all liberation theologies, including women's theologies of liberation from all social and cultural locations, is that they are dependent on the personal experience of individuals. Revelation is seen through the eyes of women's experience, which is taken to be a valid criteria for truth. In addition, some critics who are uncomfortable with images of God drawn from nontraditional sources, such as Native American or African sources, raise charges of syncretism.

In response to these charges, it should be noted that including experience in the hermeneutical process is not completely new. Experience has been taken seriously in biblical hermeneutics and theology for some time, including Hermann Lotze's assertion that history is not objective, Søren Kierkegaard's insistence that truth is subjectivity, Ernst Troeltsch's relativism, and Paul Tillich's passionate engagement and "ultimate concern." However, when Latin American liberation theology began to address the experience of the poor, when Black theology started talking about Black experience, and when feminist theology focused on women's experience, many people objected to the priority of experience in these theologies. No doubt, as women doing liberation theology continue to challenge church traditions, and particularly as they insist on the validity of conceptions of God/dess that take seriously ancient indigenous and African memories of the sacred, they will be subject to criticisms that they offer experiential rationales for their understandings without being rooted in "objective truth." In the Catholic church, male theologians have been silenced by the Vatican for liberation perspectives that challenge church teaching and authority. As women such as Ivone Gebara challenge the teachings of the church, their work is now similarly being scrutinized. It will only be a matter of time before Rome catches on to the creative, powerful, and life-changing work being done by other Catholic women theologians who will then be forced to exercise a new kind of resistance.

Biblical Language and Racism

Other challenges also face women's theological efforts. First, Delores Williams and others have called for a radical rethinking of images of light and dark, black and white. In a chapter of *Sisters in the Wilderness* entitled "Color Struck: A State of Mind," she captures the essence of the problem of color discrimination:

> In North America popular culture, religion, science and politics have worked together to assign permanent negative value to the color black. This has led to the formation of an American national consciousness that considers black frightening, dangerous and/or repulsive—especially when this is the color of human bodies.[38]

In pointing to the racism inherent in connotations of white and black in U.S. vernacular, and in pointing to those scriptural passages that inherently condone the practice of slavery, she exposes the need for a constructive *theological* rethinking of color. A hermeneutical principle for reflection on those scriptural passages that condone the institution of slavery was necessary for U.S. churches in the 1800s. Similarly, today, we need to develop hermeneutical principles for reflection on images of light and dark in scripture and church tradition that contribute to racist ideology. Grant begins this work by asserting that Jesus is a Black woman. Williams offers the image of the wilderness to include the experience of Black women in theological reflection. In order for all liberation theologies to advance, it may be that differing marginalized groups can begin to develop their own hermeneutical principles for dealing with images of light and dark in the Gospel of John and in other problematic areas. A joint conversation between white feminists, *mujeristas,* Latin American women, womanists, and others would presumably be profitable in attempting to construct new images of God that do not contribute to racist stereotyping.

Christology

An issue that white feminists, *mujeristas*, Latin American women, and womanists may want to give more attention to, both separately and collectively, concerns christology. Many issues are involved in developing a twentieth-century christology that takes seriously the results of historical critical New Testament study. A problem emerges when we look at christology from a historical critical view. Historical critical study, and in particular the insights of Albert Schweitzer, tell us that it is impossible to depict a historically verifiable view of Jesus.[39] However, some liberation theologians, for whom the man Jesus is central, develop an image of Jesus as liberator without fully addressing the complexities raised by Schweitzer and others.

Gustavo Gutiérrez focuses attention on Jesus as a liberator who is in solidarity with the poor and oppressed. He and others bring the exodus motif to life in a New Testament context by focusing on Jesus as the one who brings about radical socio-economic change. Following Gutiérrez, the christologies of some Latin American women doing theology also show Jesus as liberator. Elsa Tamez and Nellie Ritchie use this image for Jesus. While liberationists want to be able to assert that God liberates, we do not want the Jesus of liberation theology to be dismissed, as other images of Jesus have been, even if our Jesus appears dressed in the clothes of a contra fighter, an African-American working mother or a *Ms.* magazine editor. And yet womanists, *mujeristas*, and Latin American women, in particular, insist that no cosmic Christ is capable of effecting the liberation that is needed. Many white feminists, *mujeristas*, Latin American women, and womanists have asserted that Jesus, as present in "the least of these," is in some real, rather than purely symbolic, sense present in the faces of poor and oppressed women. The problem of christology is even further complicated by the fact that for some women, particularly for some U.S. Hispanic and white feminist women, christology plays a minor role in their God-thought. As Isasi-Díaz and Tarango have noted, for many U.S. Hispanic women, christological questions are peripheral, partly because these women look to Mary and the Virgin of Guadalupe for sources of revelation as much as they look to Jesus. In addition, some white feminists have rejected the possibility of a male savior. How to address the complexities of this christological problem, the problem of God's presence through Jesus Christ in, with, and among women, is a challenge that will no doubt face liberation theologies for some time to come. It is likely to be one area in which considerable difference of opinion will remain, but it is also an area for rich discussion.

Authority and Charges of Syncretism

A fourth issue facing women deals with the relationship between traditional images of the Christian God and images of God/dess which stem from older forms of African, Native American, and European spirituality. White North American women who understand the Sacred One as Goddess, referring to earlier faith traditions of Europe, have raised questions about the relationship of the Goddess to the Christian God. Some Christian women have been criticized for re-imagining God as Sophia, relying on biblical wisdom traditions for source material. We have also seen that related questions about spirituality are being asked by some *mujerista* theologians and Latin American scholars in reference to indigenous and African beliefs, such as when Tamez refers to Quetzalcoatl as the "God of Life" or when Peruvian Christian women of the Andes call on their God, Pachamama, to bring abundance and harmony to the people, or when Hispanic women pray to La Morenita, the brown-skinned Virgin of Guadalupe. Among womanists, the complex history of the development of Christianity in the United States under the conditions of slavery provides a distinct context for theologizing about God as spirit and for questioning the relationship of the Christian Spirit to African-based spirit(s). At issue for women in these distinct contexts is the question of authority. Who has the authority to determine whether these understandings of God/dess are legitimate or whether they are Christian? One helpful course of inquiry might be to follow Ada María Isasi-Díaz and Yolanda Tarango's suggestions for addressing the issue of authority:

> The history of Christianity shows that orthodox objections to syncretism have to do not with the purity of faith, but with who has the right to determine what is to be considered normative and official. For the articulation of religious understandings, beliefs, and practices to be an act of liberation, it has to be an act of self-determination and not an attempt to comply with what the "official" church says.[40]

It is crucial that women begin to claim the authority to decide for themselves the names by which they will call on God/dess without fear of being branded heretical.

Religious Pluralism

A fifth set of common questions bears on the relationship of white feminist, *mujerista* and Latin American feminist, and womanist theologies to other religions. This problem can be set in the larger context of religious pluralism within the academy. In traditional theology, classic exclusivist arguments, ecclesiocentric in nature, have largely been replaced with chris-tocentric inclusivist arguments such as those of Paul Tillich and Karl Rahner. More recently, the pluralistic theologies of John Cobb *(Christ in a Pluralistic Age* and *Beyond Dialogue: Toward a Mutual Transformation of Christianity and Buddhism*), John Hick (*The Myth of God Incarnate),* and Paul Knitter (*No Other Name*) offer a theocentric view of Christianity as offering the best possibility for dialogue.[41] Cobb, Hick, and Knitter reject the inclusivist stance of Rahner's "anonymous Christianity" or Tillich's christocentrically grounded notions of ultimate concern as offensive to other religions and impeding of any real dialogue.

How some women's liberation theologies will retain the centrality of Christ and/or Jesus and also meet the challenges of interfaith dialogue remains to be seen. While to date, this has not been a major focus of discus-sion, some women, such as Carter Heyward, have clearly rejected any exclu-sivist claims. Womanist theologians have begun to ask questions about how the Holy Spirit of Christianity relates to the spirit of African religious beliefs and, more generally, to the spirituality of African-American women's lives. Much more discussion is likely to take place as womanists do further research on this topic.

While the issue of religious pluralism has not been a central concern of Latin American women's liberation theology, it has begun to receive some treatment. As noted above, Tamez has recently begun to address this ques-tion, particularly as it relates to indigenous expressions of spirituality. Her earlier work tends to be more rigid in its polarization of the Christian God and the God of the pagans, whom she describes as conquering idolaters who valued gold more than God. In a twist on the usual use of the word "pagan" or "infidel" to denote non-Christians, Tamez ironically asserts that it is the rich Christian who supports acts of oppression against the poor who is "pagan" or "infidel," because an act of oppression against another is to be treated as "an action directed against Yahweh himself [sic]."[42] Tamez is cor-rect in her class analysis that worship of riches and power is idolatrous because it refuses to put love of God and love of neighbor at the center of human existence. Here Tamez cites Proverbs 14:31: "He who oppresses a poor man insults his Maker, but he who is kind to the needy honors him." Missing from Tamez's earlier analysis of the gods of the "pagans" is a femi-nist critique of the term "pagan" by those proclaiming a patriarchal God, an act that was used to silence the goddess traditions of indigenous and African spirituality. Given Tamez's recent interest in the development of a theology that is respectful of indigenous and African traditions, one would expect that Tamez would give further thought to the use of the term "pagan."

Another Latin American scholar, Luz Beatriz Arellano, is also concerned about religious pluralism. She refers to Nicaragua's "new spirituality" as one which reaches beyond Christian boundaries:

> The new spirituality of Nicaraguan women that I am trying to reflect is a truly ecumenical spirituality, a spirituality shared not only with Christians who belong to the various churches but also between Christians and non-Christians.[43]

In addition, Arellano speaks of "a church without borders."[44] This understanding of a broad spirituality, which encompasses both Christians and non-Christians while perhaps also targeting Marxist atheists as well as persons of non-Christian faith backgrounds, contains the seed of germination for further discussion. While Arellano does not make the explicit claim that this broad understanding of spirituality is rooted in an understanding of God/dess that incorporates both Christian and indigenous understandings of the divine—as can be seen in the use of the image of Corn Mother, for example—one could certainly posit that this understanding of divinity cannot but be helpful as peoples of different faith traditions come together in a pluralistic age. Perhaps some insight can also be gained from Paul Knitter's suggestion that a liberation theology *of religions* could provide a critique to injustice in a global context while providing hope for the future.[45] At least at the level of praxis, committed persons of faith from differing traditions ought to be able to unite in their effort to fight against injustice. Certainly this question could lead to fruitful discussion across the lines of cultural difference.

5

Clues for Doing Theology across the Boundaries of Difference

Feminist Theory Meets Feminist Theology

Introduction

Rosemarie Tong is a feminist theorist whose work I find helpful. Her *Feminist Thought: A Comprehensive Introduction* (1989) outlines the major types of feminist thought that have helped to shape the field of Women's Studies to date. She identifies these as liberal feminism, Marxist feminism, radical feminism, socialist feminism, psychoanalytic feminism, existentialist feminism, and postmodern feminism. The strength of this work lies in its clear differentiation of the scope of each type of feminism and in her own attempts to see how these various types of feminist thought can contribute to a program of action which will lead to liberation. In the introductory section, Tong holds out the hope that women of varying and diverse backgrounds can meet the challenge to develop community. She offers a model for cross-cultural conversation that deserves to be considered by women doing theology.

> It is a major challenge to contemporary feminism to reconcile the pressures for diversity and difference with those for integration and commonality. We need a home in which everyone has a room of her own, but one in which the walls are thin enough to permit a conversation, a community of friends in virtue, and partners in action.[1]

Feminist theory clearly has something to say to feminist and liberation theologians. We need to develop a methodology for doing theology across the boundaries of our differences if we are to meet the challenge raised by Tong.

Already such conversations have begun under the rubric of "appropriation and reciprocity."[2] Women doing theology[3] must develop an ethic that insists on mutuality and respects difference if we are to engage in shared, multicultural theological reflection. In looking to the work of feminist theorists interested in issues of difference and commonality, such as Elizabeth Spelman, bell hooks, Patricia Hill Collins, and Elizabeth Potter, it is clear that theologians will need to acknowledge those obstacles to multicultural dialogue that must be addressed as we work across the boundaries of difference. In addressing these obstacles to cross-cultural theologizing, we can begin to lay the foundation for the home that Tong envisions, one in which each of us has our own room and yet where conversation can begin.

Obstacles to Theologizing across the Boundaries of Difference

The Problem of False Unity

At least four major issues present obstacles to multicultural dialogue among women doing theology. The first is false unity or the masking of real differences that separate women of different cultural backgrounds. In looking at some of the dynamics involved in the tensions among women doing theology, and in particular in reference to racial tensions, Elizabeth Spelman's concept of the "inessential woman" is helpful. This notion is intended to demonstrate the importance of seeing difference among women. She critiques those who posit an "essential woman" who functions generically and masks real differences among diverse groups of women.

Spelman argues that the generic use of the word "man" has functioned in Western language to obscure the heterogeneity of men and women and to cut off "examination of the significance of such heterogeneity for feminist theory and political activity."[4] Similarly, argues Spelman, dominant Western feminist thought has largely ignored real differences of race and class and has posited the experience of white, middle-class women as normative for all women. She pointedly argues her case against the "essential woman" in the following statement:

> Don't misunderstand me: I've never met a generic woman I didn't like. But I wouldn't want my brother or my sister to marry one. And I certainly wouldn't want to be one: generic women don't eat rice and beans, collard greens, samosa, challah, hot dogs, or Wonder Bread; even in Cambridge, Massachusetts, I've never seen one eating a croissant. And while it is true that generic women don't have bad breath, that is hardly any consolation, I should think, for having no breath at all.[5]

Spelman insists that in order for women to work together across the boundaries of difference, attention must be given to the unique fabric of each woman's life and to the racial, ethnic, class, sexual orientation, and language backdrop of each particular situation.

The Perception of Anger as Unreasonable

A second obstacle to women being able to engage in critical conversation revolves around the taboos associated with emotion and anger in scholarship. This obstacle stems from the traditional dualistic split between reason and emotion that labels anger as irrational and unproductive. For those white women whose Christian training under patriarchy has taught them to silence their own anger and to fear that of others, it may be difficult to engage with those who are unafraid to express outrage at injustice. Audre Lorde addresses the need for anger to be expressed when she writes, "If I speak to you in anger, at least I have spoken to you: I have not put a gun to your head and shot you down in the street."[6] The need for white women to hear the angry concerns of women of color has been apparent for some time. It very well may be, in fact, that as women engage in more cross-cultural theologizing, and as more marginalized women voice their concerns, anger is an emotion that will require closer examination.[7]

In looking more closely at the emotional, often angry exchanges between women of color and white women, Alison Jaggar's concept of "outlaw emotion" may be helpful. Jaggar reminds us that feminist theorists "have pointed out that the Western tradition has not seen everyone as equally emotional. Instead, reason has been associated with members of dominant political, social, and cultural groups and emotion with members of subordinate groups."[8] If Jaggar is correct, then this may be why women of color are perceived by white women as angry and emotional, while white women fail to recognize the emotional or passive-aggressive content of our own disguising, despirited discourse. Therefore, it may be that lesbian women, disabled women, or women of color are not *more* emotional or *more* angry than straight, white, able-bodied women, but rather that they are simply perceived to be so at times.

While in white culture, many women have been conditioned to view displays of anger as negative or even "un-Christian," there may be an instructive aspect to anger. In discussing what she describes as "outlaw emotions," Jaggar refers to those emotions that "are distinguished by their incompatibility with the dominant perceptions and values."[9] They are generally the emotions of oppressed persons "who pay a disproportionately high price for maintaining the status quo."[10] These "outlaw emotions," because they are based in an understanding of oppression that is not experienced by dominant groups, may provide the basis for a subculture that challenges dominant patterns and becomes "politically because epistemically subversive."[11] Here Jaggar refers to the notion of the "epistemic privilege of the oppressed," which she describes as "the perspective on reality available from the standpoint of the oppressed . . . that offers a less partial and distorted and therefore more reliable view."[12]

The alternative epistemological model proposed by Jaggar replaces the dualistic split between emotion and reason in traditional philosophical categories with an understanding that our emotions inform our perceptions and ethical actions. These emotions can lead us to rethink our theoretical perspectives. Further, she gives priority to the knowledge possessed by those who feel most sharply the injustice of our society, arguing that their firsthand experience of oppression grants an understanding of the dynamics of oppression that those in positions of power may not fully appreciate.

According to Jaggar's view, one can understand the emotional encounters between white women and women of color doing theology together as a sign of healthy movement. As emotions inform our understanding of systemic, institutionalized racism, our perceptions can be reformulated and actions generated based on new understandings. By applying Jaggar's epistemological model to a new model for doing theology across the lines of cultural difference, we may begin to address issues of personal and institutional racism, along with other forms of oppression, which have limited the theological enterprise of women to date.

A Singular World View

A third obstacle facing women doing theology is the tendency toward a singular world view, which may take the extreme form of xenophobia, or fear of the "foreign," or which may simply result in a lack of information about the theological resources of others whose backgrounds are different from ours. We may know and understand our own situation and the theology that has developed out of its context, and we may be able to deconstruct the oppressive features of our own heritage and develop new, constructive, liberating theologies. However, we are much less likely to speak another's language or understand the linguistic shorthand, culture, and theology that develop out of another's own particular context. To confront this obstacle, Ada María Isasi-Díaz has proposed a new "multi-world view" that will lead to a new world order based on critical conscientization and liberation.[13] From the perspective of a "multi-world view," difference is perceived in positive terms. The whole cannot be understood from any single perspective; many different perspectives comprise the whole. Universalist understandings are suspect; notions of so-called neutral objectivity are demythologized and deconstructed. In contrast to a methodology that emphasizes neutral objectivity, Isasi-Díaz proposes advocacy education, which emphasizes the need to understand difference in all its particularity and the need to claims one's own biases. The goal of advocacy education is not to erase or tolerate difference, but to attempt to understand fully many differing perspectives.

Another aspect of this "multi-world view" is an understanding of power dynamics that contribute to oppression. For white women, this analysis needs to include a thorough understanding of the history of Western oppression of marginalized groups as well as an understanding of the current benefits of white women's privilege, particularly its "invisible package" of unearned assets that white women can count on, to use the terminology of Peggy McIntosh.[14] It involves understanding the ways in which white women consciously and unconsciously contribute to the oppression of women of color. It also involves understanding the ways that privileged white women contribute to the oppression of disabled, poor, and older women of all colors. These understandings are critical in avoiding the paralysis of white women's guilt, a syndrome that can all too easily prevent white women from engaging in the tough work of multi-world traveling or in correcting injustice. According to Isasi-Díaz, it is only when we take into account multiple perspectives regarding a particular problem or issue, including the history of power dynamics of race, class, and gender that have contributed to the problem, that we have a chance of forming coalitions across boundaries of difference, working toward common goals.

The Temptation of Silence

Elizabeth Potter takes up the problems inherent in trying to develop coalitions of solidarity and support across race, ethnic, and class lines. She points to a fourth obstacle to working across boundaries of difference, which she terms "the temptation of silence." The problems of racism have become so complex that sometimes we fear saying anything at all. During a presentation to faculty, staff, and students of Mills College, Potter began by asking such basic questions as, "Can we ever speak for or about someone else? When is it appropriate, if ever, to speak about someone whose identity is in some way different from our own? How? Under what circumstances?"[15] Our ethics and our common sense have led us to understand that we cannot speak for everyone. To universalize is to dehumanize. Yet Potter's question challenges us to think carefully about the issue of advocacy education. She continued her presentation by raising the problem of group identity. If I can speak only for my group, how narrowly is my group defined? Maybe I can speak only for myself. Equally problematic is "the temptation of silence," because to say nothing is safer than entering into the rough waters of a multi-world view. Nevertheless, we have been commissioned to be "world travelers," in the words of María Lugones.[16] What guidelines do we have for when to speak for or about someone or a group whose identity may be quite different from our own?

Several years ago at the annual meeting of the American Academy of Religion in New Orleans, I met a Ph.D. student from Colombia.[17] Together we spoke of the marked absence of Latin American or U.S. Hispanic men and women from the conference program. At that point, she and I wondered together if there were ways that I, a white feminist liberationist, might make constructive use of my knowledge of Latin American liberation theology in a more public way. But I still had questions about the appropriateness of an Anglo woman speaking on Latin American liberation theology. The questions about the ethics and responsibility of knowledge nagged at me then and continue to do so as I work through my own philosophical and pedagogical issues with advocacy education.

Elizabeth Potter, in her presentation mentioned above, indicated one of the real paradoxes of advocacy education. She hinted that one of the basic requirements for speaking on behalf of another group is that one must understand that group. Second, it is a given that as a nonmember of the group, it is impossible to fully understand the group. This is the dilemma in which I find myself as a student of liberation theologies. While Potter is careful to warn of the dangers of entering the waters of a multicultural world view, her observation about the paradox of never being completely able to understand the "other" is not intended to circumvent discussion between those whose circumstances differ. For those of us teaching in small colleges or in small departments, it would be irresponsible to teach only the material of our own experience and background. At Mills College, for example, in an Introduction to Religion class, if I do not teach womanist or *mujerista* theology, they simply will not be taught. Rather than falling into the temptation of silence, Potter suggests that one must exercise a certain caution when trying to speak about the "other." We do not presume to have all the answers, for we may have misunderstood the question, or we may be ignorant of the answer all together.

Feminist theorist Uma Narayan offers two suggestions that may be helpful. First, she suggests that the outsider exercise "methodological humility," in which the outsider conducts herself "under the assumption that, as an outsider, she may be missing something."[18] Second, she urges "methodological caution," in which the outsider attempts "to carry out her attempted criticism of the insider's perceptions in such a way that it does not amount to, or even seem to amount to, an attempt to denigrate or dismiss entirely the validity of the insider's point of view."[19]

From Silence to Advocacy

Elsa Tamez offers additional help in designing a means for doing theology across the boundaries of difference. In her 1992 address to the American Academy of Religion in San Francisco, Tamez spoke of the need to develop indigenous voices within Latin American liberation theology. Tamez, a Mexican of mixed heritage, said that it is not the task of mestizos or whites to develop Indian or African-American hermeneutics. Rather, her task is to prepare the hearts and minds of those who are not Indian or Black[20] to receive the spiritual practices of others "with joy and equality."[21]

Tamez's suggestion offers the hope that advocacy education can help us understand the realities of those whose theological context is quite different from our own. If I understand Tamez correctly, it is my task, then, to try to create an environment in which those of us who are Anglo, and particularly those who are in positions of power, are more ready to receive others' points of view, not with suspicion, but rather with "joy and equality."

Rosemarie Tong has suggested another principle that may be helpful. The metaphorical "home in which everyone has a room of her own" is key to our future theological endeavors; this metaphor recalls the heavenly mansion in which there are "many rooms." Yet the home that Tong metaphorically constructs is built so as to allow conversations to take place between the people she describes as "a community of friends in virtue, and partners in action."[22] To borrow Tong's analysis, if my teaching and my scholarly, political, and activist work are to be successful, the walls containing my own perspectives as a white, educated woman from a working-class background in the United States will be thin enough that the voices of Tamez, Isasi-Díaz, Lapiedra, Cannon, Williams, and Grant, as well as the voices of white feminist women, can be heard.

If we are to begin treading the treacherous waters of advocacy education on the way to critical awareness and a new world order, as Isasi-Díaz has suggested, then we must begin to confront the real obstacles inhibiting our progress. We must be open to risk and try to understand something of the lives of those whom we will never completely understand. We must not think that the task of multicultural theological reflection on God will be easy. Feminist theorist Chela Sandoval suggests how this activity might proceed: "Mistakes must be forgiven. Every day repeats an opportunity for beginning anew."[23] María Lugones offers the following suggestion: "Love has to be rethought, made anew."[24]

Just as feminist theory has something to say to feminist theology, feminist theology can inform feminist theory; at least some feminist theorists are making use of *theological* language, as noted in the references to the solutions proposed by Sandoval and Lugones. Women doing theology know something about mistakes. We call them sin. We also know something about forgiveness. We surely know about every day repeating an opportunity for beginning anew. This we call hope. These are theological categories. More important, they are the words of our faith. I do not propose that we substitute our words for those of Sandoval or Lugones. Theirs may well be better. What is important is that we recognize the theological issues being raised in feminist and womanist theory and that we remain open to dialogue with those theorists who are interested in women's religious thought.[25]

What can women's theologies offer to feminist, *mujerista,* and womanist theorists? We know that while we may not share the same faith stance, we have in common the goals of bringing about justice. Together we can engage in projects to that end. From women's theologies we learn that we need not fear the storm that surrounds our work against racism, classism, sexism, and homophobia, for we have learned of the God Who Is Present in the Midst of the Storm.[26] To our sister world travelers in the struggles for justice, who like ourselves may be weary of the constant battle against racism, sexism, and homophobia, we can make clear our belief that there is a God Who Knows the Truth[27] as together we try to dismantle the lies of patriarchal, racial, class, and sexual oppression so that we can all come to a better place, the home with many rooms, which we might call the realm of God.

On Building Our Own Rooms

I began this chapter with a reference to Rosemarie Tong's metaphor of home, the place with many rooms, the place where conversation can begin. I want to suggest here that we white women have some work to do in making home in our own room, even as we venture out into the living room and kitchen to talk to others from different rooms. It is not necessary for us to have our room completely decorated and pictures hung on the wall before venturing out; in fact, it is critical that we move back and forth from our room to common living spaces even as we deepen our own wellspring. One suggestion I have made about the work needed in the theological room of white women is that we need to construct a history of white feminist liberationist theology and ministry in the nineteenth and twentieth centuries. It is important for us to remember that liberation takes place in the churches, in institutions, in grassroots organizations, and on the streets, an important contribution learned from Hispanic, Latin American, and African-American theologies. A comprehensive account of our history should include the works of academic theologians; those writing spiritual autobiographies, sacred hymns, and poetry with a spiritual bent; women religious, lay leaders, and clergy preaching in local churches; and grassroots organizers developing policies advocating justice at the local, regional, national, and international levels. This project deserves further attention.

As an example of one way we white feminists might look to our own histories, I have begun to examine the theologies of various women hymn-writers.[28] Frances Dana Gage is one example of a white woman whose theological contributions should not be lost to our memory. Frances Dana Gage was born in 1808 in Marietta, Ohio. Her parents were among the first white settlers of Washington County, Ohio. Her only formal education consisted of a few years in a frontier school.

Gage's devotion to three causes dominated her life. She thought of temperance/prohibition, the abolition of slavery and the rights of freed people after the Civil War, and women's suffrage/liberation as one single cause. A devout Universalist early on in life, Gage left the church because she felt that the institution was not doing enough in her "triune" cause. Although not a member of an organized church in later life, she continued to speak, write, and think in profoundly spiritual terms. She became so notorious as an abolitionist and radical that her home and the family business in St. Louis were burned three times. Gage was a close associate of many of the foremothers of the women's suffrage movement: Elizabeth Cady Stanton, Susan B. Anthony, Lucy Stone, Lucretia Mott, and Matilda Joslyn Gage. As president of the 1851 Women's Rights Convention, Frances Dana Gage championed the right to speak of Sojourner Truth. It was Gage who introduced Sojourner Truth when she gave her legendary "Ain't I a Woman" speech. Gage continued to write and lecture tirelessly about temperance and women's rights. She and one of her daughters worked as volunteers in South Carolina for five years after the Civil War teaching and helping to relocate freed people.

One of Gage's hymns serves as a source for theological reflection for white women. "One Hundred Years Hence" was written in 1852 and was sung as the closing piece of the convention that the National Women's Suffrage Association had called to mark the nation's centenary in 1876. The suffragettes had been denied the opportunity to be a part of the official centennial celebrations.

> One hundred years hence, what a change will be made,
> In politics, morals, religion and trade,
> In statesmen who wrangle or ride on the fence,
> these things will be altered a hundred years hence.
>
> Our laws then will be uncompulsory rules,
> Our prisons converted to national schools,
> the pleasure of sinning 'tis all a pretense,
> And people will find that, a hundred years hence.

All cheating and fraud will be laid on the shelf,
Men will not get drunk, nor be bound up in self,
But all live together, good neighbors and friends,
As Christian folks ought to, a hundred years hence.

Then woman, man's partner, man's equal shall stand,
While beauty and harmony govern the land,
To think for oneself will be no offense,
The world will be thinking a hundred years hence.

Oppression and war will be heard of no more,
Nor blood of a slave leave his print on our shore,
Conventions will then be a useless expense,
For we'll go free-suffrage a hundred years hence.

Instead of speechmaking to satisfy wrong,
We'll all join the chorus to sing Freedom's song;
And if the Millenium is not a pretense,
we'll all be good brothers/neighbors a hundred years hence.[29]

Gage demonstrates in the text of this hymn that she holds multiple commitments to working against racism, sexism, militarism, and the penal system. She provides an early example of a white woman working across boundaries of difference. The theological and ethical commitments of such women as Frances Dana Gage can provide white feminist theologians with important material for theological reflection as we seek to find our own history in the process of doing liberation theology.

Taking the Methodology Bull by the Horns

I want to offer a second suggestion about our white feminist "homework." We teach and preach feminist liberationist theology, and yet we hesitate to employ the methodology we advocate in our writing. I want to invite students of theology to begin to question the accepted methods of theological scholarship. Of course, there are good reasons why we follow the accepted style of the academy, writing conceptual pieces such as this one, with footnotes from books out of our libraries as our source material. Tenure depends on scholarship, which is all too often defined in "academese." We need to be creative about developing our own avenues for publication that are accessible to the communities to which we are accountable and find ways to use the voices of our families and friends as one source for our theological reflection. Just as Isasi-Díaz and Tarango discovered in their interviews with Hispanic women, we too will find that grassroots women are developing a spirituality that is remarkably different from orthodox tradition. If our work is to be relevant to the "folk," we need to be closer in touch and unafraid to make these voices be heard. We can learn not only from Isasi-Díaz and Tarango, but also from Zora Neale Hurston, who discovered that she had to leave behind her academic dialect and speak intelligibly to folks in language they understand. I will use a true story from Kentucky to illustrate my point.

While I was home one fall day visiting family in Gravel Switch, Kentucky, I took a walk with a friend over to Miss Settie's place back on the Fork. We had climbed up one of the knobs and had returned to a pasture where a herd of cattle was grazing. Before we knew it, a bull started chasing us, followed by a couple dozen cows. The only choice was to run fast. As I came to the edge of the field, I had to cross a creek. Midway through the creek I realized that in order to get out of the pasture, I was going to have to jump an electric fence. With feet wet in the middle of the creek, I realized there was no turning back. My only hope was that the electric fence was not turned on, or if it was, that the voltage would be low enough that I would not suffer serious consequence. I was fortunate. I got over the fence unharmed and so did my friend. The bull and the cows decided not to chase us any farther.

The point I wish to make is this: bulls are used to having their own way, dominating their turf, and leading any cows who will follow to chase away those who might want to do something different in the pasture. In the case of theology, the methodology bull—the one that has placed primacy of theory over praxis—has succeeded for far too long in chasing away those who want to do theology differently. Serious heifer (trans: young cows who have not calved) theologians may be tempted to follow the methodology bull. We must, I believe, resist this temptation. Even when we are chased by the bull and its harem, we have no choice but to cross the creek, jump the fence if need be, and develop our own style of doing theological reflection.

As we women begin to develop our own methodology for doing theological reflection, we must find ways to "practice what we preach," in other words to allow the primacy of women's stories to guide our theological reflection process. Much of what we have internalized from the academic, intellectual tradition, which gives primacy to sacred "givens"—such as theory over praxis—must be resisted. We must take the methodology bull by the horns.[30]

Saying It Plain: Class and Social Location

The recent elections in this country and the swing to the right of the past twenty years, with their substantial backlash against feminism, should let us know that our brand of liberationist theology is not reaching "the folk."

We need to become multilingual in addressing our people, conscious of the language we use in differing contexts. Here is an example. I was invited to address a national convention of the National Telephone Cooperative Association. I hesitated to go, because the convention planners told me that most of these folks were from the Midwest—rural, conservative, and Republican. But I realized I had an opportunity to try to reach them. I began my sermon, consciously using language that would let them know that they were my people:

> Each year as school begins and fall draws near, I find myself thinking of home and what it means—for me sweet peas and ironstone, rocking chairs, black kettles and cast iron skillets, hand made quilts and ham and greens, front porch swings, and iced tea with sweat pouring down the glass, fishing and fish frys, fishing and fishing lies, corn bread and biscuits, fried chicken, fried apples, fried anything . . . green beans cooked with ham hocks four hours at least.
>
> Home, for me, though, is a mixed bag. Tobacco—way too much of it. Relatives trying to make a living growing it. Everybody smoking, some chewing, spitting, and drooling it. And more, family feuds, Hillbilly ways, secrets, too many of them, too long shut away, bitterness disguised as southern pride.
>
> And yet with all its ambiguities, I found myself going home at the end of one summer. It really wasn't so hard. I bought a hand made porch swing for Aunt Gloria's place and put up an iron rail fence with my cousin David so that John could sit on the porch in his wheelchair and not roll off. And then proceeded to sit on that swing and one just like it at my brother Danny's—wooden slats, chain hanging from two hooks on the porch roof—every day I was there. It was a busy time, in between porch sitting. We canned 30 quarts of sauerkraut, put up 25 pints of apple butter and 11 pints of pear butter and froze about 30 quarts of apples. Picked the tomatoes and made spaghetti sauce for the winter, dug the potatoes in the heat of the day. Went by Gravel Switch and then fishing out Black Lick back on Jean Whitlock's place. Got skunked. Aunt Gloria caught a huge bass, though. Gave me an excuse to go fishing again, this time on Dry Branch back of Danny's in Dixville. Caught something all right—a large snapping turtle that scared me to death. Tried my luck in a kayak on the Chaplin River one evening with my sister-in-law. Didn't catch any fish, but heard the crickets and the katydids and the hoot owls loud and clear. Heard big bullfrogs jump in ahead of the boat and tried not to be scared of the southern night noises.
>
> We went to a turtle cooking. Jerry caught 32 or was it 38 turtles during the year and had them in the freezer and invited everybody

over. He and Millie live a mile up the road from Danny in an old school bus. Cars and old beat up pick-ups were lined up and down the road everywhere. That's because Danny went down with his tractor and bushhogged—cut down all the weeds along the road—so people would have a place to park. Folks appreciate having the weeds mowed off. That way they could at least see the rattlesnakes or the copperheads lying in the grass. They did tease Danny about being a little redneck for driving to the "Dixville Doin" on a tractor. Well, that's really my fault, because I had his pick-up truck hauling a load to Aunt Gloria's. Now it was a sight when we got to Millie and Jerry's. Old and young people, skinny little hillbilly kids, a guy who had a speech impediment, my cousin Johnny in his wheelchair. Everybody looking out for him; Millie filling him a plate. My sis-in-law Denise strumming her guitar, David playing the dobro with steel finger picks, somebody playing the harmonica, all sitting on the tailgate of a pick-up. Now why am I telling you all this?

In part because coming home is part of my spiritual journey. I went to remind myself of why I wanted a Ph.D. degree in theology in the first place. I went also to remember my roots, to be with my people. What do I know about home? That home is making peace with our past, in all its brokenness. Accepting it in all its ambiguity, accepting people for who they are, and trying to understand their ways.

Home too is making peace with our present. With where we are now and where we are going, even if we're not sure where that is. Home for many of us takes us away from what we used to know, our blood families, into new constellations of family.

I wanted to begin here because I suspect some of us have a few things in common. Some of you probably like to fish, some like to garden, and maybe there's someone who understands about shooting Mountain Dew cans off a fence post. Some of you may be struggling with what it means to leave home and to make home when there's nothing about family that is easy. I'm not sure why you asked a woman to come to preach to you, but I know why I said yes. I believe that God was on to something when He . . . when She . . . when God said, "I will be your God and you will be my people." God did not say, "And you will be my individual person." God also did not say, "And you will be my peoples" or "And you will be my people and they will not." Somehow, at least in God's eyes, we are all one people. So, I'm here, knowing that some of you might find it odd to be listening to a woman.[31]

I began using the language of my people, my roots, because I wanted to make a connection with these folks as a bridge to the invitation I would extend at the end of the sermon. I stretched them as far as I thought they would go, talking to them about racism in very personal terms.

> We all want to move out of this Egypt land to the Promised Land, to the land of freedom from sorrow and enslavement to the work-a-day world, from those who would see us only as hands to make straw for bricks we are to tote on our backs to build their kingdoms of riches and glory not to Jesus but to Just One More Company Dollar. We all want to move away from the various Pharaohs holding us hostage to a mortgage we can barely meet and a car payment that straps us so bad we can never drive those wheels away on vacation. Many of us want out of Egypt and the captivity of contemporary culture to search for God's promise of a better place. We feel the face of Pharaoh breathing down our neck and don't know where to hide. . . .
>
> Friday morning the Pharaoh named Racism woke me up at 9:50 A.M. East Coast time, 6:50 A.M. West Coast time. "Dr. Moody, wake up. You people on the West Coast sleep way too late anyway. Can't you hear this message machine? Wake up!!" I stumbled out of bed, and answered the telephone more than half asleep. It was my friend, an ordained minister and professor at one of the major theological schools on the East Coast. I had tried to call her the day before and she was on her way to the airport to fly to New York and wanted to catch me before she left. She and I have been friends for fifteen years. I was telling her about a funny but weird dream I had and referred to it as "black humor." Long pause. You mean, "sick humor," don't you? My friend is African-American and I was calling to ask her a favor and here I had insulted her before we even got started. Now I know better. Using language like "black humor," referring to Africa as "the Darkest Continent," using metaphors which always make darkness bad and whiteness good only contribute to the racism of this country. I've even published articles on the importance of choosing our language carefully. So highly educated person that I am, at 6:50 in the morning before my first cup of coffee, I reverted to the language that I learned as a child, language that isn't helpful any more. What could I do but say I was sorry and go on? *We cannot let our blunders stop us from risking relationship with each other.* We reach out, make mistakes, acknowledge and learn from them, and simply go on.

I include this sermon here as an example of one of the ways that white women can be accountable to our people. I knew that I could not talk about racism with this group of people unless they felt we had something in common. They would not have been impressed with my theoretical knowledge of oppositional consciousness. They *were* willing to listen to a story. It is important that we find ways to communicate in accessible language with our people, whether in writing, or in a speech or sermon, or perhaps by video or music, or some other creative means. This accountability to our folk will keep us grounded in relationship with our people as we attempt to embody the justice our God calls us to model.

If it is not yet clear, I am talking about class issues. I am naming the work that has yet to be done in much of our theologizing. It is critical that white feminist theology begin to seriously address class issues. Rather than simply denouncing the myth of the classless society and offering a deconstruction of this mythology, I make a conscious effort to deal with class issues by speaking as one who does not come from middle-class or upper-class roots. My stories are not meant to entertain those who have never met a sow face-to-face and who don't know the difference between a cow, a sow, and a shoat. I do not speak of canning dozens of quarts of tomatoes in ninety-degree heat and humidity because I simply enjoy the nostalgia of the activity. These activities are grounded in necessity. Living close to the earth has given me an appreciation for ripe Rutgers tomatoes, young Silver Queen, a mess of perch or catfish, a pan of cornbread, and a glass of iced tea. Ours is a spirituality rooted not solely in Sunday school, but in the sweet smell of rich, dark earth. In our family, we never sit down together to eat without saying grace. While some theologians may not understand what might be humorously called "honeysuckle theology" (for the sweet yellow blooms of honeysuckle well-known to those who live along the railroad tracks—never prime real estate), the point is that many *will* understand what I am talking about. We need not only deconstruct the underpinnings of our classist society, but actually find ways to relate to those who struggle to make ends meet.

I have identified some of the work that white women need to do in building our own room. We need to look to our past, perhaps in unexpected places, for the wealth of women's theological wisdom that is available to us. We need to develop methods for theological investigation which allow contemporary women's voices to be heard. And we need to be prepared for the fact that our research may very well discover that contemporary women do not speak in traditional theological categories and do not think of God in four-syllable words. If we develop new methods of scholarship which include the life stories of real people as a legitimate source for reflection, and if we listen to the vocabulary women are using to describe their experience with God, then we have a better chance of being able to communicate across class boundaries in language accessible to the people we hope to reach. This is some of our homework.

Just as white feminists need to spend time in our own room, recollecting our histories and developing our own sources for theological reflection, we need to remember that women of color and other different contexts at times need to do the same. Sometimes this is frustrating, and it seems like we are in different time zones. When I am ready to move into the living room, you may be asleep. When you are ready to talk over lunch, I just want to rest. On occasion, however, there may be times when we both hear God calling us to move from our own rooms to common space, where we can attend to each other's concerns, needs, hopes, and dreams.

Hearing God Calling: The Covenant of Ruth and Naomi

In searching for ways to begin to do theology across the boundaries of difference, it may be helpful to develop a biblical model for cross-cultural theological dialogue about God. I offer the story of Ruth and Naomi as a possible model for contemporary cross-cultural dialogue among women who share a vision for a future free of oppression based on race, class, gender, sexual orientation, and other forms of marginalization. I believe that within the notion of a covenanting God and within the covenant between Ruth and Naomi, women theologians have the basis for mutual, shared theological reflection across the boundaries of difference. All of us would do well to hear again the words Ruth said to Naomi:

> Do not ask me to abandon you, or to turn from following you; for where you go I will go, and where you lodge I will lodge; your people shall be my people, and your God my God; where you die I will die, and there will I be buried. (Ruth 1:16, 17a, translation mine)

In the introduction, I posed several questions for reflection about the appropriateness of using the covenant between Ruth and Naomi as a constructive model for doing theology across the boundaries of difference. I asked whether or not this text suggests that Ruth experienced a conversion to the God and the culture of Israel while leaving her own Moabite God, history, family, and culture behind. I asked whether or not this text implies the negation of Ruth's own theological heritage in favor of that of Naomi. I asked whether this covenant is one-sided rather than reciprocal, leaving Ruth without an equal commitment from Naomi. Similarly, I asked whether or not this model can be helpful for constructing theology across the boundaries of difference. If women of color and white women, if women of varying racial, ethnic, and cultural backgrounds were to make a similar commitment to one another today, would one culture dominate the others? What would be the power dynamics between the groups? Could we ever get away from the white male God? Would we literally sacrifice our own God/dess(es) at the altar of multiculturalism? Is there significant textual evidence to suggest that this covenantal model could be one of mutuality without sacrificing self?

It seems impossible to answer these questions definitively, for there is no record in the text of Ruth or Naomi directly addressing these questions. However, the story of Ruth and Naomi suggests clues for a model of covenantal love that can lead white feminists, *mujeristas*, Latin American women, womanists, and other liberationists toward fruitful dialogue.

While one would wish the narrator had recorded the complete text of all the conversations that took place between Ruth and Naomi, a hermeneutics of suspicion tells us that the narrator's own interests, theological and otherwise, may have governed the lines recorded and preserved as sacred text. Naomi does not respond in kind to Ruth's famous words, at least in the version we have today. However, we have glimpses of a mutual, reciprocal relationship of love between these two women. Naomi continually addresses her daughter-in-law with the term of endearment, "my daughter."[32] In addition, on several occasions she refers to the relationship between Ruth and her as one of kinship. For example, in Ruth 2:20 and 3:2, Naomi speaks of Boaz as "our kinsman," a relative "of ours," indicating that she considers Ruth to be part of her family, her "people." Further, it is Naomi who devises the scheme in which Ruth asks Boaz to live up to his duty of being the "redeemer." Ruth's prophecy, "Your people will be my people," comes true in part because Naomi wills it to be true by telling Ruth of the existence of Boaz.

As to the question about whether or not Ruth gives up her own family, culture, and God, I believe it is possible to answer the question in the negative. When Ruth promises Naomi, "Your people will be my people," we do not have to automatically assume that Ruth gives up her love for her own mother, or father, or her sister-in-law Orpah, who chooses to stay in Moab. Rather, we are able to imagine that Ruth continues to love her blood family while making the choice to go to Bethlehem and love Naomi and her people. Second, we need not automatically assume that Ruth gives up her culture. The text, in fact, continues to refer to Ruth as "the Moabite" even after she goes to Bethlehem. Finally, I believe it is possible that Ruth does not necessarily give up her own God when she vows to honor the God of Naomi. Although it may have been in the theological interest of the narrator to demonstrate Ruth's conversion to Yahwist theology (see 1:16), nowhere does Ruth explicitly renounce her Moabite God/s.

In fact, some evidence exists that both Ruth and Naomi understand God to be more than the name Yahweh. According to Louise Pettibone Smith, the God Shaddai of whom Naomi speaks in 1:20 may have been Moabite in origin.[33] What is certain is that Naomi ascribes to God both the names Yahweh and Shaddai. In addition, Smith, Francis Landy, and others have suggested that there is some textual evidence to support the notion that the threshing floor rite, which Naomi suggests Ruth participate in with Boaz, may have had cultic significance and/or was perhaps connected to a barley festival tribute to an ancient grain goddess of Bethlehem.[34] While neither Smith nor Landy makes definitive judgments about whether or not the event has cultic significance, it is important for a hermeneutics of remembrance to know that at least on the level of folk culture and folk religion, a syncretistic understanding of God may well have existed at the time. What I am suggesting—for only a suggestion is possible based on the text as it has been preserved—is that perhaps Ruth and Naomi were able, in their own wisdom, to honor a multitude of Gods simultaneously, or perhaps they understood God to have many names.

In sum, in answer to the question of whether or not Ruth gives up her own family, culture, God, and identity, I do not believe any explicit textual evidence suggests a renunciation of her heritage. Naomi's travel to Moab does not entail giving up her heritage from Judah. Likewise it seems entirely possible that Ruth is able to travel to Naomi's "world" without giving up her own. In fact, the two women seem to be making every effort to forge a culture of their own, demonstrating a kind of cultural and theological flexibility that allows these women to engage in the serious business of working out their salvation.[35] In the prophetic words of covenant that Ruth says to Naomi, we may have an early glimpse of the "multi-world view" that Ada María Isasi-Díaz believes is a key to liberation.

The covenant between Ruth and Naomi is important because it provides a relational link between God and these two women. Its covenantal formula harkens back to the covenantal formula that God has consistently used, "I will be your God and you will be my people." These two women of differing cultural backgrounds make a commitment to each other to relate to one another just as God makes a relational commitment to humanity. The model I offer is that Ruth and Naomi's relatedness in friendship across the boundary of difference *is* the embodiment of the covenanting God.

Two aspects of this covenant are significant for the proposed model for doing theological reflection on God across the boundaries of difference. First, Ruth promises to accept Naomi's people as her people, altering the usual boundaries of familial and cultural allegiance. If we are to adapt this promise for our own purposes, we will find ways to say to one another, "Your people are my people." These are not words that can be uttered without the praxis of learning another's language and culture and without the commitment of a life-long struggle to doing justice and righting relationships. Second, Ruth promises to honor the God of Naomi. In order for women doing theology to make similar commitments to each other, we must make the effort to read and hear each other's theological understandings of God and engage in conversation. Who knows, in our praxis of solidarity, committed Christian womanist, *mujerista*, Asian American, Latin American, and white feminist liberationist theologians might do well to worship with each other and pray together. Finally, we recognize that the commitment of Ruth and Naomi was a lifelong one. In the words of Huston Smith, covenant involves "the pledging of total selves" and "lasts till death."[36]

The covenant between Ruth and Naomi can serve as a model for relationship in the home suggested by Rosemarie Tong, a home with many rooms, a home in which the walls of our own agendas, perspectives, and biases are thin enough to permit a conversation. If we are to begin building a theological home together, we need to confront the obstacles to its construction described in this chapter. We need to speak in our distinct theological dialects, and we need to become multilingual so that we can understand each other. We need to speak our anger, listen in patience, and learn from each other. We need to develop world-traveling skills and form multi-world views. We need to speak of each other's lives in those places where it is appropriate and keep silent on other occasions. These are some of the conditions necessary for us to enter into covenant together, to relate to each other in mutually loving and liberating ways. In Kentucky, where my family lives and my roots are, when we speak of "our people," we mean our kin. Perhaps if we accept the invitation of the covenanting God to enter into life-long, committed covenant with each other to work out our salvation together, as did Ruth and Naomi, we will find ways to become more human, literally to become "people" to one another.

As Ruth and Naomi, you and I may not know the way to our shared future. But if we take the time to listen to each other, we may glean some clues. We know with certainty that we will not find our way into the future together without the hard work of a life-long commitment to justice. Perhaps we should simply pause for a while and thank God in the midst of the storm that surrounds us, to use one of the insights of womanist theology. We might pray that God would serve as the bridge drawing us near to one another, to use the insights of white feminist theology. And then we might simply throw a party, to use the insights of Hispanic and Latin American women.

After the Jewish people had been in slavery, we would expect that God would tell Moses to tell Pharoah, "Let my people go so they can rest." Or "Let my people go so they can draw up plans for how they will strategize to get to the Promised Land." But instead, God's words to Moses were, "Let my people go so that they can have a feast unto me in the wilderness." Not at the end of the journey but right in the midst of the struggle—risk a party? What if I never learned to dance? And how will we decide which music? Who will lead and who will follow? Can't I just sit still and tap my toe? You mean move my hips? Touch each other? All in the name of God? Why didn't God suggest anything else but a party—a feast in the wilderness? Maybe that is the next step in becoming "people" to each other.

Notes

Introduction

1. Mary Daly, *The Church and the Second Sex* (Boston: Beacon Press, 1968; reprint, With the Feminist Postchristian Introduction and New Archaic Afterwords by the Author. Boston: Beacon Press, 1985), 214.

2. Audre Lorde, "An Open Letter to Mary Daly," in *This Bridge Called My Back: Writings By Radical Women of Color*, ed. Cherríe Moraga and Gloria Anzaldúa (New York: Kitchen Table Press, 1983), 94–97.

3. For further discussion, see bell hooks, *Ain't I a Woman* (Boston: South End Press, 1981), *Feminist Theory: From Margin to Center* (Boston: South End Press, 1984), and *Yearning: Race, Gender and Cultural Politics* (Boston: South End Press, 1990); and Patricia Hill Collins, *Black Feminist Thought: Knowledge, Consciousness, and the Politics of Empowerment* (London: HarperCollins Academic, 1990).

4. Ada María Isasi-Díaz and Yolanda Tarango's *Hispanic Women: Prophetic Voice in the Church* (San Francisco: Harper and Row, 1988) and Jacquelyn Grant's *White Women's Christ and Black Women's Jesus: Feminist Christology and Womanist Response* (Atlanta: Scholars Press, 1989) are two examples of works by racial/ethnic women which provide a critique to white feminist theology by seeking to point to the particularities of their own experience.

5. For her definition of "womanist," see Alice Walker, *In Search of Our Mothers' Gardens: Womanist Prose by Alice Walker* (San Diego: Harcourt Brace Jovanovich, 1983), xi.

6. Ada María Isasi-Díaz, "Mujeristas: A Name of Our Own," in *Yearning to Breathe Free: Liberation Theologies in the United States*, ed. Mar Peter-Raoul and others (Maryknoll, New York: Orbis Books, 1990), 121–128.

7. Chela Sandoval prefers to use the term "United States Third World feminist." See Chela Sandoval, "Comment on Krieger's 'Lesbian Identity and Community: Recent Social Science Literature,'" *Signs: Journal of Women in Culture and Society* 9, no. 4 (1984): 728.

8. Mary E. Hunt, *Fierce Tenderness: A Feminist Theology of Friendship* (New York: Crossroad, 1992), 74; Delores Williams, "Breaking and Bonding," *Daughters of Sarah* (May–June, 1989), 20, 21; Tereza Cavalcanti, "The Prophetic Ministry of Women in the Hebrew Bible," in *Through Her Eyes*, ed. Elsa Tamez (Maryknoll, New York: Orbis Books, 1989), 127. For further treatment, see also *Reading Ruth: Contemporary Women Reclaim a Sacred Story*, ed. Judith A. Kates and Gail Twersky Reimer (New York: Ballantine Books, 1994).

9. Welch describes an ethic of risk as follows: "Within an ethic of risk, actions begin with the recognition that far too much has been lost and there are no clear means of restitution. The fundamental risk constitutive of this ethic is the decision to care and to act

although there are no guarantees of success. Such action requires immense daring and enables deep joy." Sharon D. Welch, *A Feminist Ethic of Risk* (Minneapolis: Fortress Press, 1990), 68.

10. Jacquelyn Grant, "The Sin of Servanthood," in *A Troubling in My Soul: Womanist Perspectives on Evil and Suffering*, ed. Emilie M. Townes (Maryknoll, New York: Orbis Books, 1993), 215.

11. This panel presentation has been published as Toinette M. Eugene and others, "Special Section on Appropriation and Reciprocity in Womanist/Mujerista/Feminist Work," *Journal of Feminist Studies in Religion* 8, no. 2 (Fall 1992): 91–122.

12. Sharon D. Welch, *Communities of Resistance and Solidarity: A Feminist Theology of Liberation* (Maryknoll, New York: Orbis Books, 1985); Susan Thistlethwaite, *Sex, Race, and God: Christian Feminism in Black and White* (New York: Crossroad, 1991); Ann Kirkus Wetherilt, *That They May Be Many: Voices of Women, Echoes of God* (New York: Continuum, 1994).

13. For Elisabeth Schüssler Fiorenza's feminist treatment of "hermeneutics of suspicion," see Elisabeth Schüssler Fiorenza, *Bread Not Stone: The Challenge of Feminist Biblical Interpretation* (Boston: Beacon Press, 1984), ch. 1.

14. See especially Gustavo Gutiérrez, *The Power of the Poor in History* (Maryknoll, New York: Orbis Books, 1983), 18–22 and 101–107. Originally published as *La fuerza histórica de los pobres*, (Lima, Peru: Centro de Estudios y Publicaciones, 1979). See also Ivone Gebara, "Doing Theology in Latin America" in *With Passion and Compassion: Third World Women Doing Theology*, ed. Virginia Fabella and Mercy Amba Oduyoye (Maryknoll, New York: Orbis Books, 1988), 129–130.

15. See Benjamin A. Reist, who, in arguing that theology must take seriously the issue of race, also noted that W. E. B. Du Bois, as early as 1903, proclaimed the problem of the twentieth century to be the issue of race. Benjamin A. Reist, *Theology in Red, White, and Black* (Philadelphia: Westminster Press, 1975), ch 1. See also Jacquelyn Grant, *White Women's Christ and Black Women's Jesus*.

16. For further discussion, see Elizabeth Cady Stanton, *The Woman's Bible* (New York: European Publishing Company, 1898, repr. Seattle: Coalition Task Force on Women and Religion, 4759-15th Ave. NE, Seattle, Washington 98105, 1974), 7–13; Elisabeth Schüssler Fiorenza, *In Memory of Her: A Feminist Theological Reconstruction of Christian Origins* (New York: Crossroad, 1983), 32, 33; Elsa Tamez, "Women's Rereading of the Bible," in *With Passion and Compassion*, 78.

17. See Gustavo Gutiérrez, *A Theology of Liberation* (Maryknoll, New York: Orbis Books, 1971), xxix; and Marta Benavides, "My Mother's Garden is a New Creation" in *Inheriting Our Mother's Gardens: Feminist Theology in Third World Perspectives*, ed. Letty Russell, et al. (Philadelphia: Westminster Press, 1988), 132.

18. Chela Sandoval, "Comment on Krieger's 'Lesbian Identity and Community: Recent Social Science Literature,' " 728.

19. Ibid.

20. Ibid.

21. Chela Sandoval, "U.S. Third World Feminism: The Theory and Method of Oppositional Consciousness in the Postmodern World," *Genders* 10 (Spring 1991): 14.

22. Delores Williams, *Sisters in the Wilderness: The Challenge of Womanist God-Talk* (Maryknoll, New York: Orbis Books, 1993), ix.

23. Harriette Arnow, *The Dollmaker* (New York: Macmillan, 1954).

24. María Lugones, "Playfulness, 'World'-Traveling and Loving Perception," in *Making Face, Making Soul: Haciendo Caras*, ed. Gloria Anzaldúa (San Francisco: Aunt Lute Books, 1990), 390–402.

25. Mary E. Hunt, in a lecture on feminist spirituality given at the Church Divinity School of the Pacific, Berkeley, California, March 7, 1987.

26. Sylvia Marcos, "Toward Permanent Rebellion," *Speaking of Faith: Global Perspectives on Women, Religion, and Social Change*, ed. Diana L. Eck and Devaki Jain (Philadelphia: New Society Publishers, 1987), 260.

27. Mary E. Hunt, lecture on feminist spirituality.

28. Linda A. Moody, "Women and the Church Grow by Caring," *Women and the Church (WATCHword)*, a publication of National Ministries, American Baptist Churches, USA, Valley Forge, Pennsylvania, 11, no. 2 (June/July 1987): 5.

29. Mary E. Hunt, lecture on feminist spirituality, 6.

30. Mary E. Hunt, *Fierce Tenderness*, 143.

31. Will Coleman, "Conjuring: African American Slave Women, 'Literacy,' and the Reconstruction of Reality," Baccalaureate Address given at Mills College, Oakland, California, May 21, 1994.

Chapter 1. Contemporary White Feminist Conception of God

1. Mary Daly, *Beyond God the Father* (Boston: Beacon Press, 1973), xi.

2. In a speech given upon receiving the Peace Prize of the German Publishers Association, Tillich reminded his listeners "of the boundaries (or limits) that lie within and between all persons, ideas, and nations—boundaries which must first be acknowledged, then conquered." Wilhelm Pauck and Marion Pauck, *Paul Tillich: His Life and Thought,* Vol. I (New York: Harper and Row, 1976), 267.

3. Mary Daly, *Beyond God the Father*, 6.

4. See Paul Tillich, "Protestant Principles," *The Protestant* 4, no. 5 (April–May 1942).

5. Charles William Kegley and Robert W. Bretall, ed. *The Theology of Paul Tillich*, Vol. I (New York: Macmillan, 1952), 34.

6. Ibid., 37.

7. Wilhelm Pauck and Marion Pauck, *Paul Tillich: His Life and Thought,* 34, 229–230.

8. These trips caused him to reflect near the end of his life that he would like to rewrite his entire *Systematic Theology* "oriented toward, and in dialogue with, the whole history of religions." See John Dillenberger and Claude Welch, *Protestant Christianity*, 2d edition (New York: Macmillan, 1988), 331.

9. Paul Tillich, *Systematic Theology*, Vol. I (Chicago: University of Chicago Press, 1967), 235, 236.

10. Mary Daly, *Beyond God the Father*, 20.

11. Ibid., 32.

12. Ibid., 33, 34.

13. Ibid., 34.

14. Mary Daly, *Gyn/Ecology: The Metaethics of Radical Feminism* (Boston: Beacon Press, 1978), 34.

15. Paul Tillich, *Systematic Theology*, Vol. I, 239.

16. Ibid., 240.

17. Mary Daly, *The Church and the Second Sex* (Boston: Beacon Press, 1968), 165.

18. Mary Daly, *Beyond God the Father*, 15.

19. Paul Tillich, *Systematic Theology*, Vol. III, 293.

20. Ibid., 294.

21. Daly, *Beyond God the Father*, 72.

22. Rosemary Radford Ruether, *Sexism and God-Talk: Toward a Feminist Theology* (Boston: Beacon Press, 1983), 48.

23. Ibid., 49.

24. Ibid.

25. Ibid., 70, 71.

26. Ibid., 71.

27. Paul Tillich, *Systematic Theology*, Vol. I, 294.

28. Rosemary Radford Ruether, *Sexism and God-Talk*, 137.

29. Ibid.

30. Ibid., 186.

31. Delores Williams, "The Color of Feminism," *Christianity and Crisis* (April 29, 1985): 165.

32. Ibid.

33. Ada María Isasi-Díaz, *En La Lucha/In the Struggle: Elaborating a Mujerista Theology* (Minneapolis: Fortress Press, 1993), 171.

34. This section of the chapter is a revised version of a paper presented at the American Academy of Religion Western Chapter annual meeting, Santa Clara University, March 25, 1994. Portions of this also appear in "Constructive Theological Understandings of Sallie McFague," *New Theology Review* 8, no. 3 (August, 1995).

35. Sallie McFague, *Speaking in Parables* (Philadelphia: Fortress Press, 1975), 2.

36. Ibid., 3.

37. Ibid., 4.

38. Ibid., 3, 4.

39. Ibid., 3.

40. Ibid., 16.

41. Ibid., 17.

42. Ibid., 7.

43. Ibid., 15, 16.

44. Ibid., 33.

45. Sallie McFague, *The Body of God: An Ecological Theology*, (Minneapolis: Fortress Press 1993), 48.

46. Ibid.

47. Carter Heyward, *Our Passion for Justice: Images of Power, Sexuality, and Liberation* (New York: Pilgrim Press, 1984), 11.

48. Ibid.

49. Carter Heyward, *The Redemption of God: A Theology of Mutual Relation* (Lanham, MD: University Press of America, 1982), 7.

50. Carter Heyward, *Touching Our Strength: The Erotic as Power and the Love of God* (San Francisco: HarperSanFrancisco, 1989), 67.

51. Carter Heyward, *Our Passion for Justice*, 27.

52. Ibid.

53. Ibid.

54. Ibid., 28.

55. Carter Heyward, *The Redemption of God*, 38.

56. Ibid., 40.

57. Carter Heyward, *Our Passion for Justice*, 27, 28.

58. Ibid., 36.

59. Carter Heyward, *The Redemption of God*, 11. Biblically, this norm is based in the passage from Mark 12:28–31, in which Jesus instructs the scribes that love of God and love of neighbor are the two greatest commandments.

60. Ibid., 15.

61. Carter Heyward, *Our Passion for Justice*, 227.

62. Ibid.

63. Carter Heyward, *The Redemption of God*, 13.

64. Ibid., 20.

65. Carter Heyward, *Our Passion for Justice*, 227.

66. Ibid., 227, 228.

67. Ibid, 228.

68. Ibid.

69. Ibid.

70. Carter Heyward, *The Redemption of God*, 14.

71. Sallie McFague, *Metaphorical Theology: Models of God in Religious Language* (Philadelphia: Fortress Press, 1982), 166.

72. Ibid., 187.

73. See, for example, Mary E. Hunt, *Fierce Tenderness: A Feminist Theology of Friendship* (New York: Crossroad, 1992).

74. See Josh. 1:5, Hos 2:23, John 17:21, 1 Cor 3:9, and 1 John 1:3 as further evidence for the model of God as friend.

75. Sallie McFague, *Models of God: Theology for an Ecological, Nuclear Age* (Philadelphia: Fortress Press, 1987), 113.

76. Carter Heyward, *The Redemption of God*, xviii.

77. Carter Heyward, *The Redemption of God*, 10.

78. Ibid., 203.

79. Ibid., 6.

80. The God of justice for the poor is found in Jeremiah 2–5, Amos 5:24, Matt 25:31–46, Lk 6:17–27, Jn 4:5–26, and in Gal 3:28. The God of justice for women can be seen in Mark 14:3–9; Luke 10:38–42; John 4:5–26; Galatians 3:28. The God of justice for the outcast and "the other" can be seen in Mt 25:31–46, Lk 10:25–37, Jn 4:5–26, and in Acts 10:44–11:18. See Carter Heyward, *The Redemption of God*, 10.

81. Carter Heyward, *Our Passion for Justice*, 244.

82. Ibid., 245.

83. Ibid.

84. Ibid., 246, 247.

85. Ibid., 166.

86. Ibid., 245.

87. Ibid., 166.

88. Ibid., 141.

89. Ibid.

90. Ibid., 142.

91. Carter Heyward, *Speaking of Christ: A Lesbian Feminist Voice*, ed. Ellen C. Davis (New York: Pilgrim Press, 1989), 24.

92. Ibid., 69.

93. The biblical basis for this concept of God comes from an understanding of Exodus 3:14. This is the passage in which Moses asks God by what name he should refer to God in speaking to the people of Israel. God's response, "I AM WHO I AM," is the basis for the God whom Heyward names as the "enigmatic" God. In addition to the translations, "I AM WHO I AM" and "I WILL BE WHO I WILL BE," Heyward offers an understanding of a "God who is becoming." See *Our Passion for Justice*, 48.

94. Carter Heyward, *Speaking of Christ*, 53.

95. Carter Heyward, *Our Passion for Justice*, 167.

96. Ibid., 193, 194.

97. Carter Heyward, *Our Passion for Justice*, 214.

98. Ibid., 218.

99. Carter Heyward, *Speaking of Christ*, 10.

100. Ibid., 52.

101. Ibid., 61.

102. Sallie McFague, *Models of God*, 61.

103. Ibid., 72.

104. Heyward cites Christian tradition as it appears in the prayers of Christian mystics such as Julian of Norwich, Teresa of Avila, and John of the Cross. In their prayers we encounter what Heyward refers to as the "eroticism of agape: the sexuality of spiritual love." See Carter Heyward, *Our Passion for Justice*, 45.

105. Carter Heyward, *Our Passion for Justice*, 25, emph. mine.

106. Ibid., 130.

107. Ibid., 140.

108. Ibid.

109. Carter Heyward, *Touching Our Strength*, 128.

110. McFague, *Speaking in Parables*, 79.

111. Gustavo Gutiérrez, *A Theology of Liberation*, 15th Anniversary Edition (Maryknoll, New York: Orbis Books, 1988), 110.

112. Carter Heyward, *The Redemption of God*, 10, 11.

113. Carter Heyward, *Our Passion for Justice*, 98.

114. Ibid., 119.

115. Ibid.

116. Ibid., 16.

117. Ibid., 16.

118. Ibid., 98.

119. Ibid., 124.

120. Ibid., 145.

121. Carter Heyward, *The Redemption of God*, 11.

122. Carter Heyward *Our Passion for Justice*, 211.

123. Ibid., 252.

124. Audre Lorde, "An Open Letter to Mary Daly," in *This Bridge Called My Back: Writings By Radical Women of Color*, ed. Cherríe Moraga and Gloria Anzaldúa (New York: Kitchen Table Press, 1983), 95.

125. Ibid., 97.

126. Carter Heyward, *Our Passion for Justice*, 214, 215.

127. Sharon Welch, *Communities of Resistance and Solidarity: A Feminist Theology of Liberation* (Maryknoll, New York: Orbis Books, 1985), 51.

Chapter 2. Hispanic and Latin American Women's Views of God

1. Carmen Lora de Ames, interview by Karen O'Brien (Lima, Peru: Latinamerica Press, January, 1986); repr. "Liberation Theology Faces Feminism: Church Women's Perspectives Differ," in *Latin American Church Women Challenge Patriarchy in Church and Society* (New York: Women's International Resource Exchange [WIRE], no date), 1.

2. Ibid.

3. Gustavo Gutiérrez, *A Theology of Liberation* (Maryknoll, New York: Orbis Books, 1971), xx.

4. For further clarification, see Ivone Gebara, "Women Doing Theology in Latin America," in *With Passion and Compassion: Third World Women Doing Theology*, ed. Virginia Fabella and Mercy Amba Oduyoye (Maryknoll, New York: Orbis Books, 1988), 128.

5. Fryne Santisteban, interview by Karen O'Brien (Lima, Peru: Latinamerica Press, January, 1986); repr. "Liberation Theology Faces Feminism: Church Women's Perspectives Differ," in *Latin American Church Women Challenge Patriarchy in Church and Society*, 1.

6. Nellie Ritchie, "Women's Participation in the Church: A Protestant Perspective," in *With Passion and Compassion: Third World Women Doing Theology*, ed. Virginia Fabella and Mercy Amba Oduyoye (Maryknoll, New York: Orbis Books, 1988), 155.

7. For a detailed history of Latin American Liberation Theology, see Alfred T. Hennelly, ed., *Liberation Theology: A Documentary History* (Maryknoll, New York: Orbis Books, 1990).

8. Ada María Isasi-Díaz, born in La Habana, lived in Cuba until she was eighteen years of age. Since then, she has lived in three countries and traveled extensively. She has studied in Peru, in France, and received her doctorate in ethics from Union Theological Seminary in New York. Since coming to the United States in 1960, she has served as Director of Program and as Associate General Director of Church Women United. She currently teaches theology and ethics at Drew University. Yolanda Tarango is a Chicana activist who has worked in feminist issues, and has served as national coordinator of LAS HERMANAS, a national organization of Hispanic women.

9. Ada María Isasi-Díaz, *En La Lucha/In the Struggle: Elaborating a Mujerista Theology* (Minneapolis: Fortress Press, 1993).

10. Tamez received her doctorate from the University of Lausanne, Switzerland. She has worked as Professor of Biblical Studies at Seminario Bíblico Latinoamericano in San José, Costa Rica, and has worked on the staff at Departamento Ecuménico de Investigaciones in San José. Tamez is currently President of Seminario Bíblico Latinoamericano in San José, Costa Rica.

11. Bingemer has also served as regional coordinator of the Ecumenical Association of Third World Theologians (EATWOT) for Latin America. She is co-author, with J. B. Libanio, of *Christian Eschatology* and with Ivone Gebara, of *Mary, Mother of God, Mother of the Poor.*

12. Bidegain is a lay Catholic church historian and holds a doctorate in history from the Catholic University of Louvain. She has taught at the University of the Andes, Bogotá, and has also taught at Duke University. Her books, *Nacionalismo, Militarismo, Y Dominación en América Latina*; *Iglesia, Pueblo y Política*; and *Así Actuaron Los Cristianos en La Historia de América Latina*, are important contributions to the theological arena in Latin America.

13. Gloria Loya, "Hispanic Women: Prophetic Voice in the Church," a lecture given at the Graduate Theological Union, Berkeley, California, Fall 1990.

14. Ada María Isasi-Díaz and Yolanda Tarango, *Hispanic Women: Prophetic Voice in the Church* (San Francisco: Harper and Row, 1988), 4.

15. Ada María Isasi-Díaz, "Mujeristas: A Name of Our Own," in *Yearning to Breathe Free*, ed. Mar Peter-Raoul et al., (Maryknoll, New York: Orbis Books, 1990), 122. For a more complete treatment of mujerista theology, see Ada María Isasi-Díaz, *En La Lucha/In the Struggle.*

16. See Elsa Tamez, ed., *Through Her Eyes: Women's Theology from Latin America* (Maryknoll, New York: Orbis Books, 1989), originally published as *El Rostro Feminino de la Teología*, ed. Elsa Tamez (San José, Costa Rica: DEI, 1986); and Thomas Melville and Marjorie Melville, *Whose Heaven, Whose Earth?* (New York: Knopf, 1971).

17. Ivone Gebara, "Women Doing Theology in Latin America," 126.

18. Ada María Isasi-Díaz and Yolanda Tarango, *Hispanic Women*, 21.

19. Ibid., 29.

20. Ana María Bidegain, "Women and the Theology of Liberation," in *Through Her Eyes*, 28.

21. Ibid., 27.

22. Elsa Tamez, "Introduction: The Power of the Naked," in *Through Her Eyes*, 2.

23. "Final Statement: Latin American Conference, Buenos Aires, Argentina, Oct. 30–Nov. 3, 1985," in *Through Her Eyes*, 151.

24. Ibid.

25. Ada María Isasi-Díaz and Yolanda Tarango, *Hispanic Women*, 2.

26. Ada María Isasi-Díaz, *En La Lucha/In the Struggle*, 174.

27. Ada María Isasi-Díaz and Yolanda Tarango, *Hispanic Women*, 5.

28. For further discussion, see Ada María Isasi-Díaz and Yolanda Tarango, *Hispanic Women*, 69.

29. Luz Beatriz Arellano, "Women's Experience of God in Emerging Spirituality," in *With Passion and Compassion*, 148.

30. María Pilar Aquino, "Women's Participation in the Church: A Catholic Perspective," in *With Passion and Compassion*, 160.

31. Ibid.

32. Ivone Gebara, "Women Doing Theology in Latin America," 129.

33. Ana María Bidegain, "Women and the Theology of Liberation," 31.

34. Ibid.

35. Ibid.

36. Elsa Tamez, "Women's Rereading of the Bible," in *With Passion and Compassion*, 78.

37. Elsa Tamez, *The Bible of the Oppressed*, tr. Matthew J. O'Connell (Maryknoll, New York: Orbis Books, 1982), 37, 71. Chapters 1 through 5 of this translation were originally published as *La Biblia de los oprimidos: La opresión en la teología bíblica* (San José, Costa Rica: DEI, 1979). Chapters 6 and 7 are taken from *La hora de la vida* (San José, Costa Rica: DEI, 1978).

38. Elsa Tamez, "Introduction: The Power of the Naked," in *Through Her Eyes*, 4.

39. Elsa Tamez, "Amada Pineda: A Woman of Nicaragua," in *Speaking of Faith: Global Perspectives on Women, Religion and Social Change*, ed. Diana L. Eck and Devaki Jain (Philadelphia: New Society Publishers, 1987), 38.

40. Elsa Tamez, *Against Machismo* (Oak Park, Illinois: Meyer Stone Books, 1987), 144. Originally published as Elsa Tamez, *Teologos de la Liberación Hablan Sobre la Mujer* (San Jose, Costa Rica: DEI, 1986).

41. Elsa Tamez, "Women's Rereading of the Bible," 176.

42. Raquel Rodríguez, interview by Elsa Tamez, in *Teólogos de la Liberación Hablan Sobre La Mujer*, 165.

43. Robert McAfee Brown, *Theology in a New Key: Responding to Liberation Themes* (Philadelphia: Westminster Press, 1978), 88.

44. Beatriz Melano Couch, in *Theology in the Americas*, ed. Sergio Torres and John Eagleson (Maryknoll, New York, Orbis Books, 1976), 305–306; cited in Robert McAfee Brown, *Theology in a New Key*, 88.

45. Ada María Isasi-Díaz and Yolanda Tarango, *Hispanic Women*, 25.

46. Ibid., 29–31.

47. Ibid., 15–17.

48. Ibid., 33.

49. Ibid., 41.

50. Ibid.

51. Ibid., 22.

52. Ibid.

53. Elsa Tamez, *The Bible of the Oppressed*, 2.

54. Ibid.

55. Ibid., 4.

56. Ibid., 12.

57. Ibid., 24. For further examination of Tamez's treatment of the identification of God with the poor, see also Elsa Tamez, *The Scandalous Message of James* (New York: Crossroad, 1990), 43–50; originally published as Elsa Tamez, *Santiago: Lectura latinoamericana de la epístola* (San José, Costa Rica: DEI, 1985).

58. Elsa Tamez, *The Bible of the Oppressed*, 25.

59. Raul Vidales, *Cristianismo Anti-burgués* (San José: DEI, 1978), 116, 117; cited in Elsa Tamez, *The Bible of the Oppressed*, 35. The biblical passages central to Tamez's analysis here are Ex. 20:2 ("I am the Lord your God, who brought you out of the land of Egypt, out of the house of bondage") and Ex. 22:21 ("You shall not wrong a stranger or oppress him, for you were strangers in the land of Egypt").

60. Ibid., 77.

61. For further discussion, see Elsa Tamez, *The Scandalous Message of James*, 62–69.

62. Elsa Tamez, *The Bible of the Oppressed*, 39.

63. Ibid., 39.

64. Elsa Tamez, *The Scandalous Message of James*, 21.

65. María Clara Bingemer, "Reflections on the Trinity," in *Through Her Eyes*, 57.

66. Ivone Gebara, "Women Doing Theology in Latin America," 129.

67. Ibid., 128.

68. Tepedino has taught theology at the Catholic University and at St. Ursula's University, both in Rio de Janeiro, Brazil.

69. Ana María Tepedino, "Feminist Theology as the Fruit of Passion and Compassion," in *With Passion and Compassion*, 167. See also Consuela del Prado, "I Sense God in Another Way," in *Through Her Eyes*, 140–149. Originally published as "Yo Siento a Dios De Otro Modo," in *El Rostro Feminino de la Teología*, 73–84.

70. Ana María Tepedino, "Feminist Theology as the Fruit of Passion and Compassion," in *With Passion and Compassion*, 167.

71. Ibid.

72. Elsa Tamez, *The Bible of the Oppressed*, 58.

73. Ibid., 61.

74. Elsa Tamez, "The Woman Who Complicated the History of Salvation," in *New Eyes for Reading: Biblical and Theological Reflections by Women from the Third World*, ed. John S. Pobee and Barbel Von Wartenberg-Potter (Geneva: World Council of Churches, 1986, 16; repr. Bloomington, Indiana: Meyer Stone Books, 1987). This article, translated by Betsy Yeager, was originally published in Spanish in *Media Development*, journal of the World Association for Christian Communication, Vol XXXI, no. 2: May 1984.

75. Elsa Tamez, "Letter to Job," in *Doing Theology in a Divided World*, ed. Virginia Fabella and Sergio Torres (Maryknoll, New York: Orbis Books, 1985), 175; originally given as a paper for the Sixth International Conference of the Ecumenical Association of Third World Theologians, January 5–13, 1983, Geneva, Switzerland.

76. Elsa Tamez, *The Bible of the Oppressed*, 83.

77. Ibid., 60.

78. Luz Beatriz Arellano, "Women's Experience of God in Emerging Spirituality," in *With Passion and Compassion*, 142.

79. Ibid., 138.

80. Ibid., 144.

81. María Pilar Aquino, "Women's Participation in the Church: A Catholic Perspective," in *With Passion and Compassion*, 162.

82. Luz Beatriz Arellano, "Women's Experience of God in Emerging Spirituality," 136, 137.

83. Ibid.

84. A native of Holland, Verhoeven was ordained in the Argentine Methodist Church and has worked there for many years. The first woman accepted in the pastoral ministry of the Argentine Methodist Church, Verhoeven has lived in Mendoza, working with a group of women victims of human rights violations. To promote this work, she helped to organize the Ecumenical Foundation of Cuyo, which assists these women and their children. See Elsa Tamez, ed. *Through Her Eyes*, 164.

85. Alida Verhoeven, "The Concept of God: A Feminist Perspective," in *Through Her Eyes*, 55.

86. Translation as provided in María Teresa Porcile, "El Derecho de la Belleza en America Latina," in *El Rostro Feminino de la Teología*, 86.

87. English translation of Exodus 5:1 is from the New Revised Standard Version.

88. María Teresa Porcile, "El Derecho de la Belleza en America Latina," 86.

89. María Pilar Aquino, "Women's Participation in the Church," 162.

90. Luz Beatriz Arellano, "Women's Experience of God in Emerging Spirituality," 137.

91. Ada María Isasi-Díaz and Yolanda Tarango, *Hispanic Women*, 22.

92. Ibid., 68.

93. Ibid., 69.

94. Nellie Ritchie, "Women and Christology," in *Through Her Eyes*, 85.

95. Luz Beatriz Arellano, "Women's Experience of God in Emerging Spirituality," 137.

96. María Pilar Aquino, "Women's Participation in the Church," 162.

97. Elsa Tamez, "Amada Pineda," 38.

98. Ibid., 39.

99. María Pilar Aquino, "Women's Participation in the Church," 162.

100. Ibid.

101. Luz Beatriz Arellano, "Women's Experience of God in Emerging Spirituality," 148.

102. Carlos Mejia Godoy, "Mary Virgin Bird," cited in Luz Beatriz Arellano, "Women's Experience of God in Emerging Spirituality," 148.

103. Ignacio Bernal, *Tenochtitlan en una isla* (Mexico: Fondo de Cultura Economica, SEP, 1984), 84–86; cited in Elsa Tamez, "Introduction: The Power of the Naked," 1.

104. Elsa Tamez, "Introduction: The Power of the Naked," 2.

105. Ibid., 3.

106. Ibid., 7.

107. Ibid., 9.

108. Ibid., 13.

109. Ibid., 13.

110. Ibid., 14.

111. Elsa Tamez, "Quetzalcoatl Challenges the Christian Bible," paper presented at the annual meeting of the American Academy of Religion and Society for Biblical Literature Joint Conference, November 1992, San Francisco, California; see also Elsa Tamez, "Reliving Our Histories: Racial and Cultural Revelations of God," in *New Vision for the Americas: Religious Engagement and Social Transformation*, ed. David Batstone (Minneapolis: Fortress Press, 1993).

112. Elsa Tamez, "Quetzalcoatl Challenges the Christian Bible."

113. Aurora Lapiedra, "Religiosidad popular y mujer andina," in *El Rostro Feminino de la Teología*, 50.

114. Ibid.

115. Ibid., 57, 58.

116. Ibid., 55.

117. Norma Alarcon, born in Mexico and raised in Chicago, earned her Ph.D. in Hispanic literature in 1981 from Indiana University. Gloria Evangelina Anzaldúa is a Chicana lesbian feminist poet and fiction writer. Anzaldúa has been active in the migrant farm workers movement, has taught at several universities, is co-editor with Cherríe Moraga of *This Bridge Called My Back: Writings by Radical Women of Color* (New York: Kitchen Table Press, 1983), and is author of *Borderlands/La Frontera* (San Francisco: Aunt Lute Books, 1987), among other works.

118. See also Norma Alarcon, "Chicana's Feminist Literature: A Re-Vision Through Malintzin/or Malintzin: Putting Flesh Back on the Object," in *This Bridge Called My Back*, 182–190; and Gloria Anzaldúa, "Entering into the Serpent," in *Weaving the Visions: New Patterns in Feminist Spirituality*, ed. Judith Plaskow and Carol Christ (San Francisco: Harper and Row, 1989), 77–86.

119. Mirta Quintanales, "I Paid Very Hard for My Immigrant Ignorance," in *This Bridge Called My Back*, 154.

120. Ada María Isasi-Díaz, "A Platform for Original Voices," in *Christianity and Crisis*, June 12, 1989: 192.

121. Luz Beatriz Arellano, "Women's Experience of God in Emerging Spirituality," 148.

Chapter 3. Womanist Theological Reflections on God

1. Jacquelyn Grant, "Black Women and the Church," in *All the Women Are White, All the Blacks Are Men, But Some of Us Are Brave: Black Women's Studies*, ed. Gloria T. Hull et al. (Old Westbury, New York: The Feminist Press, 1982), 148.

2. Katie Geneva Cannon, "Christian Ethics and Theology in Womanist Perspective," *Journal of Feminist Studies in Religion* 5, no. 2 (Fall 1989): 93, 94.

3. Delores Williams, *Sisters in the Wilderness: The Challenge of Womanist God-Talk* (Maryknoll, New York: Orbis Books, 1993), xiv.

4. Ibid.

5. Emilie Townes points out that on occasion "the multiracial and gender inclusive nature of a womanist social ethic means strained dialogue." *Womanist Justice, Womanist Hope* (Atlanta: Scholars Press, 1993), 188.

6. See Alice Walker, *In Search of Our Mothers' Gardens* (San Diego: Harcourt Brace Jovanovich, Publishers, 1983), xi and xii for her complete definition.

7. Delores Williams, "Womanist Theology: Black Women's Voices," *Christianity and Crisis* 47 (March 2, 1987): 67.

8. Ibid.

9. Cheryl J. Sanders, "Christian Ethics and Theology in Womanist Perspective," *Journal of Feminist Studies in Religion* 5, no. 2 (Fall 1989): 86.

10. Delores Williams, "Womanist Theology," 69.

11. Ibid.

12. For a more complete treatment of the methodology outlined here, see Delores Williams, "Womanist Theology," 69, 70.

13. Delores Williams, *Sisters in the Wilderness*, 246.

14. Harold A. Carter, *The Prayer Tradition of Black People* (Valley Forge, Pennsylvania: Judson Press, 1976), 50; cited in Jacquelyn Grant, *White Women's Christ and Black Women's Jesus: Feminist Christology and Womanist Response* (Atlanta: Scholars Press, 1989), 212.

15. Jacquelyn Grant, *White Women's Christ and Black Women's Jesus*, 212.

16. Cannon feels there is some question as to the exact date of Hurston's birth. See Katie Geneva Cannon, *Black Womanist Ethics* (Atlanta: Scholars Press, 1988), 8.

17. Zora Neale Hurston, *Dust Tracks on a Road* (Philadelphia: J. B. Lippincott Co., 1942; reprint ed. 1971), 21; cited in Katie Geneva Cannon, *Black Womanist Ethics*, 99.

18. Zora Neale Hurston, *Dust Tracks on a Road*, 21; cited in bell hooks, *Yearning: Race, Gender, and Cultural Politics* (Boston: South End Press, 1990), 136.

19. bell hooks, *Yearning*, 142, 143.

20. Katie Geneva Cannon, *Black Womanist Ethics*, 8.

21. Zora Neale Hurston, "John Reading Goes To Sea," *Opportunity* 4 (January 1926): 19; cited in Katie Geneva Cannon, *Black Womanist Ethics*, 8.

22. Katie Geneva Cannon, *Black Womanist Ethics*, 169.

23. Ibid., 174.

24. Jacquelyn Grant, *White Women's Christ and Black Women's Jesus*, 211.

25. Ibid., 212.

26. Jacquelyn Grant, "Subjectification as a Requirement for Christological Construction," in *Lift Every Voice: Constructing Christian Theologies from the Underside*, ed. Susan Brooks Thistlethwaite and Mary Potter Engel (San Francisco: HarperSanFrancisco, 1990), 209.

27. Delores Williams, *Sisters in the Wilderness*, 146.

28. Ibid., 148.

29. Ibid., 149, 150.

30. Ibid., 152.

31. Ibid., 161.

32. Harold A. Carter, *The Prayer Tradition of Black People*, 49; cited in Jacquelyn Grant, *White Women's Christ and Black Women's Jesus*, 213.

33. Olive Gilbert, ed., *Sojourner Truth: Narrative and Book of Life* (1850, 1875; reprint, Chicago: Johnson, 1970), 118; cited in Jacquelyn Grant, "Subjectification as a Requirement for Christological Construction," 211.

34. Jacquelyn Grant, "Subjectification as a Requirement for Christological Construction," 211, 212.

35. Delores Williams, *Sisters in the Wilderness*, 120.

36. William F. Allen, Charles P. Ware, and Lucy McKim Garrison, *Slave Songs of the United States* (New York: P. Smith, 1929), 72; cited in Delores Williams, *Sisters in the Wilderness*, 110–11.

37. Delores Williams, *Sisters in the Wilderness*, 113.

38. Ibid., 262. Delores Williams notes that this song was sung in Baptist churches, including her own when she was a child, and in Methodist camp meetings in the South during the late nineteenth century.

39. Katie Geneva Cannon, "Kate and the Color Purple," in The Mudflower Collective, *God's Fierce Whimsy* (New York: Pilgrim Press, 1985), 105.

40. Katie Geneva Cannon, "Surviving the Blight," in *Inheriting Our Mothers' Gardens*, ed. Letty Russell et al. (Philadelphia: Westminster Press, 1988), 88.

41. Katie Geneva Cannon, "Kate and the Color Purple," 105.

42. Ibid., 106.

43. Ibid.

44. Katie Geneva Cannon, "Surviving the Blight," 88.

45. Ibid., 89.

46. Katie Geneva Cannon, *Black Womanist Ethics*, 18.

47. Ibid., 19.

48. Ibid., 78.

49. Ibid.

50. Phillis Wheatley, "On Being Brought from Africa to America," in Roger Whitlow, *Black American Literature: A Critical History* (Totowa, New Jersey: Littlefield, Adams and Co., 1974), 23; cited in Katie Geneva Cannon, *Black Womanist Ethics*, 79.

51. Katie Geneva Cannon, "Surviving the Blight," 87.

52. Jacquelyn Grant, *White Women's Christ and Black Women's Jesus*, 214.

53. Olive Gilbert, ed., *Sojourner Truth*, 122; cited in Jacquelyn Grant, *White Women's Christ and Black Women's Jesus*, 214.

54. Jacquelyn Grant, *White Women's Christ and Black Women's Jesus*, 214.

55. Katie Geneva Cannon, *Black Womanist Ethics*, 10.

56. Zora Neale Hurston, *Dust Tracks on a Road*, 177; cited in Katie Geneva Cannon, *Black Womanist Ethics*, 11.

57. Zora Neale Hurston, "How It Feels to Be Colored Me," *The World Tomorrow* (May 1928): 17; cited in Katie G. Cannon, *Black Womanist Ethics*, 11.

58. Zora Neale Hurston, *Jonah's Gourd Vine* (Philadelphia: J. B. Lippincott, 1934; repr., with a new foreword by Rita Dove, New York: Harper and Row, 1990), 175, 176.

59. Zora Neale Hurston, *Mules and Men* (Philadelphia: J. B. Lippincott, 1935; repr., preface by Franz Boas, with a new foreword by Arnold Rampersad, New York: Harper and Row, 1990), 141, 142.

60. Zora Neale Hurston, *Their Eyes Were Watching God* (Philadelphia: J. B. Lippincott, 1937; repr., with a new foreword by Mary Helen Washington, New York: Harper and Row, 1990), 14.

61. Ibid.

62. Zora Neale Hurston, *Their Eyes Were Watching God* (Philadelphia: J. B. Lippincott, 1937; repr., Urbana: University of Illinois Press, 1978), 20; cited in Katie Geneva Cannon, *Black Womanist Ethics*, 133.

63. Zora Neale Hurston, *Their Eyes Were Watching God* (Philadelphia: J. B. Lippincott, 1937; repr., with a new foreword by Mary Helen Washington, New York: Harper and Row, 1990), 183.

64. See Barbara Christian, *Black Women Novelists: The Development of a Tradition, 1892–1976* (Westport, Connecticut: Greenwood Press, 1980), 57.

65. Katie Geneva Cannon, *Black Womanist Ethics*, 144.

66. Ibid., 143.

67. Ibid., 145.

68. Jacquelyn Grant, "Black Women and the Church," in *But Some of Us Are Brave*, 149.

69. Jacquelyn Grant, *White Women's Christ and Black Women's Jesus*, 213.

70. Ibid.

71. J. D. Roberts, *A Black Political Theology* (Philadelphia: Westminster Press, 1974), 133; cited in Jacquelyn Grant, *White Women's Christ and Black Women's Jesus*, 215.

72. Jacquelyn Grant, *White Women's Christ and Black Women's Jesus*, 215.

73. James Cone, *God of the Oppressed* (New York: Seabury Press, 1975), 136; cited in Jacquelyn Grant, *White Women's Christ and Black Women's Jesus*, 216.

74. Jacquelyn Grant, *White Women's Christ and Black Women's Jesus*, 217.

75. Ibid., 220.

76. Ibid.

77. Delores Williams, "Black Women's Surrogacy Experience," in *After Patriarchy: Feminist Transformations of the World Religions*, ed. Paula M. Cooey, William R. Eakin, and Jay B. McDaniel (Maryknoll, New York: Orbis Books, 1991), 8, 9.

78. Ibid., 9.

79. Ibid., 10.

80. Delores Williams, *Sisters in the Wilderness*, 162.

81. Ibid., 164.

82. Delores Williams, "Black Women's Surrogacy Experience," 11.

83. Ibid., 12, 13.

84. Cheryl J. Sanders, "Christian Ethics and Theology in Womanist Perspective," 90.

85. Emilie M. Townes, "Christian Ethics and Theology in Womanist Perspective," *Journal of Feminist Studies in Religion* 5, no. 2 (Fall 1989): 95.

86. Alice Walker, *The Color Purple* (New York: Washington Square Press, 1982), 177; cited in Emilie M. Townes, "Christian Ethics and Theology in Womanist Perspective," 95.

87. Emilie M. Townes, "Christian Ethics and Theology in Womanist Perspective," 96.

Chapter 4. Women's Theologies in Dialogue

1. See Toinette M. Eugene, et al., "Special Section on Appropriation and Reciprocity in Womanist/Mujerista/Feminist Work," *Journal of Feminist Studies in Religion* 8, no. 2 (Fall 1992): 91–122, for the papers presented by Toinette M. Eugene, Ada María Isasi-Díaz, Kwok Pui-lan, Judith Plaskow, Mary E. Hunt, Emilie M. Townes, and Ellen M. Umansky.

2. Donna Haraway, "A Manifesto for Cyborgs: Science, Technology, and Socialist Feminism in the 1980s," originally published in *Socialist Review* 80 (1985); also in *Feminism/Postmodernism*, ed. Linda J. Nicholson (New York and London: Routledge, 1990), 197.

3. Chela Sandoval, "Feminism and Racism: A Report on the 1981 National Women's Studies Association Conference," originally published in 1982 by the Center for Third World Organizing, Oakland, California, and Washington, D.C.; also in *Making Face, Making Soul: Haciendo Caras: Creative and Critical Perspectives by Women of Color*, ed. Gloria Anzaldúa (San Francisco: Aunt Lute Foundation Books, 1990), 55.

4. Chela Sandoval, "Comment on Krieger's 'Lesbian Identity and Community: Recent Social Science Literature'," *Signs: Journal of Women in Culture and Society* 9, no. 4 (1984): 728.

5. Chela Sandoval, "Feminism and Racism," 65.

6. Ibid., 66.

7. Ibid., 70.

8. Chela Sandoval, "U.S. Third World Feminism: The Theory and Method of Oppositional Consciousness in the Postmodern World," *Genders* 10 (Spring 1991): 17.

9. Rauschenbusch served a congregation of German immigrants for eleven years in the area of New York known as "Hell's Kitchen." His writings often concern issues of the working class. Niebuhr served in a pastorate in Detroit from 1915 to 1928 and observed firsthand many of the abuses of the automotive industry. See John Dillenberger and Claude Welch, *Protestant Christianity: Interpreted Through Its Development*, Second Edition (New York: Macmillan, 1988), 225, 235.

10. Carter Heyward, *Touching Our Strength: The Erotic as Power and the Love of God* (San Francisco: Harper and Row, 1989), 67.

11. See Phyllis Trible, *God and the Rhetoric of Sexuality* (Philadelphia: Fortress Press, 1978), ch. 1; Mary Daly, *Beyond God the Father* (Boston: Beacon Press, 1973), ch. 1; Elisabeth Schüssler Fiorenza, *In Memory of Her: A Feminist Biblical Interpretation* (Boston: Beacon Press, 1988), 130–139.

12. See Casey Miller and Kate Swift, *Words and Women: New Language in New Times* (Garden City, New York: Anchor Books, Anchor Press/Doubleday, 1977), 64–67; Sharon Neufer Emswiler and Thomas Neufer Emswiler, *Women and Worship: A Guide to Nonsexist Hymns, Prayers, and Liturgies*, (New York: Harper and Row, 1974), Revised and Expanded Edition (San Francisco: Harper and Row, 1984), 27–33; Leonard Swidler, *Biblical Affirmations of Woman* (Philadelphia: Westminster Press, 1979), ch. 1–3.

13. Carter Heyward, *Speaking of Christ: A Lesbian Feminist Voice*, ed. Ellen C. Davis (New York: Pilgrim Press, 1989), 11.

14. Ada María Isasi-Díaz and Yolanda Tarango, *Hispanic Women: Prophetic Voice in the Church* (San Francisco: Harper and Row, 1988), 4.

15. Elsa Tamez, *The Bible of the Oppressed*, tr. Matthew J. O'Connell (Maryknoll, New York: Orbis Books, 1982).

16. Elsa Tamez, *Against Machismo*, tr. and ed. John Eagleson (Oak Park, Illinois: Meyer Stone Books, 1987), 147.

17. Ibid.

18. Elsa Tamez, "Mujer y Varon Llamados a La Vida: Un acercamiento bíblico-teológico," *Cristianismo y Sociedad* 21, no. 3–4 (1982–83): 83.

19. Ibid.

20. Elsa Tamez, "Quetzalcoatl Challenges the Christian Bible," paper presented at the annual meeting of the American Academy of Religion and Society for Biblical Literature Joint Conference, November 1992, San Francisco, California.

21. Ibid.

22. Aurora Lapiedra, "Religiosidad popular y mujer andina," in *El Rostro Feminino de la Teología*, ed. Elsa Tamez (San José, Costa Rica: Departamento Ecuménico de Investigaciones, 1986), 71.

23. David Batstone relates other accounts of belief in Pachamama. He recounts the Inca folklore surrounding the figure of Inkarri, a "child of the Sun and of a poor woman" who suffers as do the farmworkers of the Andes, his feet bleeding "but the blood was merely mingling with Mother Earth [Pachamama], his real mother." According to Batstone, this story, as it appears in a catechism used in one of the ecclesial base communities of the Northern Andes, depicts Pachamama sharing in the suffering of her son, yearning for the day when the land would be returned to the poor farmworkers. Here the story of Pachamama is used in a revolutionary way, encouraging the peasants to resist the oppression of those who have taken away their land and their rights to its bounty. David Batstone, *From Conquest to Struggle: Jesus of Nazareth in Latin America* (Albany, New York: State University of New York Press, 1991), 199.

24. Ada María Isasi-Díaz and Yolanda Tarango, *Hispanic Women*, 67.

25. Ibid., 67–69.

26. Ibid., 66.

27. See Karen Baker-Fletcher, "Soprano Obligato," in *A Troubling in My Soul: Womanist Perspectives on Evil and Suffering*, ed. Emilie M. Townes (Maryknoll, New York: Orbis Books, 1993), 172–185. See also Emilie M. Townes, *Womanist Justice, Womanist Hope* (Atlanta, Georgia: Scholars Press, 1993), ch. 6.

28. Cheryl J. Sanders, "Christian Ethics and Theology in Womanist Perspective," *Journal of Feminist Studies in Religion* 5, no. 2 (Fall 1989): 86, 87.

29. See Delores Williams, "Womanist Theology: Black Women's Voices," *Christianity and Crisis* 47, (March 2, 1987): 70; and Emilie M. Townes, "Christian Ethics and Theology in Womanist Perspective," *Journal of Feminist Studies in Religion* 5, no. 2 (Fall 1989): 96.

30. Delores Williams, *Sisters in the Wilderness: The Challenge of Womanist God-Talk* (Maryknoll, New York: Orbis Books, 1993), 177.

31. Elsa Tamez, *The Bible of the Oppressed*, 3.

32. Ibid., 60.

33. Ibid., 63.

34. Gustavo Gutiérrez, *The God of Life*, tr. Matthew J. O'Connell (Maryknoll, New York: Orbis Books, 1991), 142.

35. This technique was first used in her work with Yolanda Tarango, *Hispanic Women: Prophetic Voice in the Church*. This method is even more clearly described in her more recent *En La Lucha/In the Struggle: Elaborating a Mujerista Theology* (Minneapolis: Fortress, 1993).

36. Gustavo Gutiérrez, *A Theology of Liberation*, 15th anniversary ed., ed. and trans. Sister Caridad Inda and John Eagleson (Maryknoll, New York: Orbis Books, 1988), 110.

37. María Clara Luchetti Bingemer, "The Difference in the Way of Knowing and Speaking About God," *SEDOS* 24 (Je 15–Jl 15, 1992): 214, 215.

38. Delores Williams, *Sisters in the Wilderness*, 85.

39. For a discussion of Schweitzer, see Claude Welch, *Protestant Thought in the Nineteenth Century*, Vol. 2 (New Haven: Yale University Press, 1985), 161–163.

40. Ada María Isasi-Díaz and Yolanda Tarango, *Hispanic Women*, 69.

41. John Cobb, *Christ in a Pluralistic Age* (Philadelphia: Westminister Press, 1975) and *Beyond Dialogue: Toward a Mutual Transformation of Christianity and Buddhism* (Philadelphia: Fortress Press, 1977). John Hick and Paul F. Knitter, ed. *The Myth of God Incarnate* (Philadelphia: Westminister Press, 1977). Paul Knitter *No Other Name: A Critical Survey of Christian Attitudes Toward the World Religions* (Maryknoll, New York: Orbis Books, 1985).

42. Elsa Tamez, *The Bible of the Oppressed*, 38.

43. Luz Beatriz Arellano, "Women's Experience of God in Emerging Spirituality," in *With Passion and Compassion: Third World Women Doing Theology*, ed. Virginia Fabella and Mercy Amba Oduyoye (Maryknoll, New York: Orbis Books, 1988), 140.

44. Ibid., 141.

45. Paul F. Knitter, "Toward a Liberation Theology of Religions," in *The Myth of Christian Uniqueness: Toward a Pluralistic Theology of Religions*, ed. John Hick and Paul F. Knitter (Maryknoll, New York: Orbis Books, 1987), 178–200.

Chapter 5. Clues for Doing Theology across the Boundaries of Difference

1. Rosemarie Tong, *Feminist Thought: A Comprehensive Introduction* (Boulder, Colorado: Westview Press, 1989), 7.

2. See Toinette M. Eugene et al., "Special Section on Appropriation and Reciprocity in Womanist/Mujerista/Feminist Work," *Journal of Feminist Studies in Religion* 8, no. 2 (Fall 1992); and Katie Geneva Cannon and Kristine A. Culp, with an introduction by Emilie M. Townes, "Appropriation and Reciprocity in the Doing of Feminist and Womanist Ethics," *The Annual of the Society of Christian Ethics* (Boston: The Society of Christian Ethics, 1993).

3. Here I have consciously chosen the term "women doing theology" in recognition that some women prefer not to use the term "feminist" to describe the cultural context for their work, given that the term "feminist" has often been used to describe the cultural context of white women. See Chela Sandoval, "Feminism and Racism: A Report on the 1981 National Women's Studies Association Conference," originally published in 1982 by the

Center for Third World Organizing, Oakland, California, and Washington, D.C. In *Making Face, Making Soul: Haciendo Caras: Creative and Critical Perspectives by Women of Color*, ed. Gloria Anzaldúa (San Francisco: Aunt Lute Foundation Books, 1990), 55. See also Chela Sandoval, "Comment on Krieger's 'Lesbian Identity and Community: Recent Social Science Literature'," *Signs: Journal of Women in Culture and Society* 9, no. 4 (1984): 728.

4. Elizabeth Spelman, *Inessential Woman: Problems of Exclusion in Feminist Thought* (Boston: Beacon Press, 1988), ix.

5. Ibid., 187.

6. Audre Lorde, *Sister Outsider* (New York: The Crossing Press Feminist Series, 1984), 130.

7. See Alison M. Jaggar, "Love and Knowledge: Emotion in Feminist Epistemology," in *Gender/Body Knowledge*, ed. Alison Jaggar and Susan Bordo (New Jersey: Rutgers University Press, 1989). See also Beverly Wildung Harrison, "The Power of Anger in the Work of Love," in *Weaving the Visions: New Patterns in Feminist Spirituality*, ed. Judith Plaskow and Carol P. Christ (San Francisco: Harper and Row, 1989), 214–225.

8. Alison M. Jaggar, "Love and Knowledge," 157.

9. Ibid., 160.

10. Ibid.

11. Ibid., 160.

12. Ibid., 162.

13. Ada María Isasi-Díaz, "Educating for a New World Order," paper presented at the annual meeting of the National Association of Women in Education, Seattle, Washington, March 6, 1993.

14. Peggy McIntosh, "White Privilege: Unpacking the Invisible Knapsack," *Independent School* (Winter 1990): 31. For further discussion of white privilege, see her article "White Privilege and Male Privilege: A Personal Account of Coming to See Correspondences Through Work in Women's Studies," in *Race, Class and Gender*, ed. Margaret Andersen and Patricia Hill Collins (Belmont, California: Wadsworth, 1992), 70–81.

15. Elizabeth Potter holds the Quigley Chair of Women's Studies at Mills College, Oakland, California. This discussion took place at a faculty seminar given on March 15, 1993.

16. See María C. Lugones and Elizabeth V. Spelman, "Have We Got a Theory for You! Feminist Theory, Cultural Imperialism and the Demand for 'The Woman's Voice'," *Women's Studies International Forum* 6, no. 6 (1983); and María Lugones, "Playfulness, 'World'-Traveling, and Loving Perception," in *Making Face, Making Soul*.

17. I am thankful to Marta Inés Castillejo C. for the conversation which led to these observations.

18. Uma Narayan, "Working Together across Difference: Some Considerations on Emotions and Political Practice," *Hypatia: A Journal of Feminist Philosophy* 3, no. 2 (Summer 1988): 38.

19. Ibid.

20. I have followed the recommendation of Emilie M. Townes that she and other womanist scholars prefer that the word "Black" be capitalized.

21. Elsa Tamez, "Quetzalcoatl Challenges the Christian Bible," paper presented at the Annual Meeting of the American Academy of Religion and Society for Biblical Literature, November 1992, San Francisco, California.

22. Rosemarie Tong, *Feminist Thought*, 7.

23. Chela Sandoval, "U.S. Third World Feminism: The Theory and Method of Oppositional Consciousness in the Postmodern World," *Genders* no. 10 (Spring 1991): 71.

24. María Lugones, "Playfulness, 'World'-Traveling, and Loving Perception," in *Making Face, Making Soul*, 393.

25. Indeed, we have evidence that the worlds of Women's Studies and feminist and liberation theologies may not be nearly so far apart as they once were. Evidence for the bridging of gaps between women in Women's Studies and Religious Studies is clear in various publications: *Women and Values: Readings in Recent Feminist Philosophy*, ed. Marilyn Pearsall (Belmont, California: Wadsworth, 1986) contains a chapter on Philosophy of Religion. *The Cross Cultural Study of Women*, ed. Margot I. Duley and Mary I. Edwards (New York: The Feminist Press at the City University of New York, 1986) contains a chapter on Women and Religion. *A Reader in Feminist Knowledge*, ed. Sneja Gunew (London and New York: Routledge, 1991) contains a chapter on Religion. *The Women's Studies Quarterly* 21, nos. 1 and 2 (Spr/Sum 1993) is a thematic issue on Spirituality and Religion.

26. The image of God in the Midst of the Storm is derived from a story told in Katie Geneva Cannon, "Surviving the Blight," in *Inheriting Our Mothers' Gardens: Feminist Theology in Third World Perspectives*, ed. Letty Russell et al. (Philadelphia: Westminster Press, 1988), 88.

27. The image of a God Who Knows the Truth relies on Katie Geneva Cannon's analysis of the theology of Nanny Crawford, a character in Zora Neale Hurston's *Their Eyes Were Watching God* (Philadelphia: J. B. Lippincott, 1937; repr., Urbana: University of Illinois Press, 1979), 20, cited in Katie Geneva Cannon, *Black Womanist Ethics* (Atlanta: Scholars Press, 1988), 133.

28. I am very grateful to the long hours devoted to this project by my research assistant, Garen Murray.

29. Frances Dana Gage, "One Hundred Years Hence," in *Singing Our History: Tales, Texts, and Tunes from Two Centuries of Unitarian and Universalist Hymns*, ed. Eugene B. Navias (Boston: Unitarian Universalist Association, 1975), 55.

30. Linda A. Moody, "Women's Theological Reflections on Reproductive Choices," paper presented at the American Academy of Religion, Western Region, University of Redlands, Redlands, California, March 31, 1995.

31. Linda A. Moody, "Let My People Go," a sermon preached at the annual convention of the National Telephone Cooperative Association, San Francisco, California, February 5, 1995.

32. Phyllis Trible concurs as to the significance of this term of endearment. See Phyllis Trible, *God and the Rhetoric of Sexuality* (Philadelphia: Fortress Press, 1978), 176.

33. Louise Pettibone Smith, "The Book of Ruth: Introduction and Exegesis," in *The Interpreter's Bible*, Volume II (New York: Abingdon-Cokesbury Press, 1953), 838.

34. Louise Pettibone Smith, "The Book of Ruth," 844, 845 and Francis Landy, "Ruth and the Romance of Realism, or Deconstructing History," *Journal of the American Academy of Religion* 62, no. 2 (Summer 1994): 287–289.

35. Phyllis Trible agrees with this interpretation in her summation, "All together they are women in culture, women against culture, and women transforming culture." Phyllis Trible, *God and the Rhetoric of Sexuality*, 196.

36. Huston Smith, *The World's Religions* (San Francisco: HarperSanFrancisco, 1991), 306.

Bibliography

Allen, William F. , Charles P. Ware, and Lucy McKim Garrison. *Slave Songs of the United States*. New York: P. Smith, 1929. Cited in Delores Williams. *Sisters in the Wilderness: The Challenge of Womanist God-Talk*. Maryknoll, New York: Orbis Books, 1993.

Ames, Carmen Lora de. Interview by Karen O'Brien. Lima, Peru: Latinamerica Press, January 1986; repr. "Liberation Theology Faces Feminism: Church Women's Perspectives Differ." In *Latin American Church Women Challenge Patriarch in Church and Society*. New York: Women's International Resource Exchange, n.d.

Aquino, María Pilar. "Women's Participation in the Church: A Catholic Perspective." In *With Passion and Compassion: Third World Women Doing Theology*, ed. Virginia Fabella and Mercy Amba Oduyoye, 159–164. Maryknoll, New York: Orbis Books, 1988.

Arellano, Luz Beatriz. "Women's Experience of God in Emerging Spirituality." In *With Passion and Compassion: Third World Women Doing Theology*, ed. Virginia Fabella and Mercy Amba Oduyoye, 135–141. Maryknoll, New York: Orbis Books, 1988.

Arnow, Harriette. *The Dollmaker*. New York: Macmillan, 1954.

Baker-Fletcher, Karen. "Soprano Obligato." In *A Troubling in My Soul: Womanist Perspectives on Suffering and Evil*, ed. Emilie Townes, 172–185. Maryknoll, New York: Orbis Books, 1993.

Batstone, David. *From Conquest to Struggle: Jesus of Nazareth in Latin America*. Albany, New York: State University of New York Press, 1991.

Benavides, Marta. "My Mother's Garden Is a New Creation." In *Inheriting Our Mothers' Gardens: Feminist Theology in Third World Perspectives*, ed. Letty Russell et al. , 123–142. Philadelphia: Westminster Press, 1988.

Bidegain, Ana María. "Women and the Theology of Liberation." In *Through Her Eyes: Women's Theology from Latin America*, ed. Elsa Tamez, 15–36. Maryknoll, New York: Orbis Books, 1989. Originally published as *El Rostro Feminino de la Teología*, ed. Elsa Tamez. San José, Costa Rica: Departamento Ecuménico de Investigaciones, 1986.

Bingemer, María Clara Luchetti. "The Difference in the Way of Knowing and Speaking about God." *SEDOS* 24 (June 15–July 15, 1992): 210–217.

Brown, Robert McAfee. *Gustavo Gutiérrez: An Introduction to Liberation Theology*. Maryknoll, New York: Orbis Books, 1990.

Buber, Martin. *I and Thou*, trans. Walter Kaufmann. New York: Charles Scribner's Sons, 1970. Cited in Carter Heyward. *The Redemption of God: A Theology of Mutual Relation*. Lanham, Maryland: University Press of America, 1982.

Cadorette, Curt. *From the Heart of the People: The Theology of Gustavo Gutiérrez*. Oak Park, Illinois: Meyer-Stone Books, 1988. Cited in David Batstone. *From Conquest to Struggle: Jesus of Nazareth in Latin America*. Albany, New York: State University of New York Press, 1991.

Cannon, Katie Geneva. "Kate and the Color Purple." In The Mudflower Collective. *God's Fierce Whimsy*, 104, 105. New York: Pilgrim Press, 1985.

———. "Surviving the Blight." In *Inheriting Our Mothers' Gardens: Feminist Theology in Third World Perspectives*, ed. Letty Russell et al. , 75–90. Philadelphia: Westminster Press, 1988.

———. *Black Womanist Ethics*. Atlanta: Scholars Press, 1988.

———. "Christian Ethics and Theology in Womanist Perspective," *Journal of Feminist Studies in Religion* 5, no. 2 (Fall 1989): 92–94.

Carter, Harold A. *The Prayer Tradition of Black People*. Valley Forge, Pennsylvania: Judson Press, 1976. Cited in Jacquelyn Grant. *White Women's Christ and Black Women's Jesus: Feminist Christology and Womanist Response*. Atlanta: Scholars Press, 1989.

Cavalcanti, Tereza. "The Prophetic Ministry of Women in the Hebrew Bible." In *Through Her Eyes: Women's Theology from Latin America*, ed. Elsa Tamez, 118–139. Maryknoll, New York: Orbis Books, 1989.

Christian, Barbara. *Black Women Novelists: The Development of a Tradition, 1892–1976*. Westport, Connecticut: Greenwood Press, 1980.

Cobb, John. *Christ in a Pluralistic Age*. Philadelphia: Westminister Press, 1975.

———. *Beyond Dialogue: Toward a Mutual Transformation of Christianity and Buddhism*. Philadelphia: Fortress Press, 1977.

Coleman, Will. "Conjuring: African American Slave Women, 'Literacy', and the Reconstruction of Reality." Baccalaureate Address given at Mills College, Oakland, California, May 21, 1994.

Collins, Patricia Hill. *Black Feminist Thought: Knowledge, Consciousness, and the Politics of Empowerment*. London: Harper Collins Academic, 1990.

Cone, James. *God of the Oppressed*. New York: Seabury Press, 1975. Cited in Jacquelyn Grant. *White Women's Christ and Black Women's Jesus: Feminist Christology and Womanist Response*. Atlanta: Scholars Press, 1989.

Daly, Mary. *The Church and the Second Sex*. Boston: Beacon Press, 1968; repr. , with the feminist postchristian introduction and new archaic afterwords by the author. Boston: Beacon Press, 1985.

———. *Beyond God the Father*. Boston: Beacon Press, 1973.

———. *Gyn/Ecology*. Boston: Beacon Press, 1978.

Dillenberger, John and Claude Welch. *Protestant Christianity: Interpreted through Its Development*, second edition. New York: Macmillan, 1988.

Duley, Margot I. and Mary I. Edwards, ed. *The Cross Cultural Study of Women*. New York: The Feminist Press at the City University of New York, 1986.

Emswiler, Sharon Neufer and Thomas Neufer Emswiler. *Women and Worship: A Guide to Nonsexist Hymns, Prayers, and Liturgies*. New York: Harper and Row, 1974. Revised and expanded edition, San Francisco: Harper and Row, 1984.

Eugene, Toinette M. et al. "Appropriation and Reciprocity in Womanist/Mujerista/Feminist Work." *Journal of Feminist Studies in Religion* 8, no. 2 (Fall 1992): 91–122.

"Final Statement: Latin American Conference, Buenos Aires, Argentina, Oct. 30–Nov. 3, 1985." In *Through Her Eyes: Women's Theology from Latin America*, ed. Elsa Tamez, 150–154. Maryknoll, New York: Orbis Books, 1989.

Gebara, Ivone. "Doing Theology in Latin America." In *With Passion and Compassion: Third World Women Doing Theology*, ed. Virginia Fabella and Mercy Amba Oduyoye, 126–134. Maryknoll, New York: Orbis Books, 1988.

Gilbert, Olive, ed. *Sojourner Truth: Narrative and Book of Life*, 1950 and 1875. Repr. Chicago: Johnson, 1970. Cited in Jacquelyn Grant. *White Women's Christ and Black Women's Jesus:*

Feminist Christology and Womanist Response. Atlanta: Scholars Press, 1989; and in Jacquelyn Grant. "Subjectification as a Requirement for Christological Construction," *Lift Every Voice: Constructing Christian Theologies from the Underside,* ed. Susan Brooks Thistlethwaite and Mary Potter Engel. San Francisco: HarperSanFrancisco, 1990.

Grant, Jacquelyn. "Black Women and the Church." In *All the Women Are White, All the Blacks Are Men, But Some of Us Are Brave: Black Women's Studies,* ed. Gloria T. Hull et al. , 141–152. Old Westbury, New York: The Feminist Press, 1982.

———. *White Women's Christ and Black Women's Jesus: Feminist Christology and Womanist Response.* Atlanta: Scholars Press, 1989.

———. "Subjectification as a Requirement for Christological Construction." In *Lift Every Voice: Constructing Christian Theologies from the Underside,* ed. Susan Brooks Thistlethwaite and Mary Potter Engel, 201–214. San Francisco: HarperSanFrancisco, 1990.

———. "The Sin of Servanthood." In *A Troubling in My Soul: Womanist Perspectives on Evil and Suffering,* ed. Emilie M. Townes, 199–218. Maryknoll, New York: Orbis Books, 1993.

Gunew, Sneja, ed. *A Reader in Feminist Knowledge.* London and New York: Routledge, 1991.

Gutiérrez, Gustavo. *A Theology of Liberation,* 15th anniversary ed. , ed. and trans. Sister Caridad Inda and John Eagleson. Maryknoll, New York: Orbis Books, 1971, 1988.

———. *The Power of the Poor in History.* Maryknoll, New York: Orbis Books, 1983. Originally published as *La fuerza histórica de los pobres.* Lima, Peru: Centro de Estudios y Publicaciones, 1979.

———. *The God of Life,* trans. Matthew J. O'Connell. Maryknoll, New York: Orbis Books, 1991.

Haraway, Donna. "A Manifesto for Cyborgs: Science, Technology, and Socialist Feminism in the 1980's." *Socialist Review,* no. 80, (1985). In *Feminism/Postmodernism,* ed. Linda J. Nicholson, 190–233. New York and London: Routledge, 1990.

Harrison, Beverly Wildung. "The Power of Anger in the Work of Love." In *Weaving the Visions: New Patterns in Feminist Spirituality,* ed. Judith Plaskow and Carol P. Christ. San Francisco: Harper and Row, 1989.

Hennelly, Alfred T. , ed. *Liberation Theology: A Documentary History.* Maryknoll, New York: Orbis Books, 1990.

Heyward, Carter. *The Redemption of God: A Theology of Mutual Relation.* Lanham, Maryland: University Press of America, 1982.

———. *Our Passion for Justice: Images of Power, Sexuality, and Liberation.* New York: Pilgrim Press, 1984.

———. *Speaking of Christ: A Lesbian Feminist Voice,* ed. Ellen C. Davis. New York: Pilgrim Press, 1989.

———. *Touching Our Strength: The Erotic as Power and the Love of God.* San Francisco: Harper and Row, 1989.

Hick, John and Paul F. Knitter, eds. *The Myth of God Incarnate.* Philadelphia: Westminister Press, 1977.

hooks, bell. *Ain't I a Woman.* Boston: South End Press, 1981.

———. *Feminist Theory: From Margin to Center.* Boston: South End Press, 1984.

———. *Yearning: Race, Gender, and Cultural Politics.* Boston: South End Press, 1990.

Hunt, Mary E. Lecture on feminist spirituality given at the Church Divinity School of the Pacific, Berkeley, California, March 7, 1987.

———. *Fierce Tenderness: A Feminist Theology of Friendship.* New York: Crossroad, 1992.

Hurston, Zora Neale. "John Reading Goes to Sea," *Opportunity* 4 (January 1926). Cited in Katie Geneva Cannon. *Black Womanist Ethics*. Atlanta: Scholars Press, 1988.

———. "How It Feels to Be Colored Me," *The World Tomorrow* (May 1928). Cited in Katie Geneva Cannon. *Black Womanist Ethics*. Atlanta: Scholars Press, 1988.

———. *Jonah's Gourd Vine*. Philadelphia: J. B. Lippincott, 1934. Repr. with a new foreword by Rita Dove. New York: Harper and Row, 1990.

———. *Mules and Men*. Philadelphia: J. B. Lippincott, 1935. Repr. with a preface by Franz Boas and a new foreword by Arnold Rampersad. New York: Harper and Row, 1990.

———. *Their Eyes Were Watching God*. Philadelphia: J. B. Lippincott, 1937. Repr. with a new foreword by Mary Helen Washington. New York: Harper and Row, 1990.

———. *Dust Tracks on a Road*. Philadelphia: J. B. Lippincott, 1942. Cited in Katie Geneva Cannon. *Black Womanist Ethics*. Atlanta: Scholars Press, 1988.

Isasi-Díaz, Ada María. "Mujeristas, A Name of Our Own." In *Yearning to Breathe Free: Liberation Theologies in the United States*, ed. Mar Peter-Raoul et al., 121–128. Maryknoll, New York: Orbis Books, 1990.

———. "Educating for a New World Order." Paper presented at the annual meeting of the National Association of Women in Education, Seattle, Washington, March 6, 1993.

———. *En La Lucha/In the Struggle: Elaborating a Mujerista Theology*. Minneapolis: Fortress Press, 1993.

Isasi-Díaz, Ada María, and Yolanda Tarango. *Hispanic Women: Prophetic Voice in the Church*. San Francisco: Harper and Row, 1988.

Jaggar, Alison M. "Love and Knowledge: Emotion in Feminist Epistemology." In *Gender/Body/Knowledge*, ed. Alison Jaggar and Susan Bordo, 146–165. New Jersey: Rutgers University Press, 1989.

Kates, Judith A. and Gail Twersky Reimer, eds. *Reading Ruth: Contemporary Women Reclaim a Sacred Story*. New York: Ballantine Books, 1994.

Kegley, Charles W. and Robert W. Bretall, eds. *The Theology of Paul Tillich*, Vol I. New York: Macmillan, 1952.

Klein, Julie Thompson. *Interdisciplinarity: History, Theory, and Practice*. Detroit: Wayne State University Press, 1990.

Knitter, Paul. *No Other Name: A Critical Survey of Christian Attitudes Toward the World Religions*. Maryknoll, New York: Orbis Books, 1985.

———. "Toward a Liberation Theology of Religions." In *The Myth of Christian Uniqueness: Toward a Pluralistic Theology of Religions*, ed. John Hick and Paul F. Knitter, 178–200. Maryknoll, New York: Orbis Books, 1987.

Landy, Francis. "Ruth and the Romance of Realism, or Deconstructing History," *Journal of the American Academy of Religion* 62, no. 2: 285–318.

Lapiedra, Aurora. "Religiosidad popular y mujer andina." In *El Rostro Femenino de la Teología*, ed. Elsa Tamez. San José, Costa Rica: Departamento Ecuménico de Investigaciones, 1986.

Latin American Church Women Challenge Patriarchy in Church and Society. New York: Women's International Resource Exchange, [n.d.].

Lorde, Audre. "An Open Letter to Mary Daly." In *This Bridge Called My Back: Writings By Radical Women of Color*, ed. Cherríe Moraga and Gloria Anzaldúa, 94–97. New York: Kitchen Table Press, 1983.

———. *Sister Outsider*. New York: The Crossing Press Feminist Series, 1984.

Lugones, María. "Playfulness, 'World'-Traveling, and Loving Perception." In *Making Face, Making Soul: Haciendo Caras*, ed. Gloria Anzaldúa, 390–402. San Francisco: Aunt Lute Foundation Books, 1990.

Lugones, María C. and Elizabeth V. Spelman. "Have We Got a Theory for You! Feminist Theory, Cultural Imperialism and the Demand for 'The Woman's Voice'." *Women's Studies International Forum* 6, no. 6 (1983): 573–581.

Marcos, Sylvia, "Toward Permanent Rebellion." In *Speaking of Faith: Global Perspectives on Women, Religion, and Social Change*, ed. Diana L. Eck and Devaki Jain, 258–265. Philadelphia: New Society Publishers, 1987.

McFague, Sallie. *Speaking in Parables*. Philadelphia: Fortress Press, 1975.

———. *Metaphorical Theology: Models of God in Religious Language*. Philadelphia: Fortress Press, 1982.

———. *Models of God: Theology for an Ecological, Nuclear Age*. Philadelphia: Fortress Press, 1987.

———. *The Body of God: An Ecological Theology*. Minneapolis: Fortress Press, 1993.

McIntosh, Peggy. "White Privilege: Unpacking the Invisible Knapsack." *Independent School* (Winter 1990): 31–34.

———. "White Privilege and Male Privilege: A Personal Account of Coming to See Correspondences Through Work in Women's Studies." *Race, Class and Gender*, ed. Margaret Andersen and Patricia Hill Collins, 70–81. Belmont, California: Wadsworth, 1992.

Melville, Thomas and Marjorie Melville. *Whose Heaven, Whose Earth?* New York: Knopf, 1971.

Miller, Casey and Kate Swift. *Words and Women: New Language in New Times*. Garden City, New York: Anchor Books, Anchor Press/Doubleday, 1977.

Moody, Linda A. "Women and the Church Grow by Caring." *Women and the Church (WATCHword)* 11, no. 2 (June/July 1987), a publication of National Ministries, American Baptist Churches, USA, Valley Forge, Pennsylvania: 5, 6.

———. "Toward a Methodology for Doing Theology Across the Boundaries of Difference: Feminist Theory Meets Feminist Theology," College Theology Society, St. Mary's College, Notre Dame, Indiana, May 27, 1994. Published in *College Theology Society 1994 Annual Volume: Women and Religion*. Maryknoll, New York: Orbis Books, 1995.

———. "Let My People Go." Sermon preached at the Annual Convention of the National Telephone Cooperative Association, San Francisco, California, February 5, 1995.

———. "Women's Theological Reflections on Reproductive Choices." American Academy of Religion, Western Region, University of Redlands, Redlands, California, March 31, 1995.

———. "Constructive Theological Understandings of God: Methodological and Epistemological Contributions of Sallie McFague," American Academy of Religion, Western Region, Santa Clara University, March 25, 1994. Published in *New Theology Review* 8, no. 3, August 1995.

Morton, Nelle. *The Journey is Home*. Boston: Beacon Press, 1985.

Narayan, Uma. "Working Together Across Difference: Some Considerations on Emotions and Political Practice." *Hypatia* 3, no. 2 (Summer, 1988): 32–46.

Navias, Eugene B. , ed. *Singing Our History: Tales, Texts and Tunes from Two Centuries of Unitarian Universalist Hymns*. Boston: Unitarian Universalist Association, 1975.

Pauck, Wilhelm and Marion Pauck. *Paul Tillich: His Life and Thought*. New York: Harper and Row, 1976.

Pearsall, Marilyn, ed. *Women and Values: Readings in Recent Feminist Philosophy*. Belmont, California: Wadsworth, 1986.

Reist, Benjamin A. *Theology in Red, White and Black*. Philadelphia: Westminster Press, 1975.

Ritchie, Nellie. "Women's Participation in the Church: A Protestant Perspective." In *With Passion and Compassion: Third World Women Doing Theology*, ed. Virginia Fabella and Mercy Amba Oduyoye, 152–155. Maryknoll, New York: Orbis Books, 1988.

Roberts, J. D. *A Black Political Theology*. Philadelphia: Westminster Press, 1974. Cited in Jacquelyn Grant. *White Women's Christ and Black Women's Jesus: Feminist Christology and Womanist Response*. Atlanta: Scholars Press, 1989.

Rodríguez, Raquel. Interview by Elsa Tamez. In *Teólogos de la Liberación Hablan Sobre La Mujer*, ed. Elsa Tamez, 159–166. San José, Costa Rica: Departamento Ecuménico de Investigaciones, 1986.

Ruether, Rosemary Radford. *Sexism and God-Talk: Toward a Feminist Theology*. Boston: Beacon Press, 1983.

Sanders, Cheryl J. "Christian Ethics and Theology in Womanist Perspective." *Journal of Feminist Studies in Religion* 5, no 2 (Fall 1989): 83–91.

Sandoval, Chela. "Feminism and Racism: A Report on the 1981 National Women's Studies Association Conference," originally published in 1982 by the Center for Third World Organizing, Oakland, California, and Washington D.C. In *Making Face, Making Soul: Haciendo Caras: Creative and Critical Perspectives by Women of Color*, ed. Gloria Anzaldua, 55–71. San Francisco: Aunt Lute Books, 1990.

———. "Comment on Krieger's 'Lesbian Identity and Community: Recent Social Science Literature'." *Signs: Journal of Women in Culture and Society* 9, no. 4 (Summer 1984): 725–729.

———. "U.S. Third World Feminism: The Theory and Method of Oppositional Consciousness in the Postmodern World." *Genders*, no. 10 (Spring 1991): 1–24.

Santisteban, Fryne. "Liberation Theology Faces Feminism: Church Women's Perspectives Differ." Interview by Karen O'Brien. Lima, Peru: Latinamerican Press, January, 1986. Repr. in *Latin American Church Women Challenge Patriarchy in Church and Society*. New York: Women's International Resource Exchange, [n. d.].

Schüssler Fiorenza, Elisabeth. *In Memory of Her: A Feminist Theological Reconstruction of Christian Origins*. New York: Crossroad, 1983.

———. *Bread Not Stone: The Challenge of Feminist Biblical Interpretation*. Boston: Beacon Press, 1984.

Smith, Huston. *The World's Religions*. San Francisco: HarperSanFrancisco, 1991.

Spelman, Elizabeth. *Inessential Woman: Problems of Exclusion in Feminist Thought*. Boston: Beacon Press, 1988.

Stanton, Elizabeth Cady. *The New Woman's Bible*. New York: European Publishing Company, 1898; reprint, Seattle: Coalition Task Force on Women and Religion, 1974.

Swidler, Leonard. *Biblical Affirmation of Woman*. Philadelphia: Westminster Press, 1979.

Tamez, Elsa. *Bible of the Oppressed*, tr. Matthew J. O'Connell. Maryknoll, New York: Orbis Books, 1982.

———. "Mujer y Varon Llamados a La Vida: Un acercamiento bíblico-teológico." *Cristianismo y Sociedad* 21, no. 3–4 (1982–83).

———. *Against Machismo*, tr. and ed. John Eagleson. Oak Park, Illinois: Meyer Stone Books, 1987.

———. "Women's Rereading of the Bible." In *With Passion and Compassion: Third World Women Doing Theology*, ed. Virginia Fabella and Mercy Amba Oduyoye, 173–178. Maryknoll, New York: Orbis Books, 1988.

———. "Introduction: The Power of the Naked." In *Through Her Eyes: Women's Theology from Latin America*, ed. Elsa Tamez. Maryknoll, New York: Orbis Books, 1989. Originally published as *El Rostro Femenino de la Teología*, ed. Elsa Tamez. San José, Costa Rica: Departamento Ecuménico de Investigaciones, 1986.

———. "Quetzalcoatl Challenges the Christian Bible." Paper presented at the annual meeting of the American Academy of Religion and Society for Biblical Religion Joint Conference, November 1992, San Francisco, California.

————. "Reliving Our Histories: Racial and Cultural Revelations of God." In *New Vision for the Americas: Religious Engagement and Social Transformation*, ed. David Batstone, 33–56. Minneapolis: Fortress Press, 1993.

————, ed. *Through Her Eyes: Women's Theology from Latin America*. Maryknoll, New York: Orbis Books, 1989.

Thistlethwaite, Susan. *Sex, Race, and God: Christian Feminism in Black and White*. New York: Crossroad, 1991.

Tillich, Paul. "Protestant Principles." *The Protestant* 4, no. 5 (April–May 1942).

————. *The Courage to Be*. New Haven: Yale University Press, 1952.

————. *Systematic Theology*, 3 vols. Chicago: University of Chicago Press, 1951–1963.

Tong, Rosemarie. *Feminist Thought: A Comprehensive Introduction*. Boulder, Colorado: Westview Press, 1989.

Townes, Emilie M. "Christian Ethics and Theology in Womanist Perspective." *Journal of Femininst Studies in Religion* 5, no. 2 (Fall 1989): 94–97.

————. *Womanist Justice, Womanist Hope*. Atlanta: Scholars Press, 1993.

Townes, Emilie M. et al. , "Appropriation and Reciprocity in the Doing of Feminist and Womanist Ethics." *The Annual of the Society of Christian Ethics*, 1994.

Trible, Phyllis. *God and the Rhetoric of Sexuality*. Philadelphia: Fortress Press, 1978.

Walker, Alice. *In Search of Our Mothers' Gardens*. San Diego: Harcourt Brace Jovanovich, 1983.

————. *The Color Purple*. New York: Washington Square Press, 1982. Cited in Emilie M. Townes, "Christian Ethics and Theology in Womanist Perspective." *Journal of Feminist Studies in Religion* 5, no. 2 (Fall 1989): 94–97.

Welch, Claude. *Protestant Thought in the Nineteenth Century*, Vol 2. New Haven: Yale University Press, 1985.

Welch, Sharon D. *Communities of Resistance and Solidarity: A Feminist Theology of Liberation*. Maryknoll, New York: Orbis Books, 1985.

————. *A Feminist Ethic of Risk*. Minneapolis: Fortress Press, 1990.

Wetherilt, Ann Kirkus. *That They May Be Many: Voices of Women, Echoes of God*. New York: Continuum, 1994.

Wheatley, Phillis. "On Being Brought from Africa to America." In Roger Whitlow, *Black American Literature: A Critical History*. Totowa, New Jersey: Littlefield, Adams and Co. , 1974, 23. Cited in Katie Geneva Cannon. *Black Womanist Ethics*. Atlanta: Scholars Press, 1988.

Wiesel, Elie. *Ani Maamin: A Song Lost and Found Again*. New York: Random House, 1973. Cited in Carter Heyward. *The Redemption of God: A Theology of Mutual Relation*. Lanham, Maryland: University Press of America, 1982.

Williams, Delores, "The Color of Feminism." *Christianity and Crisis* (April 29, 1985): 164, 165.

————. "Womanist Theology: Black Women's Voices." *Christianity and Crisis* 47 (March 2, 1987): 66–70.

————. "Breaking and Bonding," *Daughters of Sarah* (May, June, 1989): 20, 21.

————. "Black Women's Surrogacy Experience." In *After Patriarchy: Feminist Transformations of the World Religions*, ed. Paula M. Cooey, William R. Eakin, and Jay B. McDaniel. Maryknoll, New York: Orbis Books, 1991.

————. *Sisters in the Wilderness: The Challenge of Womanist God-Talk*. Maryknoll, New York: Orbis Books, 1993.

Williamson, Chris. "Waterfall." Bird Ankles Music, BMI, 1975. On the album *The Changer and the Changed*. Olivia Records, Inc. , 1975.

Women's Studies Quarterly 21, no. 1 and 2 (Spr/Sum 1993).

Index